The Lancers of Bhurtpore

16TH LIGHT DRAGOONS, 1798.

The Lancers of Bhurtpore
A Diary and History of the 16th Lancers in India
1822–1834

ILLUSTRATED

Arthur C. Lowe and Others

Edited By John H. Lewis

LEONAUR

The Lancers of Bhurtpore
A Diary and History of the 16th Lancers in India 1822-1834

ILLUSTRATED

by Arthur C. Lowe and Others
Edited by John H. Lewis

FIRST EDITION

Leonaur is an imprint of Oakpast Ltd

Copyright in this form © 2019 Oakpast Ltd

ISBN: 978-1-78282-848-8 (hardcover)
ISBN: 978-1-78282-849-5 (softcover)

http://www.leonaur.com

Publisher's Notes

Contents

Introduction and Acknowledgements by the Publishers

The principal part of the book you are now holding was drawn to our attention by Charles Radford, former commanding officer of the 16th/5th The Queen's Lancers and the Parachute Squadron, Royal Armoured Corps, and a long standing Leonaur supporter and collaborator on several projects. This gentleman has an understandable and abiding interest in the history of his own regiment including that of the 16th The Queen's Lancers (formerly the 16th (The Queen's) Regiment of (Light) Dragoons),which had earned its own illustrious record before it was combined with the 5th Royal Irish Lancers to create the 16th/5th Lancers in the amalgamation which took place shortly after the Great War in 1922.

These publishers had no prior knowledge of the book that Charles Radford discovered on this occasion which is titled, 'The Diary of an Officer of the 16th Lancers' by Arthur Charles Lowe and given it is a rare volume and long out of print our ally proposed that it was high time it was republished. We, as usual, agreed with him. This book was originally produced in India by Thacker, Spink & Company of Calcutta in 1898, apparently for private circulation, though this did not concern the diarist, since this record of his military career encompassed the eighteen years from June 1822 to June 1840 and Lowe had, some twenty one years prior to first publication, died in England in 1877.

The first of the diary date year, 1822, is particularly significant as regards this book since it was then that the 16th (The Queen's) Regiment of (Light) Dragoons (Lancers) embarked on board transports to serve in India and it is, indeed, at that point which Arthur Lowe's story begins for the reader. Lowe's regiment, as the 16th Light Dragoons, had served with distinction during the late conflict against the First

OFFICER OF THE 16TH LANCERS, 1820, BY JOHN LUARD

Empire of the French of Napoleon Bonaparte during the Peninsular War in Spain and in the south of France. It was also present at the Battle of Waterloo, 18th June 1815, which brought about the final downfall of the, by then, renegade emperor. Coincidently, that battle took place seven years to the month (actually, almost to the day!) prior to the departure of the ships carrying the regiment from their anchorages off Deal, bound for the sub-continent.

By that time the regiment had become the 16th Lancers, having been converted from a light dragoon to a lancer regiment (together with the 9th and 12th (Prince of Wales's) regiments of light dragoons) in 1816. The 19th Light Dragoons were also converted to lancers at almost the same time (having taken the place of the 23rd Light Dragoons which had been converted to lancers, but disbanded), but theirs was a short career since they too were disbanded in 1821. On board the ships leaving British shores astern in June 1822 there were those who well remembered those pivotal events in European history, since they had taken part in them personally.

Most students of the history of the British cavalry during the nineteenth century would primarily associate the 16th Lancers with the Battle of Aliwal fought during the First Anglo-Sikh War of 1845-6. Such is the abiding renown of that battle that the famous charge of the 'Scarlet Lancers' during this engagement is celebrated with an annual commemorative dinner by former members of the regiment to this day. Whilst it would be entirely wrong to detract from the achievement of the charge which broke the Sikh defensive formations at Aliwal, the fact is that the 'Sixteenth' were not always 'scarlet' lancers and its charges in the principal action that concerns this book—at Bhurtpore in 1825-6 (in which their coats were blue) are without precedent since they bear the distinction of being the very first occasions in which British Army lancers employed the lance against an enemy.

Whilst the use of the lance by mounted warriors dates to the origins of cavalry itself, no British Army cavalry regiment had used them in warfare since the English Civil War (before the creation of the 'modern' army, defined by numerically titled regiments, that began during the reign of Charles II) when the Scottish Army contained a lancer regiment. In fact, there was an increase in the quantity of lancer regiments generally among the armies of Europe after the close of the Napoleonic Wars, for despite the ultimate defeat of Napoleon's armies, every qualified observer had seen (and some had been unfortunate to experience—including men of the 16th Light Dragoons) the incredible effectiveness of the many French lancer regiments in action, particularly when employing the lance as a weapon of first contact. The influence of Napoleon's Imperial Guard lancer regiments was emphasised by the uniform selected for the new British Army regiments, for they were demonstrably similar in appearance to those worn by their former opponents, particularly as regarded the headdress which was the iconic Polish four-cornered *chapka*.

The campaign of 1825-6, which included the investment and assault of the fortress of Bhurtpore (now modern day Bharatpur in eastern Rajathstan) became known as 'The Jat War'. This small Indian campaign is little known to many military historians, especially compared to the two Anglo-Sikh Wars fought twenty years afterwards. However, the fact that many of the men of the 16th Lancers who fought at Bhurtpore were also veterans of the Peninsular War and the Waterloo Campaign of 1815 is especially interesting since we are able to track the careers of certain officers through these campaigns. To facilitate this continuity of events the present publishers have drawn on the short history of the 16th Lancers prepared by Richard Cannon.

So, the history of the 16th Light Dragoons from its departure to fight in Spain against the French Army in 1808 until the fall of Napoleon in 1815 appears in this edition before Arthur Lowe's diary. The events which included 'The Jat War' of 1825-6 (augmented by extracts from the journal of John Luard, a fellow officer of Lowe's during this period) appear after the diary to give the Lowe account wider historical context. This section concludes in 1832. By this time Lowe had temporarily left the regiment on detached duty, but the 16th Lancers remained in India and it was in this year that it assumed the scarlet coat which, in due course, would instantly identify it when all other British Army lancer regiments were once again returned to blue uniforms.

Lieutenant A. C. Lowe, had been an officer of the 16th Light Dragoons since April of 1815 when he is listed as a cornet, though records reveal he did not take part in the Battle of Waterloo with the regiment three months later. He became a lieutenant in the regiment in August of the same year and remained holding that rank until 1827, when he became a captain. His diary reveals he received his promotion to major, without purchase, in 1839.

Readers will immediately note that the years covered by the Lowe diary (and therefore the published work of 1898) do not correspond with the dates covered in this book which is confined to a portion of Lieutenant Lowe's career. Diaries are, of course, centred around the lives of individuals rather than the events in which the diarists took part or witnessed. If that person is a well-known personality then this consideration is less significant since the work is, in measure, elevated and evaluated as autobiography. Equally, when the contents of the diary concern a single theme (The Peninsular War, for example) the stage upon which the diarist relates his story provides the cohesion of the work and there are ready readers for that subject and others like it, almost irrespective of the identity or stature of the author.

For the publisher, the issue becomes problematic when the source material has been written by a mostly unknown author, covers a long period of time and embraces more than one theme since, in the main, that is not (experience has taught us) what those who purchase military history books are seeking. Almost all those kinds of readers focus on particular historical periods, units or places and the books they purchase reflect that inherent focus.

The Lowe diaries (which were originally spread over three hand-written volumes) covered nearly twenty years of the author's life, comprising an initial period of service in India, (including the 'Jat War' of 1825-6, which is related in this book), followed by a period of detached service in Australia and thereafter by his return to India when Lowe took his part in the First Afghan War with the 16th Lancers as the British attempted to install the unpopular puppet ruler Shah Shuja on the throne of Afghanistan. The diary ends as Lowe returns to England.

Combined, these writings not only encompass a considerable period of time, but, inevitably, create a sizeable tome in the 1898 edition. Those familiar with this kind of material will possibly not be surprised to learn that the original text is, since it is a diary, some way from being a structured narrative. It is littered with navigational readings (which may be of interest to students of the age of sail), compositions of doggerel verse for which the author had some enthusiasm and various other distractions which are not the principal focus for students of military history. Indeed, Lowe's diaries are inevitably far from confined to his experiences on the campaign and battlefield.

In that aspect of their content, however, we can find little to criticise, because they provide the modern reader with invaluable insights into virtually every aspect of life—from the significant to the trivial—within a British cavalry regiment and all those associated with it on transports, in garrison life, and travelling through India during the first decades of the nineteenth century. Through Lowe's observations the reader is given fascinating and sometimes humorous insights into the scenes, people and personalities—both British and Indian—of that period in the rise of the British Empire on the sub-continent.

So, the present publishers believed that there was sufficient material concerning the first period that the 16th Lancers and Arthur Lowe spent in India to form a book in its own right, especially if that material was supported by other texts to give the diary context and included supporting illustrations. To assist in the achievement of that objective, this edition contains a brief overview of the Bhurtpore Campaign of 1825-6 edited by Sir Evelyn Wood (1915). No doubt, in the future, the other aspects of the Lowe diary will be treated in a similar fashion by this publisher.

These considerations constituted Leonaur team's plan for a book that became this book from the time that they first examined its potentials. However, it was immediately recognised that the project contained a stumbling block. On virtually every page of the Lowe diary, published in 1898, information was demonstrably missing—excised as if by a censor. This made the text inherently unattractive and less appealing to read whilst impacting on the value of the work as history. Ultimately, the Leonaur team, in concert with Charles Radford and with the assistance of research material from the military historian John Rumsby, solved that problem and in so doing created an entirely original published version of the Lowe text which has, in the opinions of those involved, quite literally brought it to life. How that occurred is, perhaps, interesting since we believe it has made this edition exceptional.

At first examination it was clear that practically every person's name that appeared in the text was identified only by a capital letter followed by a long dash. The reader was prevented from knowing who these people were in their relationship to the author and the events in which they took part. Did Lowe, who of course knew very well what these names were, simply abbreviate them to save time in the writing or to prevent embarrassment if the diary fell into the wrong hands whilst he was actually making entries into it? Alternatively, did a later editor (at the time of the publication of the work in 1898) make this decision for reasons we cannot now fathom, since everyone mentioned in the diary was almost certainly dead by that time? Perhaps, it was considered, the removal of names was done at that time, if at all, out of deference to the descendants of those people. In any event, it was felt the matter was quite academic a century and more later and had become an unequivocal obstruction to valuable recorded history.

Irrespective of motive, if a later person (other than Lowe) was responsible for this edit, it had been executed in a most extraordinary and inclusive fashion, because even on those occasions when the text was clearly referring to Lowe himself—that name was also quite unnecessarily expunged. These instances, at least, made it clear that complete anonymity was not the objective of the culling of names, since the correct initial letter had been employed. The same treatment had been applied, quite ludicrously, to people who were well known and whose initial letter followed a rank or title which made it perfectly simple, given a rudimentary knowledge of time and place, to identify the individual. Accordingly, the Leonaur team decided it was worthwhile to attempt to discover the identities of the personalities in Lowe's diary and replace the dashes with accurate names in a new edition.

That task transpired, initially, to be less difficult than may be imagined. Most of the people referred to in the diary were officers of the 16th Lancers. Richard Cannon's, 'Historical Record of The Sixteenth, or The Queen's Regiment of Light Dragoons, Lancers', published in London in 1842 covers the history of the regiment from its formation in 1759 until the year before publication, 1841. Thus, it covers the entire period of Arthur Lowe's diary. This book is one of an extensive series concerning the individual regiments of the British Army and though each volume is usually not large, they are exceptionally thorough. Particularly useful are comprehensive lists of officers ordered by rank at pivotal stages of the regiment's services including embarkations, battles etc.

Similarly, for the purposes of this book, 'A Narrative of the Siege and Capture of Bhurtpore' by J. N Creighton published in 1830 by Allen & Co, London was especially useful, because in that book the author has provided comprehensive lists of officers who served in that campaign, not only of the 16th Lancers, but of all the regiments who served in the British and Indian force under Combermere. Additionally, Charles Radford's association with the author and historian, John Rumsby, who has written the excellent, 'Discipline, System and Style—The Sixteenth Lancers and Soldiering in India, 1822-1846' published by Helion & Company, 2016, gave us access to the author's very thorough research notes as they bore on the information needed to complete this project.

Armed with all this material the task began and names fell readily into place, especially among those identified by higher ranks for there

A SELF PORTRAIT BY JOHN LUARD, 1820.

Note the unusual undress jacket worn by Luard. This style appears to have been short lived. It can be seen in the illustration of the lancer officer on page 8, and the same jacket can be found on a print of the uniform of the 19th Lancers.

are few colonels and majors and even fewer candidates for staff officers in the text. A combination of factors came into play. For example, at its most straightforward, Riding Master Blood was the only 16th Lancers officer aboard a transport in 1822 whose name began with the letter 'B'. Surgeons and others were also readily identifiable. Whilst other initial letters were more common, the context of a passage eliminated certain candidates since, for example, one might readily assume that captains would not engage in high jinks escapades with cornets and so forth. The most problematic issues arose among the largest group by rank—the lieutenants—since the same initial letter applied to several of them. When the initial letter was repeated in the text so that it covered all of them the conclusion was obvious, but occasionally there were instances where one could only say with certainty that the diarist was referring to this person OR that person. It was decided when those situations arose, both names would be given covered by an explanation.

A further key to the entire puzzle came from an entirely different source. Everyone involved in this project was aware of the books written by James Lunt. For Colonel Charles Radford the association was closer yet because he knew Major-General Lunt personally, since he had been a commanding officer and colonel of the 16th/5th The Queen's Royal Lancers. Indeed, his son Robin Lunt, had also been a 16th/5th Lancer officer during the period of Charles Radford's own service with the regiment. James Lunt wrote a highly regarded history of the regiment, 'The Scarlet Lancers—the story of 16th/5th Queens Royal Lancers: 1689-1992' published in 1993. However, some thirty years previously he had also written, 'Scarlet Lancer' (Rupert Hart-Davis, 1963) which followed the career of, John Luard, an officer of the 16th Light Dragoons and later 16th Lancers. Notably, the Luard family also remained associated with the 16th/5th in modern times. Richard Luard served in the regiment and was also a contemporary of Charles Radford.

The late James Lunt's interest in John Luard is an understandable one because this officer left for posterity a journal of his own military career which included his service in the Peninsular War (4th Dragoons), during The Waterloo Campaign (16th Light Dragoons) and, as a contemporary of Arthur Lowe, in the 'Jat War' of 1825-6. Indeed, Luard was a passenger on the same ship that carried Lowe on the journey to India in 1822 and, inevitably, he is readily identifiable in the Lowe diary by the combination of the letter 'L' and his rank. James Lunt utilised short passages of the Lowe diary in his own book and cited as his reference the published edition of 1898. However, in one of those passages contained in 'Scarlet Lancer', full names (not initial letters with dashes) appeared without qualification as to their authenticity, which from our own perspective (in a few cases) remained less than completely certain. This suggested that James Lunt had access to information we did not currently possess, for his source could not have been the 1898 edition of the Lowe diary.

In any event, access to John Luard's journal was much desired by all concerned and some efforts have been made to discover its whereabouts, most especially so that a copy of it might be deposited at the 16th/5th The Queen's Lancers archive at Stoke-on-Trent, a project in which Charles Radford is closely involved. Luard, incidentally, was also an excellent artist and he produced a series of drawings of—among other subjects—his time in India. Some of these images are held in the 16th/5th archive and among the subjects Luard illustrated is a depiction of the 16th Lancers in action in cooperation with helmeted troopers of Skinner's Horse and *sowars* of the Bengal Light Cavalry at Bhurtpore against Jat cavalry in the forest outside the bastion. Two officers appear in the illustration and it is possible that John Luard is one of them, ensuring that this image is a unique and accurate record of the 'Sixteenth' in action at this singular moment—the first charge of British Army lancers. At time of writing, incidentally, John Luard's very important historical journal remains undiscovered by those who seek it.

More pertinently for the current project the question was, 'From where did James Lunt procure the full names in the Lowe diary passages, he used in 'Scarlet Lancer'? Little online research was required to discover that Arthur Lowe's original diaries were kept at the National Army Museum in Chelsea, London. The following question was, 'Are the names within the diary shown as capital letters followed by dashes or are they written in full?' Charles Radford visited the museum and there, with the assistance of the museum staff including Robert Fleming, Templar Study Centre Manager, he discovered that Lowe had, indeed, written every name in his diary in full. We may confidently assume that Major-General Lunt had access to the same resource for his own book published in 1963, though at that time the diaries were kept elsewhere. Accordingly, we were able, as a result of this research, to verify our own investigative work and remove any doubt regarding the identities of those personalities who had not only the same first letter to their names, but also a similar rank or position.

So simply put, whilst this edition covers only a portion of Arthur Lowe's diary, its publication is notable since it is the first time a complete section of the diary has been published inclusive of the full names of those who appear within its pages.

The reader will appreciate, without further emphasis here, that bringing this book into being has been something of a combined effort by 'a coalition of the willing' whose names have appeared in this introduction and so, in many ways, it seems to me almost inappropriate to thank them for their contributions, since this has been a team effort made by those dedicated to preserving the historical record of this exceptional regiment. Nevertheless, I do thank them all and most sincerely.

Perhaps, one might safely say that this book came about in the infectious positive spirit of the 16th/5th—past and present. May these pages do justice to the regiment and all who served in it which included, incidentally, the father of two members of the Leonaur team.

John H Lewis
July, 2019

A Brief History of the 16th Light Dragoons, 1809-1815

Richard Cannon

By 1809, Napoleon Buonaparte had added Italy and Genoa to his dominions; the unsatiated ambition of this chieftain thirsted for universal empire, and he was endeavouring to reduce the Iberian Peninsula to submission to his yoke. British troops were sent to aid the Spaniards and Portuguese, and on the 31st of March, 1809, the Sixteenth Light Dragoons, commanded by Colonel George Anson, embarked from Falmouth for Portugal, landed at Lisbon on the 13th of April, and were formed in brigade with the Fourteenth Light Dragoons, under Major-General Stapleton Cotton.

★★★★★★

The following officers proceeded abroad with the regiment in 1809.

Colonel, George Anson; *Major*, the Honourable Lincoln Stanhope; *Captains*, Raymond Pelly, James Hay, George Home Murray, Robert Ashworth, John Henry Belli, Honourable Henry B. Lygon, Honourable Edward C. Cocks, Clement Sweetenham; *Lieutenants*, Robert Lloyd, William Glasscott, Ralph B. Johnson, George Thompson, William Persse, Richard Weyland, Hugh Owen, William Hay, John P. Buchanan, William J. Alexander, Henry Van Hagen, William Tomkinson, Thomas Penrice, Henry B. Bence, William Osten, Charles Sawyer; *Cornets*, William Lockhart, Charles T. Bishop, George Keating; *Paymaster*, John Burnet; *Surgeon*, Isaac Robinson; *Assistant Surgeons*, James O'Meally, R.T. Healde; *Adjutant*, John Barra; and *Veterinary Surgeon*, John Peers.

★★★★★★

After ten days' march the regiment joined the army assembling at Coimbra under Lieut.-General Sir Arthur Wellesley, to drive the French under Marshal Soult from Oporto.

Advancing upon this enterprise, the regiment crossed the Vouga before daylight on the 10th of May, and approaching Albergaria Nova, arrived in the presence of four regiments of French cavalry, a battalion of infantry, and some artillery, under General Franceschi. The enemy was driven from his post; "the superiority of the British cavalry was evident throughout the day" (*London Gazette*); and the Sixteenth Light Dragoons were commended for their spirited conduct on this occasion. Several men and horses were wounded; and Major the Honourable Lincoln Stanhope received a sabre wound while leading a charge of the regiment on this occasion.

After the enemy was driven from his post, the regiment moved forward in pursuit, and halted that night at Oliveira; on the following morning it was again in motion, and about eight o'clock came up with the French, who were strongly posted on the heights above Grijon; they were again forced to make a precipitate retreat, and two squadrons of the Sixteenth and Twentieth Dragoons, darting forward in pursuit, killed many and took some prisoners. The spirited conduct of the regiment, on this occasion, was commended by Sir Arthur Wellesley, in his public despatch. It lost several men and horses, and, among the wounded, were Captain Sweetenham and Lieutenant Tomkinson.

The French continued their retreat and arrived at Oporto during the night, but were driven from that place, with severe loss, on the following day. The Sixteenth pursued the enemy, one squadron proceeding by way of Guimaraens, and the other three by Braga; on the 16th of May, the advance-guard of the regiment, with the leading companies of the brigade of Foot Guards, came up with the rear of the enemy, which was formed on a strong position near Salamonde. This post was attacked, and the French fled in dismay, and with loss, particularly at the bridge of Ponte Nova, over which they endeavoured to escape.

From Salamonde the pursuit was continued, and the advance-guard of the army, of which the Sixteenth formed part, arrived at Montalegre on the 19th of May, much fatigued from long marches through an exhausted country, and from incessant rain. The enemy having been chased beyond the confines of Portugal, and forced to abandon his artillery and baggage, the pursuit terminated; the Sixteenth retraced their steps to Oporto, halted at that city one day, and afterwards proceeded to Coimbra.

On the plains of Coimbra, the British cavalry were reviewed by Sir Arthur Wellesley on the 16th of June; they afterwards proceeded towards Abrantes; and Colonel Anson having been placed at the head of a brigade, with the rank of brigadier-general, the command of the regiment devolved on Major the Honourable Lincoln Stanhope.

Advancing from the vicinity of Abrantes, the Sixteenth passed the frontiers of Portugal, to co-operate with the Spaniards under General Cuesta; but the British commander being, from the neglect and apathy of the Spanish authorities, unable to procure provisions for his troops, halted at Talavera de la Reyna. The French advanced in force under Joseph Buonaparte, and on the 27th and 28th of July, the valley of the Tagus at Talavera, resounded with the roar of cannon and musketry, and the Sixteenth Light Dragoons were at their post in the line of battle, supporting the infantry, and manoeuvring to hold the French cavalry in check. On this occasion the sterling qualities of the British troops were proved; the furious onsets of their opponents were repulsed with dreadful slaughter, and the allied army stood victorious on the field of battle.

The loss of the Sixteenth was limited to six rank and file killed; Lieutenant Bence and five rank and file wounded; two men missing. Its commanding officer, Major the Honourable Lincoln Stanhope, obtained a gold medal, and the gallant bearing of the regiment was afterwards rewarded with the royal authority to bear the word "Talavera" on its guidons and appointments.

This display of British skill and prowess was followed by the advance of French armies having so great a superiority of numbers, that the English general was obliged to withdraw behind the Tagus; and Assistant Surgeon O'Meally, being employed with the medical staff in charge of the wounded, was made prisoner and sent to France. The Sixteenth were afterwards employed on the Guadiana; they subsequently occupied quarters in Estremadura and the Alentejo. Extraordinary fatigue, want of food, and the climate of the banks of the Guadiana, proved fatal to the British troops, and many officers and soldiers died of a malignant fever. Assistant Surgeon Healde, of the Sixteenth, died at Estremos; and of the thirty-six officers of the regiment present, nineteen were attacked with the prevailing disease.

During the winter the Spanish armies were defeated, captured, or dispersed; the British remained in Portugal; their commander was created Viscount Wellington; and in December, the Sixteenth Light Dragoons marched from the Alentejo to Portuguese Estremadura, oc-

FRANCE

Sebastian
Bayonne
Fuenterrabia
Durango
Roncevalles
Pyrenees Mts.
Vitoria Pampeluna
Figueras
gos
Calahorra
Gerona
Barcelona
Tudela Ebro
Saragossa
Lerida
ro
Mts Siguenza
ss of Somo Sierra
Tortosa
Tarragona
ADRID
Ucles
40
ana
Majorca
acid SPAIN
Murviedro
Valencia
Iviza
ina R.
Castalla
orena
ss dela
rolina
Alicante
Murcia
C. Palos
Cartagena
ranada
C. Gata

Map of the
SPANISH CAMPAIGN.

English Miles

0 20 40 60 80 100   200

cupying quarters at Abrantes on the banks of the Tagus.

Additional French troops, flushed with their recent victories in Germany, crowded into Spain, and in the campaign of 1810, the British had to contend with such an immense superiority of numbers, that their operations were limited to the defence of Portugal. The Sixteenth advanced, in February, to the frontiers; but afterwards withdrew to Carbadao; in April they again moved forward to the Sierra d'Estrella, a lofty range of mountains in the province of Beira, and were reviewed, on the 19th of June, by Lord Wellington.

Advancing with overwhelming numbers, the enemy besieged Ciudad Rodrigo, and the English general, hoping the enemy would, by detaching troops, give him an opportunity of relieving the place, reinforced Brigadier-General Craufurd, who commanded the outposts behind the Agueda, with the Fourteenth and Sixteenth Dragoons; the enemy pushed some troops forward, and the British cavalry in advance were posted at Gallegos, with the infantry in the wood of Almeida.

On the 4th of July the enemy passed the river, and drove back the outposts; the British retired skirmishing upon Alameida, a troop of the Sixteenth, a troop of the First German Hussars, and two guns covered the movement, and, after some sharp fighting in which the French were repulsed, the British light infantry and the guns took post in a wood near Fort Conception, and the Sixteenth Light Dragoons, and other cavalry, were stationed higher up, on the Duas Casas. The French withdrew behind the Azava, leaving only a piquet at Gallegos; their marauding parties, however, entered the villages of Barquillo and Villa de Puerco on three successive nights, and Brigadier-General Craufurd, thinking to cut them off, formed two ambuscades, in one of which were the Sixteenth Light Dragoons.

At daybreak on the morning of the 11th of July, a body of French infantry was discovered near Villa de Puerco, and a party of cavalry at Barquillo. The British advanced along a difficult defile between stone enclosures, and the French infantry, having time to form square on a steep rise of land, were enabled to repulse their opponents and to effect their retreat. The French dragoons were charged, broken, and two officers and twenty-nine men made prisoners.

During the night of the 23rd of July, the vedettes and piquets of the Sixteenth were exposed to a heavy storm of wind and rain; as daylight approached, they discovered the advance of the enemy in force, and the regiment took part in covering the retrograde movements of the light division across the River Coa.

The French besieged Almeida, which surrendered towards the end of August; on the 28th of that month the enemy attacked the outposts, the Sixteenth were sharply engaged, and Captain the Honourable Henry B. Lygon was severely wounded while in command of the skirmishers.

Having gained possession of one of the principal fortresses of Portugal, the French Marshal, Massena, urged forward his numerous legions; the British fell back fighting; the Sixteenth, taking a most active part in covering the retreat, were frequently engaged with the enemy. On the 3rd of September their outposts were attacked; on the 24th the French skirmished with the piquets in front of Mortagao, when a squadron of the Sixteenth distinguished itself, leaving a number of opponents dead on the field, and bringing off several prisoners.

On the 25th of September the cavalry skirmishers exchanged a few shots, and the regiment was employed in covering the retreat of the light division to the position on the rugged rocks of Busaco; it had several men and horses killed and wounded; Captain George Home Murray was also slightly wounded, and Cornet George Keating severely wounded.

At the Battle of Busaco, on the 27th of September, the regiment was commanded by Major Clement Archer, but the ground was too mountainous and rugged for the use of cavalry, and the regiment had no opportunity of distinguishing itself. The enemy having turned the position by a flank movement, the army retired towards the fortified lines; when the Sixteenth were again at the post of honour confronting the enemy and covering the retrograde movement.

On the 1st of October the outposts were driven from the hills bounding the plain of Coimbra to the north, and the British fell back, fighting, across the Mondego. Leaving Coimbra on the 4th of October, Marshal Massena advanced and drove the English piquets from Pombal. On the following morning he pushed so suddenly upon Leyria as to create some confusion; some brilliant fighting took place, and the Sixteenth particularly distinguished themselves in action with the Third French Hussars and the Fifteenth French Dragoons. The regiment lost several men and horses, and Captain Murray was slightly and Captain Sweetenham severely wounded.

At this period skirmishing took place every day, and on the 8th of October, a squadron of the Sixteenth charged the head of a French column in the streets of Alcoentre, slew seven or eight of the en-

Cavalry skirmish in the Peninsular War.

emy, and took twelve men and horses, of the Second and Fourteenth French dragoons, prisoners.

The French, confident in their superior numbers, pressed boldly forward, and the temerity of their cavalry was again punished on the 9th of October, near Quinta de Torre, when a squadron of the Sixteenth distinguished itself.

On the 10th of October the skirmish was resumed, and the British took post in the lines of Torres Vedras, where they opposed a resistance which arrested the progress of the numerous legions of Buonaparte. The Sixteenth were posted at Mafra; and on the 22nd of October the brigade to which they belonged took the outpost duty at Ramalhal, which was occupied as a post of reserve and support to Obidos, where a garrison was placed to restrain the French on that side.

Marshal Massena, who had vaunted he would drive the English into the sea, and plant the eagles of France upon the towers of Lisbon, became convinced of the hopelessness of the task he had undertaken, and, in the middle of November, he retired to a position at Santarem. The Sixteenth moving forward in pursuit, formed part of the advance-guard of the allied army, and many prisoners were captured. Sergeant Baxter and six men of the regiment, being in advance, came suddenly upon a piquet of fifty French infantry, who were cooking, but they instantly ran to their arms. The sergeant led his little band to the charge with heroic gallantry, and broke in among the enemy with such resolution, that, with the assistance of some countrymen, he made prisoners a French officer and forty-one soldiers, with the loss of one man of the Sixteenth killed. Sergeant Baxter had distinguished himself on former occasions, and in this advance, Sergeants Blood, Biggs, and Liddle, were conspicuous for bravery in presence of the enemy.

A board of officers assembled to decide upon the disposal of two thousand one hundred and eleven dollars, the produce of horses captured from the enemy, and awarded nine hundred and eighty-five dollars to the Sixteenth Light Dragoons.

During the early part of the year 1811, the two opposing armies confronted each other; and Captain the Honourable Edward Charles Cocks was detached with a squadron of the Sixteenth to Caldos to watch the enemy's movements, and to harass and attack his foraging parties. While thus employed, Captain Cocks and the men of the regiment under his orders, distinguished themselves on several occasions, and took many prisoners; and, on the 25th of January, Sergeant Blood and six men charged the rear of a French squadron, in the act of crossing a bridge, and cut off fifteen men and horses, thus affording another instance of the superiority of the British cavalry.

On the 24th of January a reconnoissance was made by the enemy, when the Sixteenth were engaged.

The enemy had a custom of sending a strong patrol almost every night to Arrada; on the 19th of February, thirty men of the Sixteenth Light Dragoons and First German Hussars, under Cornet Strenuwitz, formed an ambuscade near Ferragoas, but waited two days without seeing the French detachment. A small patrol was sent up to the enemy's piquet at Alcanhede, and on retiring it was pursued by an officer and twenty French foot, and an officer and twenty dragoons. The enemy, coming within reach of the ambuscade, were charged with distinguished gallantry; the officer, and the whole of the infantry, were taken or cut down; the officer proved to be one of General Clausel's *aides-de-camp*; three of the dragoons were made prisoners, several sabred, and the remainder escaped by dispersing.

On the 5th of March the French Army retreated from Santarem, and the Sixteenth moved forward in pursuit. Lieutenant Richard Weyland commanded a detachment of the regiment in observation near Leyria, where, on the morning of the 9th of March, he made a party of thirty French dragoons prisoners. He followed the enemy from Leyria, and arrived at the table-land in front of Pombal, in time to join the German hussars in an attack upon the French cavalry, who were broken, and some prisoners were taken.

The enemy was driven from Pombal on the 12th of March; and, on the evening of the same day, his rear-guard was dislodged from a position at Redinha. The regiment skirmished with the enemy, and supported the infantry, in the action of the 14th of March; also in the action at Foz d'Aronce, on the 15th of March, when the enemy was driven into the River Ceira, and many men were drowned.

On the 26th of March, a patrol of the Sixteenth under Lieutenant William Persse, and a patrol of the Royal Dragoons under Lieutenant Foster, attacked a detachment of French cavalry between Alverca and Guardia, with signal gallantry; killed and wounded several, and took the officer and thirty-seven men prisoners. In his public despatch. Lord Wellington designated this a "gallant action;" and the conduct of Lieutenant Persse of the Sixteenth was applauded.

The cavalry and light troops continued to hover round and assail the enemy's rear; the Sixteenth were become conspicuous for their daring and success; and on the 29th of March they formed part of the force which drove the enemy from Guardo, back upon Sabugal, on which occasion Sergeants Baxter and Greaves, being at the head of a few men, greatly distinguished themselves, charging the enemy on two separate occasions, and taking many prisoners.

Some sharp fighting took place at Sabugal on the 3rd of April; the French divisions were driven from thence, and the brigade of which the Sixteenth formed part, took a quantity of baggage; Lieutenant William Lockhart of the regiment distinguished himself on this occasion.

Advancing towards Fort Conception, on the 7th of April, to the support of a corps of Portuguese militia under Colonel Trant, the Sixteenth, the Royal Dragoons, and a troop of artillery, came suddenly upon a large body of French infantry, which was attacked, when about three hundred of the enemy were killed, wounded, and taken prisoners. A squadron of the Sixteenth, led by Captain Murray, charged the French rear-guard, which had formed square, cut many men down, and took one officer and fifty-six soldiers prisoners.

Having chased the French Army over the frontiers of Portugal, the British blockaded Almeida; and the Sixteenth Light Dragoons went into quarters of refreshment, the horses being exhausted by continual marches and skirmishing. Marshal Massena reinforced and re-organized his discomfited army, and advanced to relieve Almeida, when the regiment left its cantonments and once more confronted the enemy in the vicinity of Fuentes d'Onor, where some sharp fighting took place on the 3rd and 5th of May, in which the Sixteenth took part, and the enemy was repulsed and forced to retire back into Spain.

The regiment had one horse killed on the 3rd, and on the 5th, Lieutenant Blake, seven rank and file, and four horses killed; Lieutenant Weyland, sixteen rank and file, and five horses wounded; Captain Belli and one sergeant taken prisoners. The commanding officer, Lieut.-Colonel Clement Archer, received a gold medal, and the gallant conduct of the officers and soldiers was subsequently rewarded with the honour of bearing the word "Fuentes d'Onor" on the guidons and appointments.

After this repulse of the enemy, the Sixteenth were allowed a short period of repose in cantonments among the Portuguese peasantry; they were formed in brigade with the Fourteenth Light Dragoons under Major-General Anson, and were reviewed by Lord Wellington on the 19th of July.

In the autumn the allied army blockaded Ciudad Rodrigo, and the French troops advanced to relieve that fortress. The Sixteenth were

16TH LIGHT DRAGOONS; ENEMY SIGHTED.

posted at Espejo, on the Lower Azava, with advanced posts at Carpio and Marialva. Soon after daybreak, on the 25th of September, fourteen squadrons of the Imperial Guards drove the outposts from Carpio, across the Azava, and the Lancers of Berg, crossing that river in pursuit, were charged by two squadrons of the Sixteenth and a squadron of the Fourteenth Light Dragoons, and driven back. The enemy attempted to rally and to return, but they were checked by the light infantry posted in a wood, and were driven across the river by the cavalry. The regiment afterwards fell back, and the army was eventually concentrated behind Soito. The conduct of the Sixteenth, on this occasion, excited admiration; and the behaviour of Captain James Hay, and of Captain (Brevet-Major) the Honourable Edward Charles Cocks, was commended in the public despatches.

A favourable opportunity occurring, the British troops moved forward in the depth of winter and besieged Ciudad Rodrigo, the Sixteenth forming part of the covering army, and this important fortress was wrested from the enemy in January, 1812.

From the Agueda the regiment proceeded by easy stages to the Alentejo, and crossing the Guadiana River, penetrated into Spanish Estremadura, to join the covering army during the siege of Badajoz. Marshal Soult assembled a numerous body of troops and advanced to raise the siege, when the covering army fell back, and while the French Army was advancing in haste to fight for Badajoz, this fortress was, by a mighty effort, captured by storm during the night of the 6th of April. The French marshal, confounded by this sudden stroke, faced about and retired towards the frontiers of Andalusia.

The Sixteenth regiment of Light Dragoons was one of the corps which followed the retiring enemy, and during the night of the 10th of April, it marched from Villa Franca upon Usagre, to take part in cutting off a body of French cavalry encamped between Villa Garcia and Usagre. The enemy, however, fell back upon Llerena, and formed for battle behind the junction of the Benvenida road. The opposing horsemen mustered about nineteen hundred sabres on each side; but the British soon decided the action, by charging the enemy in front and flank with such resolution, that he was instantly broken and chased from the ground with the loss of many officers and soldiers.

After charging the French squadrons in front, the Sixteenth pursued the enemy a considerable distance and took many prisoners. Captain the Honourable Edward Charles Cocks signalising himself in a particular manner.

★★★★★★

Captain the Honourable Edward Charles Cocks, (eldest son of the Earl Somers) whose deeds of gallantry are recorded in this history, was promoted from the Sixteenth Light Dragoons, by purchase, to a majority in the Seventy-Ninth Regiment, in February, 1812, and was killed at Burgos on the 8th of October, 1812.

> The enemy made two sorties on the head of the sap, between the exterior and interior lines of the castle of Burgos, in both of which they materially injured our works, and we suffered some loss. In the last, at three on the morning of the 8th, we had the misfortune to lose the Honourable Major Cocks, of the Seventy-Ninth, who was field-officer of the trenches, and was killed in the act of rallying the troops who had been driven in. I have frequently had occasion to draw your Lordship's attention to the conduct of Major Cocks, and in one instance, very recently, in the attack of the horn work of the castle of Burgos, and I consider his loss as one of the greatest importance to this army and to His Majesty's service.— *Lord Wellington's despatch*, dated 11th October, 1812.

★★★★★★

The regiment was commanded, on this occasion, by Captain George Home Murray, whose conduct was commended in the public despatch of Lieut.-General Sir Stapleton Cotton, who stated:—

> I cannot say too much in praise of the gallantry and regularity of the four regiments (Fifth Dragoon Guards, Twelfth, Fourteenth and Sixteenth Light Dragoons,) which attacked and pursued the enemy; nor could anything have exceeded the steadiness and good discipline displayed by the Third and Fourth Dragoons who supported them.

The loss of the regiment, in consequence of the sudden and spirited manner in which the attack was made, was only one horse killed; one man and two horses wounded.

Leaving Estremadura, the regiment marched to Beira, and the French troops which had penetrated that province under Marshal Marmont, withdrew into Spain.

The regiment was reviewed by Lord Wellington on the 12th of June, and on the following day it advanced upon Salamanca; from whence the French withdrew, and the allied army took up a position in the mountains of St. Christoval during the siege of the forts. Marshal Marmont put his army in motion, but being unable to save the forts, he fell back beyond the Douro, and the British Army advanced to the opposite bank of the river.

Having obtained reinforcements, the French commander suddenly crossed the Douro in the middle of July, when the allied army retired; but Lord Wellington ordered the light division, and Major-General Anson's brigade of cavalry, to halt on the Trabancas at Castrejon. On the morning of the 18th of July, the enemy appeared in force, and some sharp fighting took place, in which the Sixteenth were hotly engaged, and had three men and five horses killed; Lieutenant Baker, eight rank and file, and two horses wounded; three men and four horses missing.

Lord Wellington, having arrived at Castrejon, ordered the troops to retire behind the Guarena River; a series of movements followed in which the commanders of both armies showed great abilities; the Sixteenth Light Dragoons took part in covering the operations, and, finally, the British were once more formed in position in the mountains near Salamanca. On the 22nd of July, the French marshal manoeuvred to gain the Ciudad Rodrigo road, and Lord Wellington, watching the opposing army from one of the rocks called Arapiles, saw his adversary's left wing separated from his centre, and instantly seizing the opportunity which this faulty movement offered, he ordered the British divisions forward, and the battle commenced.

The Sixteenth Light Dragoons, with the other regiments of Major-General Anson's brigade, formed on the right of the sixth and seventh divisions, and afterwards advanced on the left of the third division when it made its brilliant and successful attack on the enemy's left wing. Galloping forward, the regiment flanked Major-General Le Marchant's brigade of heavy cavalry in its spirited charge upon the French infantry. The rapid advance of the cavalry upon a light soil, with a strong breeze at their back, soon enveloped them in a cloud of dust; their charge was, however, successful, and two thousand prisoners were taken.

The Sixteenth continued to advance, and, after passing through a wood, arrived at some ploughed fields, where the dust was so great, they could see nothing, and the brigade halted. When the dust cleared, the regiment retired a short distance to be out of the range of the fire of a large body of infantry and artillery in its front. The battle con-

16TH LIGHT DRAGOON ON PATROL.

tinued to rage; for a short period, the victorious career of the British was checked; but, after a desperate effort, the changing current of the fight once more flowed in favour of the allied army, and the French were driven from the field with severe loss. Captain George Home Murray commanded the regiment on this occasion, and was rewarded with a gold medal; and the royal authority was afterwards given for the Sixteenth to bear the word "Salamanca" on their guidons and appointments, in commemoration of their conduct on this occasion.

Moving forward in pursuit of the enemy, on the following day, the Sixteenth, and four other regiments, overtook the French rear-guard, at a small stream, at the foot of a height, near the village of La Serna; the five regiments charged; the French cavalry fled before the British horsemen, and the First and Second German Dragoons broke a square of infantry and made many prisoners; the Sixteenth charged, on this occasion, with great gallantry.

Continuing to form part of the advance-guard in the pursuit of the broken remains of the French army, the regiment arrived, on the 31st of July, at the ancient city of Valladolid, where a quantity of cannon and military stores was captured.

At Valladolid the pursuit was discontinued, and the Marquis of Wellington undertook a march of one hundred miles to Madrid, with the main body of the army, leaving the Sixteenth and several other corps, on the Douro. The brigade occupied extensive cantonments; but in the middle of August, a French force under General Clausel advanced down the Pisuerga stream, and the brigade was concentrated at Tudela, a small town on the Douro five miles from Valladolid, where above twenty thousand French troops had arrived on the 18th of August. On that day the brigade was attacked by very superior numbers, and after some fighting, it fell back behind the Douro, and occupied quarters along the bank of that river from Tudela to a station opposite to Valladolid.

About this period Sergeant-Major Blood, whose conduct on former occasions reflected credit on the regiment, returned from an incursion, in which he had penetrated to the neighbourhood of Astorga, in the rear of the French Army, and the Marquis of Wellington rewarded the zeal and address which the sergeant-major had evinced on this service, with a donation of a hundred dollars, and offered to recommend him for a commission.

The army returning from Madrid, the Sixteenth crossed the Douro and advanced upon Valladolid on the 6th of September; the French retreating with the loss of a piquet, which was captured by the Eleventh Dragoons.

As the enemy retreated up the beautiful Pisuerga and Arlanzan valleys, which were carefully cultivated and filled to repletion with corn, wine, and oil, the Sixteenth were at the head of the allied army, which followed the French; day after day the opposing legions manoeuvred, the French offering battle in strong positions, and the allies turning them by flank movements; repeated rencounters took place between the outposts, and at Torquemado, the piquets were attacked on the 13th of September, when a squadron of the Sixteenth, under Captain Buchanan, distinguished itself, making many prisoners. At length the army arrived at Burgos; the Sixteenth passed the Arlanzan River below the town, on the 19th of September, and the siege of the castle was commenced.

The regiment, commanded by Lieut.-Colonel Hay, covered the siege of Burgos Castle, furnishing outposts at Monasterio, sixteen miles in advance of Burgos. A numerous French Army, under General Souham, advanced to force the allies to raise the siege, and on the 13th of October the outposts were attacked. Captain Persse of the Sixteenth was twice forced from the bridge beyond Monasterio, and twice recovered it in the most gallant manner, and Colonel F. Ponsonby brought forward the reserves. Captain Persse and several men of the regiment were wounded. This demonstration was followed by others; the outposts fell back on the 19th of October, and during the night of the 21st, the British raised the siege and retired; the Sixteenth taking part in covering the movement.

On the 23rd of October the infantry crossed the Pisuerga River. The French attacked the rear-guard under Lieut.-General Sir Stapleton Cotton, and drove the piquets from the bridge of Baniel; the British horsemen rallied upon their reserves, and gained the Hormaza stream, where they disputed the ground for some time, and Captain Persse led a squadron of the Sixteenth to the charge, against very superior numbers, with a degree of valour and resolution seldom witnessed, which excited great admiration. Eventually, the British withdrew behind Cellada del Camino, and took post on a large plain. Major-General Anson's brigade formed the rear-guard, and after some severe fighting between the Eleventh Light Dragoons and the French cavalry, the brigade fell back, covered by the Sixteenth.

As the regiment was retiring, a multitude of Spanish irregulars came rushing from the hills, upon its flank, pursued by a crowd of

French hussars, at the same moment it was charged in front by a large body of dragoons. Thus attacked, the regiment sustained a serious loss; its commanding officer, Lieut.-Colonel Pelly, who joined on the preceding day, had his horse killed under him, was wounded, and taken prisoner. The regiment retired by the bridge of Venta de Pozo; the enemy's squadrons, pressing forward in pursuit, came within the range of some British infantry and artillery, when a tempest of bullets emptied the French saddles by scores, and the survivors drew off to the hills.

Two sergeants, six rank and file, and thirty-eight horses, of the Sixteenth, were killed on this occasion; Lieutenant Lockhart died of his wounds; Captain Murray, four sergeants, thirty-five rank and file, and twenty-four horses wounded; Lieut.-Colonel Pelly, Lieutenant Baker, one sergeant, ten rank and file, and five horses missing: Lieutenant Beauchamp had two horses killed under him. Sergeant-Majors Blood, Baxter, and Grindrod, distinguished themselves in this day's fighting.

Continuing to take part in covering the retreat to Salamanca, the regiment underwent much fatigue and privation, and in the retreat from thence to the Agueda, incessant rains, with a deficiency of provision for the soldiers, and of forage for the horses, rendered the sufferings of the army severe beyond what had been experienced in the preceding campaigns.

During the winter the regiment occupied quarters at Aveiro, thirty-three miles from Oporto; and it received one thousand and seventeen dollars—its share of the produce of horses captured from the enemy.

Moving forward from its winter quarters, the regiment crossed the Douro, in May, 1813, and penetrating the Tras-os-Montes, traversed those mountainous regions to the banks of the Esla, which river was passed towards the end of May; the French abandoning the line of the Douro and falling back.

A series of retrograde movements brought the French Army to the vicinity of Burgos; the British pressing forward, the French blew up Burgos castle and withdrew behind the Ebro. Moving towards the sources of this celebrated stream, the British commander poured his columns through deep narrow valleys and rugged defiles, traversed wild regions heretofore deemed impracticable for an army, and turning the French position on the Ebro, forced them back into the valley of Vittoria, where a general engagement was fought on the 21st of June.

The Sixteenth were attached to the troops under Lieut.-General

Sir Thomas Graham, who attacked the enemy's right wing and drove them from their position above Abechuco. The allied army succeeded at every part of the field; the French were overthrown, their artillery and baggage captured, and their numerous legions forced to make a precipitate flight to the Pyrenean mountains.

The Sixteenth supported the infantry during the action, and took part in forcing the enemy from the field. Their loss was seven men and eleven horses killed; Lieutenant Arnold, Adjutant Barra, two sergeants, ten rank and file, and eleven horses wounded: Lieutenant Thelluson of the Eleventh Light Dragoons, attached to the Sixteenth, was killed, Lieut.-Colonel Hay, commanding the regiment, was rewarded with a gold medal, and the royal authority was afterwards given for the word "Vittoria" to be inscribed on its guidons and appointments, to commemorate its gallant bearing on this occasion.

From Vittoria the regiment was detached, under Lieut.-General Sir Thomas Graham, by the pass of Adrian, to the district of Guipuscoa in the province of Biscay, and arrived, on the evening of the 24th of June, at the vicinity of Villa Franca, at the moment when the rear-guard of General Foy's division, which was escorting a valuable convoy towards France, was entering the town. The enemy took up a strong position; some fighting occurred; and the British having recourse to flank operations, the French retreated to Tolosa, where they again offered battle, and were driven from thence with the loss of four hundred men; but the convoy entered France in safety.

In the beginning of July, Sir Thomas Graham invested St Sebastian, and the Sixteenth Light Dragoons were attached to the troops employed in the siege of this fortress. When Marshal Soult advanced to relieve Pampeluna, which was blockaded by the allied army, the regiment communicated with the centre divisions through the mountain passes. The enemy having been repulsed, the siege was resumed, and the regiment covered this operation until the surrender of the castle of St. Sebastian, in the early part of September.

After the capture of St. Sebastian, the regiment advanced to the confines of Spain, and it was at the passage of the Bidassoa on the 7th of October, but did not sustain any loss.

To arrest the torrent of invasion which menaced France, Marshal Soult took up a position on the Nivelle River, which he fortified with labour and art; but on the morning of the 10th of November, as the sun arose in splendour, and the rays of light gleamed upon the Pyrenean mountains, ninety thousand combatants, accompanied by ninety-five pieces of artillery, rushed to battle, and breaking through the barrier constructed by the French commander, carried their conquering arms into the plains of France. The Sixteenth Light Dragoons supported the infantry; as they approached St. Jean de Luz, the bridge was on fire, when Sergeant Maloney led the advance-guard through the flames at a gallop dispersed the incendiaries, and partly saved the bridge from destruction.

Continuing its career of victory, the allied army passed the River Nive, and gained advantages in action on the 9th, 10th, 11th, and 12th of December, in which the Sixteenth took part, and distinguished themselves. Lieut.-Colonel Hay was rewarded with a medal, and the word "Nive" was afterwards added to the inscriptions authorised to be borne on the guidons and appointments. The regiment had four horses killed; Captain Persse, Lieutenant Nepean, one trumpeter, seven rank and file, and six horses wounded.

In the second week of February, 1814, the enemy's left wing was menaced to draw the enemy's attention to that quarter, while the passage of the River Adour was effected below Bayonne, the Sixteenth being attached to the troops selected to effect the passage of the river. On the night of the 22nd of February, a body of troops moved towards the Adour, and at daylight on the following morning they approached the bank, when the British artillery compelled the French flotilla, and a sloop of war, to retire up the river.

A few men passed the stream in a boat, and forced the French piquet to retire; a raft was formed, a hawser stretched across, and by the evening of the following day, the first division of infantry and some cavalry were on the right bank: on the 26th of February, a floating bridge was constructed, and on the 27th the town was blockaded. The Sixteenth forming part of the force which was stationed before Bayonne, they were prevented sharing in the other operations of the army. In April hostilities terminated with the abdication of Buonaparte, and the restoration of the Bourbon family to the throne of France.

Thus ended a war in which British skill and British valour, being exerted for the promotion of the well-being of mankind, had delivered the inhabitants of Spain and Portugal from the power of a chief who sought to rule them with Asiatic despotism; a war in which the Sixteenth, the Queen's regiment of Light Dragoons, had evinced intrepidity and firmness in action, and regularity in quarters: these qualities were rewarded with the royal authority to display the word "Peninsula" on its guidons and appointments.

BATTLE OF WATERLOO
at 5 min. past 8 o'clock, p.m.
Scale ⅛ ¼ ½ Mile.
English.
Prussians.
French.

Mont St. Jean · Le Voye · RODER · MERLE · BYLANDT · LÜTZOW · LÜTZOW · PACK · BESKOW · KEMPT · BEST · ALIX · Papelotte · La Haye · MARCOGNET · STEINMETZ · Smohain · CALIX · ALIX · DONZELOT · MARCOGNET · Frischermont · IMPERIAL GUARD · SUBERVIE · To Lasne and St. Lambert · elle Alliance · JEANNIN · RIDLEY & SOWA · Domon · TRÜMER · SCHULDBURG · Hanotelet · RYSSEL · HILLER & TIPPELSKIRCHEN · KRAFFT · To Ajrien · VDOW · WALZDORF · ANCHENOIT · From Maison du Roi · Wood of Virere · Lasne Stream · Wood of Hubermont

Charge of the 16th Light Dragoons at Waterloo.

★★★★★★

The following non-commissioned officers and soldiers of the regiment particularly distinguished themselves during this war:—*Sergeant-Majors* Blood, Baxter, Drawbridge, Greaves, Maloney, Kearney, Blythe, Ashworth; *Sergeants* Lincoln, Collins, Jolly, Lakin; *Corporals* Cox, Yates; *Privates* Arthur, Hurst, Fitzpatrick, Weedon, Mitchell, Daley, Castans, Bulpot, Pemberton.

★★★★★★

After reposing a short period in cantonments, the regiment commenced its march from Bayonne to Calais, which it accomplished in five weeks, and embarked for England in July; having sustained a loss of three hundred and nine men, and fourteen hundred and sixteen horses, during the six campaigns it had served in Portugal, Spain, and France.

After its arrival in England, the regiment was stationed at Deal and Hounslow, and in February, 1815, it was ordered to London, to aid in suppressing the riots, which took place on the introduction into parliament of a bill, to regulate the importation of grain. The public excitement having subsided, the regiment marched into Kent, the headquarters being at Canterbury.

In the meantime, Napoleon Buonaparte had invaded, with a few followers, the kingdom from which he had been exiled. The armies of France instantly forsook their sovereign, and elevated the invader to the throne of that kingdom. Against Buonaparte and his adherents, the nations of Europe declared war, and while the din of hostile preparation resounded in every quarter, three, squadrons of the Sixteenth Light Dragoons embarked for Flanders, under the command of Lieut.-Colonel James Hay: having landed at Ostend, they marched to the banks of the Dender, where they were formed in brigade with the Eleventh and Twelfth Light Dragoons, under the command of Major-General Sir John Vandeleur, the headquarters being at Denderwyndick.

They were reviewed, with the British cavalry, on the 29th of May, by Field-Marshal His Grace the Duke of Wellington, and Prince Blücher; and when Buonaparte suddenly passed the frontiers with his *armée d'élite*, and attacked the British and Prussian advance-posts, the regiment advanced upon Quatre Bras, and arriving at that post on the evening of the 16th of June, skirmished with the French cavalry, but was too late to take a decisive part in the action.

Having overthrown the Prussian Army at Ligny, Buonaparte turned the main body of his numerous bands against the British, who fell back on the 17th of June, from Quatre Bras to Waterloo; the Sixteenth taking part in covering the retrograde movement by the open country, and fording the little River Dyle, took their station on the left of the position at Waterloo, where they passed the night exposed to violent storms of wind and rain.

The morning of the memorable 18th of June arrived, and the French legions were seen crowding the high grounds in front of the allied army, and descending in dense columns to commence one of the most important battles recorded in history, a battle in which the destiny of millions was decided by the sword, and British valour shone forth with unparalleled lustre. The Sixteenth Light Dragoons were stationed on the left of the line, and witnessed the furious onsets of Napoleon's veterans repelled by British prowess. The heavy cavalry regiments under Major-General Sir William Ponsonby, having by a gallant charge broken several columns of French infantry, were afterwards seen retiring in some disorder before a large body of lancers, when Major-General Sir John Vandeleur moved his brigade to their relief, and charging the lancers, drove them back, making many of them prisoners.

The Sixteenth charged the lancers with the same gallantry which they had evinced in the Peninsular campaigns; and their commanding officer, Lieut.-Colonel Hay, being severely wounded, the command of the regiment devolved on Major Murray. After driving back the French cavalry, the regiment resumed its post on the left, where it remained until the evening, when it was relieved by the arrival of the Prussians to co-operate with the Anglo-Belgian Army, and moving to the right of the British position, had the honour to take a distinguished part in the general attack made on the French Army, which was overthrown, cut to pieces, and driven from the field with the loss of its cannon and baggage. In this charge the brigade was exposed to a battery, which was, however, speedily turned and captured; the brigade then charged, and broke, a square of infantry of the Imperial Guard, cutting down or making prisoners the whole.

Re-forming after this charge, the brigade was led at speed against another mass of French infantry, which was also broken and cut to pieces. The infantry was supported by a body of *cuirassiers*, and as the brigade advanced to charge these steel-clad warriors, they withdrew;—some of the French officers, taken prisoners, afterwards stated that these *cuirassiers* were covering the person of the Emperor. In these attacks the brigade took about three thousand prisoners. Darkness had enveloped the field of battle; the panic-struck fugitives were flying before the conquering sabres of the British dragoons in every direction, when a regiment of German dragoons, coming up in the rear of the Sixteenth, mistook them for French, and were preparing to attack them, but the error was discovered in time to prevent serious consequences. The regiment halted on the field of battle, surrounded by the ensanguined trophies of victory; its loss was Captain J. P. Buchanan, Cornet Alexander Hay, two sergeants, six rank and file, and thirty-five horses killed; Lieut.-Colonel James Hay; Captain Richard Weyland, Lieutenants William Osten, N. D. Crichton, two sergeants, sixteen rank and file, and twenty horses wounded.

The regiment was afterwards rewarded with the honour of bearing the word "Waterloo" on its guidons and appointments; every officer and soldier received a silver medal, and the privilege of reckoning two years' service for this day; and Lieut.-Colonel Hay and Major Murray were advanced to the dignity of Companions of the order of the Bath.

The following officers of the Sixteenth Light Dragoons received silver medals for the Battle of Waterloo.

Lieut.-Colonel James Hay.
Major G. H. Murray.
Captains.
John H. Belli (Bt. Major,) Clemt. Sweetenham, Richard Weyland, William Tomkinson, Charles King, J. Barra.
Lieutenants.
William Osten, T. Wheeler, F. Swinfin, George Baker, Richard Beauchamp, N. D. Crichton, E. B. Lloyd, William Napean, J. A. Richardson, John Luard, William Harris, C. T. Monkton, A. Macdowell.
Cornets.
William Beckwith, William Polhill, George Nugent, Alexander Hay.
Paymaster George Neyland.
Surgeon Isaac Robinson.
Assist. Surgeons J. McGr. Mallock, D. Murray.
Veterinary Surgeon John Jones.
Quartermaster John Harrison.

One of the non-commissioned officers killed at the Battle of Waterloo was Sergeant-Major Baxter, who so repeatedly distinguished himself in the Peninsula, and whose fall was much regretted.

From the field of battle, the regiment advanced upon Paris, which city surrendered to the allied armies: the French troops retiring be-

BRITISH LANCER UNIFORM 1820's.

hind the Loire. On the 3rd of July, the advance-guard of the Sixteenth was fired upon, a sergeant wounded, and a horse killed; but on the brigade trotting forward, a French officer advanced and apologised, attributing the occurrence to the irritated state of the French soldiers, in consequence of the abdication of Buonaparte and the surrender of Paris. The regiment was afterwards stationed at the beautiful village of Anieres; one regiment of the brigade bivouacking in the Champs Elysées in turns. After passing in review before the Emperors of Russia and Austria and the Kings of Prussia and France, on the 24th of July, the brigade marched into Normandy, the Sixteenth occupying cantonments at Aumal, &c.

Peace being restored, the regiment left France; it embarked at Calais in December, and landing at Dover, marched from thence to Romford, where it was reviewed by His Royal Highness the Duke of York, who made known the pleasure of His Royal Highness the Prince Regent, that the Sixteenth should lay aside their carbines, and be equipped as a corps of "Lancers;" the use of the lance, which had been discontinued by the English cavalry about two hundred years, being resumed at this period.

In the beginning of March, 1816, the regiment embarked at Bristol for Ireland; in April it took the Dublin duty, and was stationed in that city until June, 1818, when the headquarters were removed to Clonmel.

On the 21st of June, 1819, the Sixteenth Lancers embarked at Waterford for Bristol, where the headquarters were stationed, with detached troops at Radipole barracks, and in South Wales.

Six troops again proceeded to Ireland in 1821, leaving one squadron and the headquarters at Manchester.

Glossary of the Terms used in Major Lowe's Diary

(Contributed by Charles Radford)

Assafoetida - Plant of the parsley family used in Indian cooking.
Baboo - A Hindu gentleman—form of address corresponding to Mr.
Banian - Hindu trader, merchant, cashier or money changer.
Berkaandoss - Policeman.
Budgerow - A large and commodious but generally cumbrous and sluggish boat for journeys on the Ganges.
Chattar - Umbrella.
Chillum - Part of a *hookah* that contains the tobacco or 'other substance' being smoked.
Chobdar - Mace bearer.
Chokedar - Night watchman.
Choprasseh - A government messenger in the Britain Raj.
Chowrie - Fly-whisk used to drive off flies, often made from the tail of a Yak!
Coss - Unit of land distance varying between 1 to 3 miles.
Darogah - Chief officer.
Daundies - Boatmen.
Dawk - Transportation by a relay of people or horses.
Dhoolie - Simple litter used to transport sick or wounded persons.
Diwan-i-Khas - Council Chamber.
Dootee - Cloth wrapped around man's waist, passing through the limbs and fastening at the back.
Embonpoint - Plumpness.
Fakir - Indian religious ascetic who lives solely on alms.
Ghaut - Wide set of steps descending to a river.
Goole - Group of men.
Hakri (Hackerie) - Cart.
Haram zaadar - Bad people.
Havildar - NCO in the Indian Army equivalent to sergeant.
Hukka, (Hookar) - Pipe (smoking).

Jagheer – Holding (of land/property).

Jampaan – Closed sedan chair for one person.

Khansama – House steward or butler.

Kitmagar – Male servant waiting at table.

Kurnaut – Canvas enclosure, wall of a tent.

Lac – One hundred thousand.

Lalla Rookh – Oriental romance by Thomas Moore, 1817.

Lattee – Staff or stick.

Mahout – Elephant driver or keeper.

Maund – Unit of weight.

Minar – Tower.

Musnud – Cushioned seat used as a throne by Indian princes

Nawab – Honorific title bestowed by reigning Mughal Emperor on semi-autonomous rulers in their states.

Nautch – 'Dancing' as in girl or woman.

Nylgai – Large Indian antelope.

Palanquin – Sedan chair.

Pashwah – Minister.

Paunchway – Dinghy.

Pice – Small change.

Pilau – Cooked in the native fashion.

Pitarah – Large covered basket.

Qui Hi – Persons who had become indolent. Aware that a servant would be perpetually nearby, they would call out '*Qui Hi*' (Is any one there?)

Rasais – 'Scent' as in perfume.

Ryot – Someone who had acquired the right to hold land for the purpose of cultivation.

Saump wallah – Fellow with snakes.

Sepoy – Soldier in the Indian Army equivalent to Private/Trooper.

Seraglio – The women's apartments in a Muslim palace.

Sirdar – Headman

Sowar – Soldier on horseback in the Native Army.

Syce – Groom, stable lad.

Tamaushau – Fun or play.

Tazziah – Replica of Muslim shrine which is assembled during the month of Muharram.

Tiffin – Snack or light meal.

Vakeel – Lawyer.

Zenana – Part of the house reserved for the women.

The Diary of an Officer of the 16th Lancers Part One—Leaving Home

Arthur C. Lowe

LEAVING HOME

On Monday night, the 10th June 1822, the baggage of four troops of the 16th Lancers, composing the left wing, quitted Romford. On the 12th at 2 o'clock a.m., the four left troops marched, and embarked at Tilbury Fort on board the *General Hewitt* on the same day. The headquarters and four right troops marched under the command of Major Persse on the 14th, at 2 o'clock a.m., arrived at Tilbury at 9, and were conveyed in a lighter to the H. C. ship the *Marchioness of Ely,* moored about two miles up the river. On going on board I found Sir John Browne who overpowered me with civil professions devoid of meaning, and Col. Grant, an old brother officer in the 18th Hussars. Between 11 and 12 o'clock turned into the great cabin amid a scene of the greatest confusion; my companions in it were Armstrong, Douglas, Collins, Havelock, Pratt, Blood, and Drs. Robinson and Murray.

The following day we dropped down the river and anchored in the Lower Hope; the ship's company were here selected and paid, and, to do them justice, I never saw a worse-looking set of fellows. Old Die, the boatswain, remarked that if he had been sent through hell with a small toothcomb, he could not have picked up a more lousy crew. Sunday, the 16th June, we dropped further down the river and anchored nearly opposite to Southend. The pilot reminded me of the Welshman in the younger days of Mr. Mathews, "Am I any thinner do you think?"

On the 17th June, weighed at 4 o'clock a.m., and anchored at 6 at

The *Marchioness of Ely.*

the mouth of the river. On the 18th got under weigh at 1 a.m., and anchored off Deal, from whence I received a welcome letter from my mother. Left our anchorage on the 19th at 2 p.m., and passed Dover at 6.

June 20.—The wind freshened, and was quite fair; lat. 50° 35' north. Our pilot now left us, and the arrangements with regard to our sitting at table were made; the number of passengers on board was so great that Kay, our captain, could not stow us all away at the cuddy table, so a party of ten was formed who used to dine in his cabin. I belonged to this set; and if we fared worse as to our eating, we made amends for it by real good humour and good fellowship. I rather like, on the whole, the appearance of the companions who I have so long to be imprisoned with. Sir Harry Darrell is a very gentlemanly old man, rather weak, and already bores you about his dear Lady Darrell, who he has left at St. Omer to educate his family. Parkes is a silent and reserved man; what he does say is to the purpose; I shall be disappointed if he does not prove a trump; his wife is an eminently beautiful woman, and appears lively and fascinating in her manners.

Smallpage, who is a lieutenant in the Company's Cavalry, is exactly the reverse of Parkes, talkative and blustering; he wishes to be thought equally well versed in the art of pugilism and dog-fighting as in the abstruse sciences of ethics and mathematics: but above all he tries to impress you with the idea of his having been quite in the first flight in Yorkshire. Mrs. Smallpage, though not pretty, is particularly pleasing in her appearance; her countenance is expressive of mildness, good humour and amiability; in her manners she is quiet, good-natured and thoroughly unassuming; unless I very much mistake the Lieutenant has the best of the bargain. Miss Garrett (who, in a way I cannot understand, comes out under the protection of Hilton and his wife, a proud, painted, scraggy Scotch woman) is a coarse, silly young woman, with an affectation of romance about her: her companion, Miss Rowe, is a half-caste, and quite harmless.

The remainder of our female society is formed in the regiment; the leader of the squadron is Mrs. Persse, who I have already ascertained to be the daughter of Judge Moore; I don't like her. The only thing I have been able to squeeze out of little Mrs. Enderby, who is also an Irishwoman, is that she is related to, and was occasionally on a visit to, an old woman of the name of Lady Roche, who resided in Dublin; she is more like a dry lemon than anything that occurs to me; but, notwithstanding this, there is a something about her that promises well. Mrs. Crossley is rather a formal well-behaved person; she was companion to Miss Halulet, and seems proud of telling you she is her relation, and was her *chaperon*. My brother officers I like extremely, but there is in Greville's appearance that makes me distrust him, and I don't think Collins will prove himself worthy of dependence. We have on board 56,000 gallons of water, 44 dozen of different kinds of poultry, 56 pigs, and 70 sheep.

June 21.—Wind fresh and fair; passed the Straits at 10 a.m., and saw the last of England at 11; lat. 49° 5' north.

June 22.—The wind fell, and the day was so cloudy that no observation could be taken. Saw a Danish brig. During the night it was very squally,—sprang our foretop-mast; as the boatswain and several of the crew were drunk, there was some difficulty in taking in canvass.

June 23.—Lat. 47° 45' north, wind became foul.

June 24.—Lat. 46° 36' north, wind fell, and we were becalmed; spoke a Danish brig from Oporto. Captain Kay, wishing to send letters by her, lowered a boat; but the Dane was particularly active in lowering his, and coming on board of us, The face of the chief mate, when he first stepped on our quarter-deck, was singularly expressive of fear; he had taken us for a Turkish frigate, and was by no means satisfied with his fate, till he assured himself of the mistake. He took our letters and sent us a present of a few limes. In the evening several small birds, Mother Carey's chickens, (Storm Petrels), were flying round the ship; this little bird is so like, that I mistook it for the swallow.

June 25.—Lat. 46° 22' north, becalmed. Several of the party sick. Poor Mrs. Persse suffered extremely, so much so that she frequently fainted, but she bore up against it heroically. Mrs. Parkes has the most exquisitely formed leg and foot I ever saw. Harris looked woefully dismal, and Collins wished he had never been born. As we were going to breakfast, a small shark was seen playing about the bows. After dinner we went out in the jolly boat. Luard, Harris, Armstrong, and I rowed. Persse, Havelock, and Douglas were of the party. Harris shot one of Mother Carey's chickens.

June 26.—Lat. 45° 47' north, wind freshened from the north-west at 12 a.m.; spoke an English schooner bound from Lyons to Elsinore. Just before dinner we spied a vessel bearing down upon us; she proved to be a South American privateer; when she perceived our strength, she crowded all her canvass and steered another course.

June 27.—Lat. 43° 57' north. By the log, we had gone 147 miles; saw a whale in the afternoon, and danced in the evening. From some mismanagement in Miss Garrett's dress, when advancing in the Ete, she dropped her flannel petticoat on deck,—a little laughter was caused by the accident; but she was so amazingly quick in picking it up, running into her cabin and concealing it, and again joining the quadrille, that some lost the fun.

June 28.—Lat. 42° 19' north, long. 11°2' wind fresh and air.

June 29.—Lat. 39° 41' north, 189 miles. Gave Havelock at dinner £90, for which he is to give me £1 a day till we anchor at Saugor,

June 30.—Lat, 36° 35' north, 212 miles. Wind quite fair.

July 1.—Lat. 32° 28' north, 186 miles. Passed Santo Porto at 4 p.m. The island is very rocky, and from its elevation has a very bold appearance; having got under its lee we becalmed during the night.

July 2.—Lat. 32° 37' north, 81 miles; becalmed in view of Madeira. This island has a bold and grand appearance. At 4 p.m. we were within three leagues of Funchall; we fired two guns, but no boat would put off. At night we burned blue lights, but with no better success. Although three vessels were in sight, we could hold no communication with the shore. I regretted the day had been so hazy, that I could not get as good a view of Madeira as I wished. At 12 p.m. Kay gave orders to stand out to sea.

July 3.—Lat. 31° 59' north; indifferent observation; 66 miles. At 5 a.m. a breeze sprung up, and by breakfast-time we were again out of sight of land; the ship's company were busily employed in getting up a new foretop-mast.

July 4.—Lat. 29° 28' north, 142 miles, therm. 74°. Saw land at 2 p.m., and at 5 passed within a league of Palma, one of the Canary Islands; its appearance is much the same as that of Santo Porto—high, bold, and rocky.

July 5.—Lat. 27° 15' north, 169 miles, therm. 75°. I amused myself the greater part of the morning, sparring, with Smallpage who is a difficult man to get at.

July 6.—Lat. 24° 54' north, long. 18° 58' west; 164 miles, therm. 80°.

July 7.—Lat. 23° 1' north, long. 20° 10' west; 183 miles, therm. 76°. Crossed the Tropic of Cancer.

July 8.—Lat.,20° 12' north, long. 21° 35' west; 125 miles, therm. 76°. Very sultry.

July 9.—Lat. 19° 6' north, long. 23° 1' west; 88 miles, therm. 86°. Wind very light.

July 10.—Lat. 18° 22' north, long. 24° 3' west; 56 miles, therm. 82°.

July 11.—Lat. 17° 37' north, long. 25° 8' west; 62 miles, therm. 78°. Passed St. Antonis, one of the Cape de Verde Islands, towards evening.

July 12.—Lat. 15° 37' north, long. 25° 8' west; 137 miles, therm. 81°. Spoke a Portuguese brig; a whale passed within a very short distance; a flying fish flew on board, it is smaller than a herring, and its wings or fins are five or six inches long.

July 13.—Lat. 14° 11' north, long. 25° 14' west; 73 miles, therm. 80°.

July 14.—Lat. 12° 13' north, long. 24° 17' west; 138 miles, therm. 81°.

July 15.—No observation; 51 miles, therm. 78°. A small shark, about 6 feet long, was caught astern; the moment he was landed the sailor hauled him forward to the forecastle; he was instantly cut up and almost eaten alive: a small piece was reserved for the cuddy table. I just tasted enough to convince me it was bad; the sailors cut the vertebrae of the backbone into rings, through which they fasten their neckcloth.

July 16.—No observation; 108 miles, therm. 82°.

July 17.—Lat. 9° 37' north, long. 20° 30' west; 102 miles, therm. 78°.

July 18.—Lat. 9° 15' north, long. 26° west; 55 miles, therm. 81°.

July 19.—No observation; 91 miles. Shoals of skip-jacks (the Bonito) passed ahead, leaping out of the water, for all the world as the sailors said, as if they were playing at leapfrog.

July 20.—Lat. 7° 31' north, long. 17° 14' west; 89 miles, therm. 86°.

July 21.—Lat. 7° 27' north, long. 18° 19' west; 107 miles, therm. 81°. Wind foul.

July 22.—Lat. 6° 56' north, long. 18° 31' west; 100 miles, therm. 78°. Spied a ship ahead. Kay fired a signal gun for her to bring to; as she did not obey it, he ordered a shot to be sent after her, on seeing which she instantly backed her topsails, and we soon came up with her; she proved to be the brig *Emma* of London, bound to Pernambuco: at sea the strongest man appears Justice of the Peace. I sent a letter to Tom by the *Emma*, dated from Madeira.

July 23.—No observation; 88 miles. Several Bonitos were pursuing the flying fish with inconceivable rapidity.

July 24.—Lat. 5° 37' north, long. 19° west; 105 miles. Parkes amused me by observing that it was singular his forehead should have broken out into a violent eruption, at the time he was married, and should not have subsided.

July 25.—Lat. 5° 15' north, long. 19° 30' west; 81 miles, therm. 78°.

July 26.—Lat. 4° 41' north, long. 20° 45' west; 94 miles, therm. 78°.

July 27.—Lat. 4° 36' north, long. 18° 5' west; 93 miles.

July 28. Lat. 4° 1' north, long. 16° 15' west; 89 miles therm. 78°.

July 29.—Lat. 2° 51' north, long. 16° 4' west; 86 miles, therm. 77°.

July 30.—Lat. 1° 18' north, long. 17° west; 82 miles, therm. 77°. Numbers of Bonitos around the ship pursuing the poor little flying fish.

July 31.—Lat. 0° 17' south, long. 18° 11' west; 93 miles, therm. 75°. At 9 o'clock a.m. Neptune hailed the ship, and was answered with all due form and respect of the captain, who gave him permission to come on board. At about 10 the procession commenced; the figures of the doctor, the coachman, the bear, and his leader were very characteristic. Neptune performed his part with some humour. On coming to the binnacle, the procession stopped, when His Majesty presented the captain with a couple of fowls; and after having sung a regular song for the occasion, the burden of which was:

> You, gentlemen and ladies, who come here to see the fun
> I hope that you will not forget to shove about the rum.

When this elegant production was finished, Neptune was drawn to the lee gangway, and amidst torrents of water discharged from the maintop, and from an engine concealed, between mid-ships and the forecastle, he commenced his interrogatories. Persse and his wife were the first trotted out, and were excused being shaved on account of the great esteem the great God Almighty, the great ruler of the seas, had for the 16th Lancers; we were each individually shewn up, and let off,

CROSSING THE LINE BY JOHN LUARD.

for the same reason, there being an understanding that we were all to book up a certain quantity of grog. The ship's company did not fare so well; some were severely shaved, and a few skulkers were operated upon with the no-grog razor, an instrument formed out of the iron hoop of a tub, having the edge teethed like a saw. Everybody was well wetted; buckets of water were shied about in all directions till we were tired of the fun, if fun it can be called.

The greatest good humour prevailed, and no one in the least degree lost their temper, unless it was little Mrs. Enderby, who was angry at her husband having been sluiced and alarmed for the consequences. But the captain richly deserved a wet skin; like an old sailor he climbed up to the mizzen-top, where he had buckets of water brought to him, and from whence he continued wetting everybody that came underneath with impunity, till Luard ran up the larboard shrouds, and Armstrong the starboard; and having caught the delinquent, he was brought on deck to receive the punishment which he merited. This happened to be Collier's birthday, and he kept it in due form. A large party met in the mate's cabin, and drank champagne, till 12 o'clock.

Harris, on leaving us, fell through the hatchway from the gun deck, and alighted on his head on the orlop, (lowest of three decks); in descending he caught hold of fat Crossley's leg. Crossley continued howling and kicking till he sent his shoe and Harris whirling to that infernal region, the orlop. Sperling almost destroying Wayland's cabin was capital. The whole day passed over pleasanter than any since I have been on board. Our bark was going forward from morning till night. A sailor caught a Bonito; the green on its back is particularly vivid; this fish might weigh 40 pounds, but was much smaller than most we saw, unless we were deceived by the water.

Aug. 1.—Lat. 1° 27' south, long. 19° 11' west; 86 miles, therm. 77°.

Aug. 2.—Lat. 1° 45' south, long. 26° 10' west; 82 miles, therm. 78°. A shark was caught, much the same size as the first that was taken, about 6 feet long; he was cut up alive and eaten almost as soon as he was dead. The moon was eclipsed at half-past 9, and was at its greatest obscurity at 20 minutes before 11. There was a difference about a cabin which Collins and I lost by our own dilatoriness; Luard wished to have exchanged his for the vacant one, and thought he had not been used handsomely in its being let to other officers. Greville contrived to get the cabin for Sperling, that he might have his own entirely for himself and Mrs. Tulley, Armstrong and Sperling get the cabin between them.

Tom wished me to take half, which I declined; we commence a friendship which I hope may last; we propose living together when we reach our destination at Cawnpore. Sir Harry Darrell fished up in a bucket some very beautiful insects, blue on the back, and white on the belly. Sir Harry caught what he said was a Nautilus; he gallantly presented this curiosity to Mrs. Persse. Several curious species of the blubber fish were taken during the day.

Aug. 3.—Lat. 3° 2' south, long. 20° 57' west; 86 miles.

Aug. 4.—Lat. 5° 5' south, long. 21° 50' west; 118 miles, therm. 76°.

Aug. 5.—Lat.7° 18' south, long. 23° 8' west; 135 miles.

Aug. 6.—Lat.9° 20' south, long. 24° 39' west; 134 miles, therm. 75°.

Aug, 7.—Lat. 11° 22' south, long. 25° 33' west; 137 miles.

Aug. 8.—Lat. 13° 16' south, long. 26° 27' west; 124 miles, therm. 75°.

Aug. 9.—Lat. 15° 30' south, long. 27° 22' west; 158 miles. Won a bet of £1 from Harris that Blood could not with one blow of a sabre cut off the head of a goose clean; though an excellent swordsman, Blood failed. For the last few days there has been a good deal of betting on the latitude, at the meeting on the poop at 12. Very good fun, everybody as shrewd as he is able; Neyland quite the essence of sharpness.

Aug. 10.—Lat. 18° 6' south, long. 27° 6' west; 169 miles, therm. 74°.

Aug. 11.—Lat. 20° 6' south, long, 26° 54' west; 101 miles, therm. 74°. At 11 we saw Martin Vas Rocks bearing S. S. W., and Trinidad bearing nearly due west. In the evening Kay lowered a boat for us, and we rowed round about the ship for an hour. Without injustice I may say I never saw a worse boat's crew than we mustered. The Martin Vas Rocks appeared six in number; the largest had the form of a castle, and two others of Martello towers.

Aug. 12.—Lat. 21° 7' south, long. 28° 7' west; 145 miles, therm. 74°. Not being quite well, I left the cuddy soon after the ladies, having resolved to abstain from wine. I lost a good deal of fun which arose from the speeches made by Sir Harry after having proposed the health of the king. In the evening extra grog was served out to the men. Sergeant-Major Drawbridge mounted the capstan; and after giving the health of the king, Colonel Newberry, and Captain Kay, he made us all laugh by giving us a final toast, a safe delivery to the *Marchioness of Ely.* When the cuddy, (small cabin), was shut a jovial party assembled on the poop, and smoked cigars and drank some whiskey-punch of Persse's, all the way from Lough Rea, till a late hour. I little regarded the good resolution I had formed at dinner.

Aug. 13.—Lat. 22° 47' south, long. 26° west; 138 miles, therm. 74°. Crossed the Tropic of Capricorn 8 p.m.

Aug. 14.—Lat. 25° 9' south, long. 20° 14' west; 217 miles. There must have been a mistake in the log.

Aug. 15.—Lat. 26° 40' south, long. —; 180 miles. Blowing very hard. At 9 a.m. the wind had increased to what I ignorantly fancied a gale; our mainsail was shivered into 50 rents; soon afterwards the mizzen-topsail, fore stay-sail, and flying jib shared the same fate, the wind soon abated. When we had got quite snug, I said to Kay, "It has been blowing quite a gale this morning" (who by-the-bye might have repeated Mr. Johnnes Knight's story of Genl. Genl.), but Kay answered, "Oh! dear, no; merely a strong puff." Coming Jack over a Landsman, this.

Aug. 16.—Lat. 27° 38' south, long. 18° 53' west; 131 miles, therm. 72°. Delightful weather.

Aug. 17.—Lat. 28° 33' south, long. 16° 26'west; 155 miles, therm. 66°.

Aug, 18.—Lat. 28° 40' south, long. 13° 37' west; 162 miles, therm. 66°.Young Biddell caught a Cape pigeon by entangling its wings on a string which hung astern. This bird is rather larger than the domestic pigeon, and resembles it in the shape of its head, which, as well as the neck, is of a dark dusky brown colour; the breast and belly are white; the wings and back are black and white-mottled. It could not rise from the deck when placed on it.

Aug. 19.—No observation could be taken; 135 miles, therm. 60°.

Aug. 20.—Lat. 26° 36' south, long. 9° 45' west; 112 miles.

Aug. 21.—Lat. 28° 26' south, long. 14° 46' west; 94 miles, therm. 65°.

Aug. 22.—Lat. 30° 35' south, long. 10° 42' west; 96 miles.

Aug. 23.—Lat. 32° south, long. 8° 42' west; 138 miles. At 10 o'clock spoke the *Nymph* of London bound to the Cape; as we were fearful least we should not touch there, the greatest bustle in the way of letter-writing took place. I wrote to Georgy.

ALBATROSS SHOOTING BY JOHN LUARD.

Aug. 24.—Lat. 32° 39' south, long. 4° 48' west; 199 miles, therm. 65°.

Aug. 25.—Rainy; dirty day; no observation; 201 miles, therm. 62°.

Aug. 26.—Lat. 32° 6' south, long. 3° 4' east; 187 miles, therm. 61°.

Aug. 27.—Lat. 32° 9' south, long. 4° 25' east; 37 miles, therm. 58°.

Aug. 28.—No observation; 16 miles. As we were becalmed, Kay lowered the jolly boat for us. Persse, Luard, Neville, Harris, Armstrong, and myself with two sailors formed the boat's crew. Persse killed an albatross which he would hibernicize into Ballytross; the albatross is a magnificent bird. This one measured from the tip of one wing to that of the other 9 feet and half. No Cape pigeons were killed. Several Cape hens, a bird larger than the pigeon, and black. Several blue birds, some of them exquisitely delicate, and a large black bird, which shewed capital fight before we could get him into the boat. We did not return to the ship till after dinner-time. Kay was beginning to get fidgety, a breeze having sprung up.

Aug. 29.—Lat. 33° 9' south, long. 7° 47' east; 124 miles, therm. 61°.

Aug. 30.—Lat. 34° 36' south, long. 12° 4' east; 200 miles, therm. 62°.

Aug. 31.—Lat. 35° 17' south, long. 16° 37' east; 136 miles, therm. 62°. In the beginning of the month Persse and Smallpage bet Millet and Persse £10 each that we should pass the Cape during August; yesterday the bets were off, or there would have been some difficulty in deciding them, as by reckoning we must have passed the longitude of the Cape as near as possible at 12 o'clock at night, we did not get a view of land.

Sept. 1.—Lat. 35° 43' south, long. 21° 2' east; 223 miles, therm. 64°.

Sept. 2.—Lat. 36° south, long. 23° 46' east; 140 miles, therm. 60°.

Sept. 3.—Lat. 36° 25' south, long. 27° 54' east; 231 miles, therm. 62°.

Sept. 4.—Lat. 36° 9' south, long. 32° 9' east; 220 miles, therm. 61°. Sergeant-Major Maloney's poor little child that had been ill nearly the whole of the voyage died, and was thrown over the sea gangway. Hilton hustled through the service.

Sept. 5.—Lat. 35° 20' south, long. 35° 30' east; by account 143 miles, therm. 63°. Blew hard.

Sept. 6.—Lat. 34° 22' south, long. 36° 57' east; 90 miles, therm. 64°.

Sept. 7.—Lat. 35° 39' south, long. 37° 18' east; 79 miles, therm. 65°.

Sept. 8.—Lat. 36°. 21' south, long. 40° 17' east; 141 miles, therm. 64°.

Sept. 9.—Lat. 36° 20' south, long. 44° 1' east; 143 miles, therm. 57°.

Sept. 10.—Lat. 36° 43' south, long, 45° 30' east; 71 miles, therm. 60°. During the morning we were becalmed. Kay lowered the jolly boat after breakfast. We killed amongst the party seven albatross, two gannetts, and several birds, the names of which we were unacquainted with. Returned to the ship by 12 o'clock. We had so many guns in the boat that we but narrowly escaped an accident. The albatross generally measured from tip to tip of the wing, 9 feet 8 inches to 9 feet 10 inches.

Sept. 11.—Lat. 37° 31' south, long. 48° 51' east; by dead reckoning 166 miles, therm. 61°.

Sept. 12.—Lat. 37° 27' south, long, 52° 33' east; 138 miles, therm. 60°.

Sept. 13.—Lat. 37° 25' south, long. 56° 4' east; 141 miles, therm. 59°.

Sept. 14.—Lat. 37° 23' south, long. 60° 4' east; 181 miles, therm. 61°.

Sept. 15.—Lat. 38° 2' south, long. 63° 41' east; 162 miles, therm. 62°.

Sept. 16.—Lat. 38° 19' south, long. 68° 15' east; 229 miles, therm. 60°.

Sept. 17.—Lat.38° 10' south, long. 71° 48' east; 139 miles, therm. 58°.

Sept. 18.—Lat. 38° 12' south, long. 73° 27' east; 51 miles, therm. 57°.

Sept. 19.—Lat. 39° 23' south, long. 75° 24' east; 90 miles, therm. 57°.

Sept. 20.—Lat. 39° 20' south; no observation for the longitude. Blew a gale of wind.

Sept. 21.—Lat. 37° 28' south, long. 80° 37' east; 183 miles, therm. 54°.

Sept. 22.—Lat. 34° 53' south, long. 83° 51' east; 194 miles, therm. 57°.

Sept. 23.—Lat. 32° 58' south, long. 86° 6' east; 158 miles, therm. 60°. At 2 o'clock a complete shoal of whales appeared in sight. As Enderby had brought from England some Congreve rockets, I was anxious to see their effect tried. The cutter was lowered, and we were soon in the midst of the shoal; a quartermaster, who had been employed in the South Sea fishery, acted as coxswain, and steered the cutter almost on the back of a fish 40 or 50 yards long, Enderby fired the rocket; it went into the water about a yard on the left side of the fish, and must have exploded in him, as it never again appeared. The whale when struck remained for an instant stationary, and then, partly turning on its back, went down head foremost; being some distance from the ship we could not follow him.

Other fish were playing about the boat, spouting the water up to a considerable height; on looking over the gunnel I saw a very large one immediately under our keel, and felt rather uncomfortable till he was clear of us. I just at this instant remembered that I cannot swim. Enderby soon readjusted his rocket gun, and got another shot at a whale about 40 yards distance; the rocket entered the water 15 yards on our side and reappeared at nearly 200 on the other side of the fish. We appeared from the ship to be in imminent danger; for a short time after the first shot we were not visible, and some anxiety was felt for our safety; a pun was made on the occasion. We should have been *bewhaled*.

Sept. 24.—Lat. 32° 22' south, long. 87° 1' east; 52 miles, therm. 60°.

Sept. 25.—Lat. 30° 17' south, long. 87° 54' east; 138 miles, therm. 60°. During the early part of the day we were nearly becalmed; our old party went out in the cutter, and killed five albatross, two blubber birds, and several pintardas or Cape pigeons.

Sept. 26.—Lat. 28° 40' south, long. 89° 16' east; 108 miles, therm. 62°.

Sept. 27.—Lat. 26° 45' south, long. 91° 14' east; 163 miles.

Sept. 28.—Lat. 23° 58' south, long. 91° 22' east; 184 miles, therm. 63°. Fell in with the south-east. The pintardas and other birds left us after having followed the ship almost six weeks from 27° south lat., long. 19° west.

Sept. 29.—Lat, 20° 32' south, long. 91° 9' east; 184 miles, therm. 69°.

Sept. 30.—Lat. 17° 35' south, long. 91° 3' east; 182 miles, therm. 74°.

Oct. 1.—Lat. 14° 25' south, long. 91° 6' east; 184 miles, therm. 78°.

Oct. 2.—No observation; 190 miles.

Oct. 3.—Lat. 9° 46' south, long. 91° 16' east; 82 miles, therm. 80°.

Oct. 4.—Lat. 7° 59' south, long. 90° 37' east; 98 miles, therm. 81°. We fell in with the *Winchelsea*, East Indiaman bound to Calcutta, having the 44th Foot on board, and, amongst the officers, the son of Dr. Robinson. The *Winchelsea* left the Downs ten days before us. The captain, who had made thirteen voyages, said he had never experienced such weather as he met with doubling the Cape. For some time, the two ships kept close company, the bands of the different regiments relieving each other.

Oct. 5.—Lat. 6° 30' south, long. 90° 43' east; 79 miles, therm. 81°.

Oct. 6.—Lat. 5° 45' south, long. 91° 9' east; 52 miles, therm. 82°.

Oct. 7.—No observation; 55 miles, therm. 82°. The sun was vertical and the heat oppressive. Some swallows were flying about the ship; one of which flew into a cabin was caught, and another suffered itself to be taken from the rigging. At 8 p.m. the rain fell in torrents, and there was soon after every appearance of a storm, Dodd, a recruit attached to Enderby's troop, who had fallen asleep in the forestay-sail netting, fell over, and was not missed till he was called for his watch.

Oct. 8.—Lat. 5° 41' south, long. 92° east; 33 miles, therm. 83°. Luard and Enderby each caught a shark. I hooked a large one and played him for half an hour. Die, the boatswain, who was in the jolly boat, was in the act of gaffing him with the boat-hook, when the chain gave way which is attached to the hook, and I lost my shark. The sailors remarked they never knew a corpse on board without seeing plenty of sharks cruising about. Moon, a private in the regiment, died this morning, having been ill the whole voyage; he was thrown overboard at 6 p.m., after Harris reading the service.

Oct. 9.—Lat. 5° 3' south, long. 92° 27' east; 44 miles, therm. 83°.

Oct. 10.—Lat. 4° 47' south, long. 92° 45' east; 23 miles, therm. 85°.

Oct. 11.—Lat. 4° 30' south, long. 93° 11' east; 11 miles.

Oct. 12.—Lat. 4° 13' south, long. —; 10 miles, therm. 85°.

Oct. 13.—Lat. 4° 6' south, long. 93° 40' east; 11 miles, therm. 83°. In the sun 130°.

Oct. 14.—Lat. 3° 22' south, long. —; 34 miles, therm. 82°.

Oct. 15.—Lat. 2° 27' south, long. 93° 50' east; 62 miles, therm. 80°.
A party rowed the cutter to the *Winchelsea*; she had daily, since we first fell in with her, continued in her company. On going on board we found her a larger but not so comfortable a ship as the *Ely*. Their sick amounted to 164. We had only twelve men on the doctor's list.

Oct. 16.—Lat. 1° 12' south, long. 92° 46' east; 64 miles, therm. 85°.

Oct. 17.—Lat. 1° 23' south, long. —; 22 miles.

Oct. 18.—Lat. 1° 21' south, long. 92° 4' east; 12 miles, therm. 83°. Some officers of the 44th returned our visit. I had rated but meanly the boat's crew we mustered among ourselves, but I never saw such a set of lubbers as paddled the *Winchelsea's* jolly boat. Captain Shelton, who has lost an arm, is a pleasing, gentlemanly person; an officer claimed a sort of acquaintance with me as having hunted with me when I was quartered with the Inniskillings at Portamna with Hearn of Hearnsbrook's hounds. The voyage having been so protracted, and as there was every prospect of the calm continuing, Kay determined to touch somewhere for water, and first thought of Penang; but, altering his mind, he resolved to water at Car Nicobar, that island not being out of his course.

Oct. 19.—Lat. —. No observation, long. 92° east; 63 miles, therm. 76°.

Oct. 20.—Lat. 0° 56' south, long. 91° 44' east; 29 miles, therm. 80°.

Oct. 21.—No observation; 59 miles on the log. Kay, fearing we might fall short of water, went to the *Winchelsea*, hoping they might have a superabundance on board; but the captain could not spare any. To the great delight of us all a breeze sprung up; everybody's spirits were exhilarated. Old Die, the boatswain, had frequently been rebuked for the extreme coarseness of his language, which the presence of the ladies in no way softened. He had to give an order aloft, and as usual commenced "Maintop there." "Aye, aye, sir." "Make fast the maintop gallant clue-garnets." "They are fast, sir."

Die on looking up at once saw that his order was not properly executed, and was beginning to let out at the captain of maintop, having just got as far as, "oh, you bl—y li—," when he turned round, and, perceiving Mrs. Parkes, he at once stopped short and altered his speech into "Oh! my heye what a story." Mrs Parkes may be proud of such a conquest over the language, of a rough seaman, re-trained, I should think, in that point for the first time. I fancy she must have appeared to Die as a reproaching angel. Instead of Parkes she should be called *La Champs Elysée.*

Oct. 22.—Lat. 1° 20' north, long. 91° 57' east; 117 miles, therm. 80°.

Oct. 23.—Lat. 3° north, indifferent observation; 104 miles, therm. 83°.

Oct. 24.—Lat. 4° 34' north, long. 92° 8' east; 105 miles.

Oct. 25.—Lat. 5° 42' north, long. 92° 21' east; 45miles, therm. 83°.

Oct. 26.—Lat. 6° 38' north, long. 92° 42' east; 74 miles, therm. 82°.

Oct. 27.—Lat. 7° 42' north, long. 92° 27' east; 31 miles, therm. 84°.

Oct. 28.—Lat. 8° 3' north, long. 92° 44' east; 71 miles. A species of hawk was caught in the rigging.

Oct. 29.—Lat. 8° 44' north, long. 92° 52' east; 68 miles, therm. 83°. At 12 a.m. land was in sight.

Oct. 30.—At daybreak we were anchored within half a league of Car Nicobar; the lat. is 9° 10' north, long. 92° 56' east. The breadth of the island is about four miles, the length not more than seven. It forms one of a cluster of islands, the appearance of which at a distance resembles a chain of wooded hills. A person who has never been for a length of time on ship-board, cannot fancy how grateful the sight of verdure is to the eye. Here the sea at high tide washes the very roots of trees covered with rich and perpetual foliage. Captain Greville, who had gone on shore early with Mangles, the 2nd Mate, returned to the ship at 8 o'clock a.m., giving a satisfactory account of the friendly disposition of the inhabitants, two of whom accompanied them.

When these natives walked up the deck, the ladies shut their eyes, and, shrieking, ran into their cabins, and well might an Englishwoman be astonished at such a sight as presented itself to her eyes. One, whose name was Lancour, wore a hat and spoke a little English; the rest of his dress, like his A. D. C.'s, consisted simply of a piece of cloth scarcely broader than tape passed tightly between his legs and fastened round his loins. These men were copper-coloured, and, though short, were both well-proportioned as far as was visible; but I imagine I may doubt the symmetry of those parts which were thoroughly concealed by a piece of tape. Their faces were hideous, the eye small, the mouth large (from chewing the betel-nut), the teeth black, and the only expression of countenance that of idiocy.

Lancour told us an abundant supply of water was procurable close to the shore, immediately all the boats were put in readiness to water. Shortly after breakfast a canoe came from the island paddled by eight men, who brought plantains, cocoa-nuts, oranges, citrons, limes, the shaddock, a kind of melon, and yams; these they readily exchanged for silver money, handkerchiefs, the gaudier the more value they placed on them, or tobacco. After dinner, Mrs. Parkes and Mrs. Enderby went ashore; I made one of the party. We landed at a village which consisted of five huts of an oval form, about 30 feet high and 80 in circumference; they were each neatly thatched. The base of these huts was open like a cart-house, you ascended to the only apartment by a bamboo ladder and opposite to the entrance was a fireplace; the floor was formed of split bamboo well laid down.

In the open part, underneath each of these huts, two or three swings were placed, on which men, women, and children are fond of sitting, keeping themselves gently moving backwards and forwards. The women had rings beaten out from dollars round their necks, wrists, and ankles, and the first joint of each finger and toe was covered with rings. No female that I saw exceeded in height 4 feet 9 or 10 inches, and all without exception were disgustingly ugly; their breasts had no covering, and girls, almost children themselves, were suckling infants. By the time a woman has arrived at the age of 20, nothing that I am aware of has a less inviting appearance, saving an older woman of Car Nicobar. No female spoke English, though several of the men had learnt a few broken sentences. In the village I perceived several of the natives with swollen limbs, and two dreadful cases of elephantiasis presented themselves.

Few of the men were more than 5 feet 2 inches, and none I think higher than 5 feet 5 inches; generally, they were well-proportioned, particularly in the shape of their limbs. At 7 the ladies and the greater share of the party returned to the ship. Parkes, Colonel Luard, and I remained on the island till a much later hour. The natives got rather tired of our company and appeared anxious to eat their supper, which consisted of small pieces of pork roasted, and which they would not partake of whilst we remained. We were much entertained with the extravagant conceit of Lancour, to whom Mangles had given an old uniform coat—the satisfaction with which he viewed himself and his strut, was a savage caricature of a dandy. By-the-bye, Lancour drank quite enough spirits to have made a more civilized man intoxicated.

Oct. 31.—I again went on shore with Kay and Newberry. On landing we found several officers of the 44th Regiment who had established a market and were bartering for pigs and fruit. The infantry had got up very early. Harris, Armstrong, and I strolled along the shore with our guns; a curlew was the only bird shot. I picked up several very curious shells from the beach. The island is covered with wood, and several of the trees are prodigiously large. In striking from the beaten path, I had much difficulty in making way through the jungle which is rendered almost impenetrable from a creeper which grows most luxuriantly. As our cloaks had got completely wet, we formed an odd resolution of hanging them up and remaining in the sea until they were dry; the plan did not quite succeed, though we were bathing and running on the sand almost two hours. I endeavoured to find out from Lancour, who spoke more English than the rest, their form of worship and if they had any idea of a God; but I could not derive any knowledge on this subject. On asking who was king, he said he was captain. During the day many canoes were paddled to the ship taking fruit and pigs, which are very small and in great abundance: from their being fed on the cocoa-nut, the flesh is delicate and delicious.

Nov. 1.—Got under weigh at 1 o'clock a.m., Lat. 10° 4' north, long. 92° 54' east; 58 miles, therm. 82°. At 1 p.m., saw the Andaman Islands bearing north, and by east. At 9 passed the South Sentinel Island.

Nov. 2.—Lat. 12° 8' north, long. 92° 3' east; 133 miles, therm. 84°.

Nov. 3.—Lat. 14° 58' north, long. 90° 53' east; 119 miles, therm. 84°.

Nov. 4.—Lat. 17° 59' north, long. 90° east.; 174 miles, therm. 85°.

Nov. 5.—Lat. 19° 30' north, long. 89° 59' east; 90 miles.

Nov. 6.—Lat. 20° 38' north, long. 89° east; 66 miles.

Nov. 7.—Scallon the pilot came on board at 10 o'clock a.m.

Nov. 8.—Saugor Island in sight at 3 o'clock p.m.

Nov. 9.—Anchored at 4 p.m. at Saugor or Kedgeree.

Nov. 15.—The brigs arrived which were to take us to Calcutta. Enderby having gone up, the command of his troop devolved upon me. Collins and I went up in the same vessel.

Nov. 21.—Collins and I went ashore to breakfast at Foultre, where an inn or tea-garden is kept by a Dutchman. On entering the house, we found Bignell, the 3rd Mate of the *Ely*, who had under his protection Miss Garrett, to whom he was betrothed, and Miss Rowe. I never saw a man appear fonder of a woman than Bignell is of his intended. Greville and Armstrong came on shore, and we formed a large party at dinner; a French captain joined us. The name of this place must have been changed from Fontre.

Nov. 23.—In the evening we arrived and disembarked at Calcutta, and then marched the men to the south glacis of the fort, where the regiment were encamped. Newberry and Enderby met us; the latter, as I had no bed and no house to go to, insisted I should accompany him to Major Vaughan's, the fort major, where he and his wife were living. This was too good an offer for a man who had only an unfurnished tent to go into to refuse. Major Vaughan was himself dining at Government House, but though the host was absent, an excellent dinner was on his table, and I found a comfortable bed in Newberry's room. I slept so sound that I was not awoke by the stings of hundreds of mosquitoes who had intruded through the curtains.

Nov. 24.—Called on James Pattler, usually known as Jemmy Blaze; he gave me a civil and pressing invitation to his house during my stay at Calcutta and ordered my boxes to be removed to his house in Chowringee. Here I remained till the regiment were ordered to embark for Cawnpore. No man kept a better table, the sporting characters were always welcome guests and as Mrs. Pattler was in England, ladies did not visit at the house. There is a difference in the manners of society that strikes you on first coming into the country, and which is not in favour of the residents in the East. The general tone of society is, I should say, worse than the same rank at home. Ladies do not pay that strict regard to decorum, which they are absolutely obliged to do in England, if they have any regard for their character. Perhaps this may be attributable to the rapidity with which marriages are frequently concluded, so that the husband has as little opportunity of discovering the imperfections of his intended, as the wife has of perceiving the faults of her husband.

Scarcely a day passed without my being engaged to some party, and, on the whole, my time passed pleasantly enough. I went to a masquerade given by Mrs. Casement in the character of a stage coachman, and had a good deal of fun, or rather 'sky,' to use the slang expression of the country. The races were a constant lounge in the morning, but the sport was bad; scarcely a well-contested race took place; there appeared to be extensive betting, and the stakes ran for were large. I had the pleasure of renewing an acquaintance with a very agreeable woman, who I had, known as a girl at Boulogne, the daughter of a Mrs. Lowe; she was married to a Mr. Dewar, a Civilian. I saw her frequently, and liked her better as a married woman than as a girl.

It was ridiculous to see the admiration that was bestowed on my fair shipmate, Mrs. Parkes; so lovely a creature must be a rare sight in Calcutta. Chowringhee, the fashionable residence of Europeans, has

Fort William, 1820's.

Old Fort Ghaut.

of late been much extended by buildings; the houses are usually good, and occasionally magnificent. The Government House is a splendid palace for the governor-general. On the 2nd of January 1823, Lord Hastings retired and the regiment was drawn up in review order to honour his departure. No man at the head of government had ever been more esteemed or more popular than the Marquis of Hastings; but, from the return of his wife to him, his popularity began to decline, and, at the time of his leaving the country, it may be said to have entirely subsided. At the end of December, Sir Edward Paget arrived as commander-in-chief. On the 30th the left wing of the regiment, which had embarked in the *Genl. Hewitt*, arrived after a tedious and hazardous voyage.

Fanny Parkes' Description of the Passage to India in 1822

In the pages of Arthur Lowe's diary that refer to the outward passage to India, we are introduced to Mrs Fanny Parkes (formerly Frances Susanna Archer 1794-1875), she of the exquisitely formed leg, who was the wife of an East India Company civil servant (writer), Charles Crawford Parkes (1797-1856). Fanny Parkes eventually wrote about her experiences in India and beyond in a well-regarded book of two large volumes published in 1850, entitled, *Wanderings of a Pilgrim in Search of the Picturesque etc.* In the opening pages of her book the voyage to India in company with the 16th Lancers is described from her perspective and that passage, until the arrival in Calcutta, has been included in this book. The authenticity of history is best served by cross referencing eyewitness statements, but perhaps more importantly Fanny Parkes provides some insights into the lives of the officers and men of the regiment on board ship from an outsider's viewpoint which is both female and civilian. However, Fanny Parkes was coincidentally also part of the wider 16th Lancers community because her father was Captain William Archer who had also served in the regiment during its period as light dragoons.

At Tournai on the 10th of May, 1794 Archer was with the 16th opposite the right flank of the French Army under Pichegru. The regiment was ordered to charge a field battery of eight guns which was supported by cavalry and infantry. The guns were captured at the cost of three troopers and two horses killed. However, two sergeants, 5 troopers and one officer—Lieutenant William Archer—were wounded in the action. Though he was subsequently promoted the wound was apparently serious enough to compel him to retire from the service. Archer's brother, Clement, also served with the 16th during the

Peninsular War and for a period commanded the regiment. He was severely wounded at Fuentes d'Onor and died in 1817.

★★★★★★

In April, 1822, *Monsieur mon mari* took me to Switzerland. For the first time, I quitted England. How beautiful was the Valley of Chamouni! how delightful our expedition on the La Flegere! The guides pronounced it too early in the year to attempt the ascent of Mont Blanc. We quitted the valley with regret, and returned to Geneva: but our plans were frustrated, and our hopes disappointed; for, on reaching the hotel, we found a letter requiring our instant return to England. The *Marchioness of Ely*, in which we had taken our passage to Bengal, was reported to be ready to sail in a few days: no time was to be lost; we started immediately, travelled night and day incessantly, and arrived, greatly harassed, in town. The illness brought on by the over-fatigue of that journey never quitted me for years. The vessel, however, was merely preparing for her departure, and did not sail until long after.

Happily, the pain of separation from the beloved home of my childhood was broken by the necessity of exertion in preparation for the voyage.

June 13th.—We went to Gravesend, to see the ship: it was scarcely possible to enter our destined abode, the larboard stern cabin; so full was it to overflowing—boxes of clothes, hampers of soda water, crates of china and glass—a marvellous confusion! After a time, the hampers and boxes were carried below, the furniture cleated and lashed, and some sort of order was established.

We had carefully selected a ship that was not to carry troops: we now found the *Ely* had been taken up to convey four troops of H. M. 16th Lancers; the remainder of the regiment was to sail in the *General Hewitt*. Some of our fellow-passengers were on board on the same errand as ourselves.

June 18th.—We had lingered with our friends, and had deferred the sad farewell until the last moment: half uncertain if we should be in time to catch the ship in the Downs, we posted to Deal, took refuge at the 'Three Kings,' and had the satisfaction of watching the *Marchioness of Ely*, and the *Winchelsea* her companion, as they bore down. At 11 p.m. we went on board, and sailed the next day. There was such a glorious confusion on deck, that those who were novices in military and naval affairs might deem, as they gazed around, it could never subside into anything approaching order.

Everyone, however, was saying it would be very different when the ship was at sea; of which, indeed, there was little doubt, for to go on as we were would have been impossible. Off the Isle of Wight, the pilot left us to our captain's guidance; the breeze was favourable; we were sailing so smoothly, there was scarcely any motion. The last farewell tears dropped as I passed the Needles and the coast of Hampshire, whilst memory recalled the happy days I had spent there, and in the Forest, the beautiful Forest!

Such thoughts and feelings it was necessary to throw aside. I joined the party in the cuddy, scrutinised the strange faces, and retired to my cabin, with as solitary a feeling as if my husband and I had been exiles for ever.

The voyage began prosperously; I was satisfied with the captain, with my cabin, with my servant, and happy with my lord and master.

We regretted we had taken our passage in a ship full of troops, and anticipated we should be debarred taking exercise on the quarter-deck, and enjoying ourselves with walk and talk during the fine moonlight nights. In the *Ely* it appeared as if it would be impossible; were you to attempt it, you would be sure to blunder over some sleeping lancer. However, the band was on board—some small consolation; and as the society was large, there was more chance of entertainment.

July 1st.—Porto Santo looked beautiful, its head enveloped in clouds. The rocky island rises boldly out of the sea; its mountains are very picturesque. The sight of land and white *chateaux* was quite charming.

I now began to recover from the *maladie de mer*, and to regain my usual good spirits. Creatures of habit, we soon grew accustomed to the small space. The stern cabin, twelve feet by ten, at first sight appeared most extremely inconvenient; but now it seemed to have enlarged itself, and we were more comfortable. Still sleep would scarcely visit me, until a swinging cot was procured. From that time, I slept calmly and quietly, whatever pranks the old *Ely* might choose to play.

The comfort or discomfort of a voyage greatly depends upon your fellow-passengers. In this respect we were most fortunate; one-half the officers of the 16th Lancers were in the *Ely*. The old 16th to me were friends; my father, who had been many years in the regiment, was forced to quit it, in consequence of a severe wound he received in action in the Pays Bas, under the command of the Duke of York. My uncle had commanded the gallant regiment in Spain, and other rela-

77

tives had also been many years with the regiment. Chance had thrown us amongst friends.

Perhaps no friendships are stronger than those formed on board ship, where the tempers and dispositions are so much set forth in their true colours.

July 4th.—We passed the Isle of Palma; it looked beautiful, rising abruptly from the sea; the trees appeared fine and numerous. We are in the trade winds, going generally about eight knots an hour; the evenings are delicious; little or no dew falls so far from land; in the evening we sit on deck, and enjoy the breeze. The moon is reflected so beautifully on the waves, the nights are so warm, the air so pure, the climate so agreeable, I could willingly turn canary bird, and take up my residence in this latitude.

Sometimes quadrilles are danced by the light of the moon; sometimes by the glare of half-a-dozen lanterns. There is little or no motion in the vessel; no events occur; yes—let me not forget—a little boy fell into the pea-soup and got a ducking; luckily for him, it was nearly cold. "*The misfortunes of the stable fall on the head of the monkey!*" (*Oriental Proverbs*, No. 9.) The deck presents a curious assemblage: Lancers at extension exercise, women working, sailors hauling, children at school, ladies reading or talking in groups—altogether an amusing scene.

On Sundays, Divine service is performed; the psalms are sung in very good style, accompanied by the Lancer band. The weather is hot; the thermometer 79° in our cabin, 81° in the cuddy, which at dinnertime contains six-and-thirty people. Today a shark was caught; it was attended by three pilot fish, which, they say, guide the shark to its prey. These small fish are very pretty, and striped like zebras. The shark was hooked and dragged up by the stern windows; he straggled manfully, but was soon despatched.

A little flying-fish flew into one of the ports to escape the pursuit of a larger fish; it was small and curious, but not so pretty as one would imagine. Two large fins spread out on its sides, like wings. It was a novelty to most of the passengers.

July 22nd.—What a strange, bustling life! This is baggage-day; all the trunks are on deck—such a confusion! I am suffering from *maladie de mer*; the wind is contrary; we tack and veer most tiresomely; the ship pitches; we cling about like cats, and are at our wits' end, striving to endure our miseries with patience.

The Bristol water is invaluable, the ship water very black, and it smells vilely. I knew not before the value of good water; and, were it not for the shower bath, should be apt to wish myself where Truth is—at the bottom of a well.

Yesterday such a noise arose on deck, it brought me to the scene of action in a minute: "Come here! come here! look! look! There they go, like a pack of hounds in full cry!" I did come, and I did look; and there were some hundred of skip-jacks leaping out of the water, and following each other with great rapidity across the head of the ship. When many fish leaped up together, there was such laughing, shouting, pointing, and gazing, from four hundred full-grown people, it was absurd to see how much amusement the poor fish occasioned. I looked alternately at the fish and the people, and laughed at both.

A kind of rash teases me; in these latitudes they call it prickly heat, now you cannot be healthy without it, and affirm that everyone ought to be glad to have it. So am not I.

Having beaten about the line for a fortnight, with a contrary wind, at length we entertained hopes of crossing it, and letters were received on board from Neptune and Amphitrite, requesting to be supplied with clothes, having lost their own in a gale of wind.

July 30th.—Neptune and his lady came on board to acquaint the captain they would visit him in form the next day. The captain wished the god goodnight, when instantly the deck was deluged with showers of water from the main-top, while a flaming tar-barrel was thrown overboard, in which Neptune was supposed to have vanished in flame and water.

July 31st.—At 9 a.m. the private soldiers who were not to be shaved were stationed on the poop with their wives; on the quarter-deck the officers and ladies awaited the arrival of the ocean-god. First in procession marched the band, playing "God save the King;" several grotesque figures followed; then came the car of Neptune—a gun-carriage—with such a creature for a coachman! The carriage was drawn by six half-naked seamen, painted to represent Tritons, who were chained to the vehicle. We beheld the monarch and his bride, seated in the car, with a lovely girl, whom he called his tender offspring. These ladies were represented by the most brawny, muscular, ugly and powerful fellows in the ship; the letters requesting female attire having procured an abundance of finery.

The boatswain's mate, a powerful man, naked to the waist, with a pasteboard crown upon his head and his speaking-trumpet in his hand, who represented Neptune, descended from his car, and offered the captain two fowls as tropical birds, and a salted fish on the end of a trident, lamenting that the late boisterous weather had prevented his bringing any fresh. A doctor, a barber with a notched razor, a sea-bear and its keeper, closed the procession.

Re-ascending the car, they took their station in front of the poop, and a rope was drawn across the deck to represent the line. Neptune then summoned the colonel-commandant of the Lancers to his presence, who informed him he had before entered his dominions. The major was then conducted, by a fellow calling himself a constable, to the foot of the car: he went up, expecting to be shaved, but the sea god desired him to present his wife to Amphitrite. After the introduction they were both dismissed.

My husband and myself were then summoned: he pleaded having crossed the line before. Neptune said that would not avail, as his lady had entered the small latitudes for the first time. After a laughable discussion, of to be shaved or not to be shaved, we were allowed to retire. The remainder of the passengers were summoned in turn. The sentence of shaving was passed upon all who had not crossed the line, but not carried into execution on the officers of the ship. The crew were shaved and ducked in form, and in all good humour.

In the meantime the fire-engine drenched everybody on deck, and the officers and passengers amused themselves for hours throwing water over each other from buckets. Imagine four hundred people ducking one another, and you may have some idea of the frolic. In the evening the sailors danced, sang, recited verses, and spliced the main brace (drank grog), until very late, and the day ended as jovially as it began. Several times they charmed us with an appropriate song, roared at the utmost pitch of their stentorian lungs, to the tune of "There's na luck about the house."

We'll lather away, and shave away.
And lather away so fine,
We always have a shaving day
Whenever we cross the line.

With sorrow I confess to having forgotten the remainder of the ditty, which ended—

There's nothing half so sweet in life
As crossing of the line.

"Rule Britannia," with a subscription for the ruler of the seas, was the finale, leaving every one perfectly satisfied with his portion of salt water. It was agreed the rites and ceremonies had never been better performed or with greater good humour.

Colonel Luard's beautiful and faithful sketches have since been presented to the public. Watching his ready pencil, as it portrayed the passing scene, was one of the pleasures of the *Ely*; and I feel greatly obliged to him for having given me permission to add copies of some of his original sketches to my journal.

Neptune was accompanied on board by a flying-fish that came in at one of the ports, perhaps to escape from an albicore: a lucky omen. The gentlemen amuse themselves with firing at the albatross, as they fly round and round the vessel; as yet, no damage has been done—the great birds shake their thick plumage, and laugh at the shot.

The favourite game is pitch-and-toss for dollars. Boxing is another method of spending time. Chess and backgammon-boards are in high request; when the evenings are not calm enough for a quadrille or a waltz on deck, the passengers retire to the cuddy, to whist or blind hookey, and dollars are brought to table in cases that formerly contained Gamble's most excellent portable soup! On the very general introduction of caoutchouc into every department of the arts and sciences, some of the principal ship-builders proposed to form the keels of their vessels of indian-rubber, but abandoned the project apprehending the *entire effacement of the equinoctial line.*

Aug. 1st.—Caught a bonito and a sea-scorpion; the latter was of a beautiful purple colour, the underpart white: also a nautilus and a blue shark; in the latter were four-and-twenty young ones. The shark measured seven feet; its young from twelve to fourteen inches. The colour of the back was blue, of the belly white; several sucking-fish were upon the monster, of which some were lost in hauling him on board: one of those caught measured nine inches and a half; it stuck firmly to my hand in an instant.

Our amusements concluded with viewing an eclipse of the moon.

A stiff gale split the mainsail and blew the foretop and mizzentop sails to pieces: no further damage was sustained. I enjoyed the sight of the fine waves that tossed the vessel as if she were a cockle-shell.

We caught two Cape pigeons, very beautiful birds; the moment they were brought on deck they suffered extremely from *maladie de mer!*

SEABIRDS FOLLOWING SHIPS BY JOHN LUARD.

Aug. 11th.—During Divine service we came in sight of San Trinidada and Martin Vas Rocks; the former distant twelve miles, the latter thirty.

Aug. 16th.—Lat. 27° S., long. 19° W.—The annexed lithograph is from an original drawing of Colonel Luard's, and the following extract from his *Views in India*—

The drawing represents the numerous birds that constantly follow ships from lat. 27° S. to lat. 40° S., constantly hovering about the ship, and picking up anything eatable which may be thrown overboard. The pintado, or Cape pigeon, a very pretty bird, black and white striped all over, is the most numerous. They fly backwards and forwards across the ship's wake, in such numbers and so carelessly, that they are frequently caught by entangling their wings in lines thrown over the stern of the ship to catch the albatross. This immense bird is also portrayed in the drawing, whose astonishing power, fierceness, and fleetness, render him formidable amongst the feathered tribe of these regions. There is an instance on record of a man having fallen overboard from a ship-of-war, when a noble-minded midshipman instantly jumped overboard, and, from his power as a swimmer, would probably have rescued the sailor from a watery grave, had not an albatross passing at the moment stooped upon the generous youth, and struck him upon the head: he sank to rise no more! Both he and the sailor were drowned.

Aug. 23rd.—There is a ship alongside! a ship bound for England! it speaks of home and the beloved ones, and although I am as happy as possible, my heart still turns to those who have heretofore been all and everything to me, with a warmth of affection at once delightful and very painful.

Aug. 27th.—Lat. 32° 9' S., long. 4° 25' E.—A dead calm! give me any day a storm and a half in preference! It was so miserable—a long heavy swell, without a ripple on the waves; the ship rolled from side to side without advancing one inch; she groaned in all her timbers: the old *Marchioness* appeared to suffer and be as miserable as myself. The calm continued the next day, and the rolling also; the captain kindly allowed the jolly-boat to be lowered, in which some of the lancers and my husband went out shooting.

This day, the 28th of August, was the commencement of the shooting season: game was in abundance, and they sought it over the long heavy swell of the glasslike and unrippled sea. The sportsmen returned with forty head of game: in this number was an albatross, measuring nine feet from the tip of one wing to that of the other; a Cape hen, a sea-swallow, with several pintado and other birds.

When the boat returned, it brought good fortune; the wind instantly sprang up, and we went on our way rejoicing. This day a whale was seen at a distance; if it had approached the vessel, a captain of the Lancers had prepared a Congreve rocket for its acceptance.

Sept 1st—We spoke a Dutchman off the Cape, looking in a very pitiable condition: the same gale which had damaged her overtook us, and blew heavily and disagreeably for three days. The weather was very cold and wet. and we felt disappointed at not touching at the Cape.

Sept. 10th.—Lat. 36° 43' S., long. 45° 30' W. ther. 64°.—Another calm, and another *battue* the gentlemen returned from the watery plain with great *éclat*, bringing seven albatross, thirty pintados, a Cape hen, and two carnets. One of the albatross, which was stuffed for me, measured thirty-three inches from head to toe, and nine feet ten inches across the wings.

Sept. 20th—In the evening we passed St. Paul's and Amsterdam, but the haziness of the weather prevented our seeing them. This, the most southerly point of our voyage, was also the coldest. The cold was really painful.

Sept. 23.—A school (technical term used in the whale fishery), of twenty or thirty whales passed near the ship; it was almost a calm: they were constantly on the surface, frolicking and spouting away. They were, the sailors said, of the *spermaceti* order, which are smaller in size, and do not spout so high as the larger race. I was disappointed. Two of the officers of the lancers rowed within ten yards of a large whale, and fired a Congreve rocket into its body; the whale gave a spring and dived instantly. The rocket would explode in a few seconds and kill him: a good prize for the first ship that falls in with the floating carcase. They fired at another, but the rocket exploded under water and came up smoking to the surface. The boat returned safely to the ship, but it was rather a nervous affair.

Sept. 25th.—Another calm allowed of more shooting, and great was the slaughter of sea game. I must make an extract from Colonel

Luard's work, speaking of a battle that took place on the 10th.—

The Cape hen was a large fierce black bird, and only having its wing broken, tried to bite even person's legs in the boat. When she was placed on the ship's quarter-deck, a small terrier belonging to one of the officers attacked her. and they fought for some time with uncertain advantage, the bloody streams from the dog proving the severity of the bird's bite at last the terrier seized his adversary by the throat, when the battle and the bird's life ended together. In lat. 4° 13' S., long. 93° 11' E., the thermometer in the sun standing at 130°, and in the shade 97°, two small birds, in every respect resembling the English swallow, came about the ship. One of them was caught, and died; the other (probably in hopes of rejoining its companion) remained with the ship fourteen or fifteen days, frequently coming into the cabins and roosting there during the night. It was at last missing; and, not being an aquatic bird, perhaps met a watery death.

During the time of the *battue* on the third day, three sharks were astern; we caught one that had a young one by her side. When opened on deck, a family of twenty-four were found, each about twelve or fourteen inches long; the mother measured seven feet. The shark is said to swallow its young when in peril, and to disgorge them when the danger has passed. The curious birds and fish we see relieve the tedium of the voyage.

We now looked impatiently for the end of our passage, and counted the days like schoolboys expecting their vacation. It was amusing to hear the various plans the different people on board intended to pursue on landing — all too English by far for the climate to which they were bound.

The birds were numerous south of the tropics; we saw few within them. The flying-fish are never found beyond the tropics.

Oct. 11th.—Lat. 4° 20' S., long. 93° 11' E.—The heat was very great; the vertical sun poured down its sickening rays, the thermometer in the shade of the coolest cabin 86°; not a breath of air; we felt severely the sudden change of temperature. The sails flapped against the mast, and we only made progress seventeen knots in the twenty-four hours! Thus passed eleven days — the shower bath kept us alive, and our health was better than when we quitted England. *M. mon mari*, who was studying Persian, began to teach me Hindostanee, which afforded me much pleasure.

In spite of the calm there was gaiety on board; the band played delightfully, our fellow-passengers were agreeable, and the calm evenings allowed of quadrilles and waltzing on the deck, which was lighted up with lanterns and decorated with flags.

We spoke the *Winchelsea*, which had quitted the Downs seven days before us and experienced heavy weather off the Cape: it was some consolation to have been at sea a shorter time than our companion. But little sickness was on board; a young private of the lancers fell overboard, it was supposed, during a squall, and was lost; he was not even missed until the next day: a sick lancer died, and a little child also; they were buried at sea: the bill of health was uncommonly good. A burial at sea, when first witnessed, is very solemn and impressive.

We passed an English ship—the Lancer band played "God save the King," the vessel answered with three cheers. It was painful to meet a homeward-bound ship; it reminded me of home, country, and, dearer still, of friends. The sailors have a superstition, that sharks always follow a ship when a corpse is on board: the night after the man fell overboard, the lancer and the child died; the day they were buried three sharks were astern. I thought of the sailors' superstition; no sharks had been seen along-side for three weeks.

The sunsets on and near the line are truly magnificent, nothing is more glorious—the nights are beautiful, no dew, no breeze, the stars shining as they do on a frosty night at home, and we are gasping for a breath of air! A sea-snake about a yard and a half long was caught—many turtle were seen, but they sank the moment the boat approached them. A subscription lottery was made; the person whose ticket bears the date of our arrival at Saugor will win the amount.

Oct. 22nd.—Becalmed for eighteen days! not as when off the Cape; there it was cool, with a heavy swell, here there is no motion, the sun vertical, not a breath of air, the heat excessive. At length a breeze sprang up, and we began to move: one day during the calm we made seven knots in the twenty-four hours, and those all the wrong way!

Day after day, day after day,
We stuck, nor breath nor motion;
As idle as a painted ship
Upon a painted ocean.

Our voyage advanced very slowly, and the supply of fresh water becoming scanty, we were all put on short allowance; anything but agreeable under so hot a sun. Captain Kay determined to make the land, and water the ship, and made signals to our companion, the *Winchelsea*, to that effect.

Oct. 30th.—To our great delight we arrived at, and anchored off, Carnicobar, one of the Nicobar Islands, lat. 9° 10' N., long. 92° 56' E. Boats were immediately sent on shore to a small village, where the landing was good, and two springs of delicious water were found for the supply of the ship.

The island where we landed was covered to the edge of the sand of the shore with beautiful trees; scarcely an uncovered or open spot was to be seen. Off the ship the village appeared to consist of six or eight enormous bee-hives, erected on poles and surrounded by high trees; among these, the cocoa-nut, to an English eye, was the most remarkable.

The ship was soon surrounded by canoes filled with natives; two came on board. The ladies hastened on deck, but quickly scudded away, not a little startled at beholding men like Adam when he tasted the forbidden fruit: they knew not they were naked, and they were not ashamed. I returned to my cabin. The stern of the vessel was soon encircled by canoes filled with limes, citrons, oranges, cocoa-nuts, plantains, yams, eggs, chickens, little pigs., and various kinds of fruit. The sight of these temptations soon overcame my horror at the want of drapery of the islanders, and I stood at the port bargaining for what I wished to obtain until the floor was covered.

Our traffic was thus conducted—I held up an empty jam-pot, and received in return a basket full of citrons; for two empty phials, a couple of fowls; another couple of fowls were given in exchange for an empty tin case that held portable soup; the price of a little pig was sixpence, or an old razor: they were eager at first for knives, but very capricious in their bargains: the privates of the lancers had glutted the market. On my holding up a clasp-knife, the savage shook his head. I cut off the brass rings from the window-curtains—great was the clamour and eagerness to possess them.

On giving a handful to one of the men, he counted them carefully, and then fitted them on his fingers. The people selected those they approved, returned the remainder, and gave me fruit in profusion. Even curtain-rings soon lost their charm—my eye fell on a basket of shells, the owner refused by signs all my offers—he wanted some novelty: at length an irresistible temptation was found—an officer of the lancers

Car Nicobar by John Luard.

cut off three of the gay buttons from his jacket, and offered them to the savage, who handed up the shells.

"*Figurez-vous*," said the lancer, "the Carnico barbarian love of that fellow, matted with straw and leaves from the waist to the knee, decked with three lancer buttons suspended round her neck by a cocoa-nut fibre, and enraptured with the novelty and beauty of the *tout ensemble!!*"

The dress, or rather the undress of the men was very simple; a handkerchief tied round the waist and passed between the limbs so as to leave the end hanging like a tail: some wore a stripe of plantain-leaf bound fillet-like round their heads; the necks of the chiefs were encircled either with silver wire in many rings, or a necklace of cowries.

One of the canoes which came from a distant part of the island was the most beautiful and picturesque boat I ever saw; it contained twenty-one men, was paddled with amazing swiftness, and gaily decorated. Of the canoes, some were so narrow that they had bamboo outriggers to prevent their upsetting. The natives appeared an honest, inoffensive race, and were much pleased with the strangers. After dinner it was proposed to go on shore in the cool of the evening: the unmarried ladies remained on board. I could not resist a run on a savage island, and longed to see the women, and know how they were treated.

Really the dark colour of the people serves very well as dress, if you are not determined to be critical. On landing, I was surrounded by women chattering and staring; one pulled my bonnet, but above all things they were charmed with my black silk apron; they greatly admired, and took it in their hands. They spoke a few words of English, and shook hands with me, saying, "How do? how do?" and when they wished to purchase my apron they seized it rather roughly, saying, "You buy? you buy?" meaning, Will you sell it? they were kind after the mode Nicobar.

The natives are of low stature, their faces ugly, but good-humoured; they are beautifully formed, reminding one of ancient statues; their carriage is perfectly erect. A piece of cloth is tied round the waists of the women, which reaches to the knee. Some women were hideous: of one the head was entirely shaved, excepting where a black lock was left over either ear, of which the lobes were depressed, stretched out, and cut into long slips, so that they might be ornamented with bits of coloured wood that were inserted. She had the elephantiasis, and her limbs were swollen to the size of her waist. They are very idle; in fact, there appears no necessity for exertion—fruits of all sorts grow wild, pigs are plentiful, and poultry abundant. Tobacco was much esteemed.

Silver they prized very much, and called coin of all sorts and sizes dollars—a sixpence or a half-crown were dollars. The only apparent use they have for silver is to beat it out into thick wire, which they form into spiral rings by twisting it several times round the finger. Rings are worn on the first and also on the middle joint of every finger, and on the thumb also. Bracelets formed after the same fashion wind from the wrist half-way up the arms. Rings ornament all their toes, and they wear half-a-dozen anklets. The same silver wire adorns the necks of the more opulent of the men also. They are copper-coloured, with straight black hair; their bodies shine from being rubbed with cocoa-nut oil, which smells very disagreeably.

Their huts are particularly well built. Fancy a great bee-hive beautifully and most carefully thatched, twelve feet in diameter, raised on poles about five feet from the ground; to the first story you ascend by a removeable ladder of bamboo; the floor is of bamboo, and springs under you in walking; the side opposite the entrance is smoked by a fire: a ladder leads to the attic, where another elastic floor completes the habitation. They sit or lie on the ground. Making baskets appears to be their only manufacture.

From constantly chewing the betel-nut, their teeth are stained black, with a red tinge, which has a hideous effect. I picked up some beautiful shells on the shore, and bartered with the women for their silver wire rings.

The colours of my shawl greatly enchanted Lancour, one of their chief men; he seized it rather roughly, and pushing three fowls, tied by the legs, into my face, said, "I present, you present." As I refused to agree to the exchange, one of the officers interfered, and Lancour drew back his hand evidently disappointed.

The gentlemen went on shore armed in case of accidents; but the ship being in sight all was safe. I have since heard that two vessels, which were wrecked on the island some years afterwards, were plundered, and the crews murdered.

Many of the most beautiful small birds were shot by the officers. As for foliage, you can imagine nothing more luxuriant than the trees bending with fruits and flowers. No quadrupeds were to be seen but dogs and pigs; there are no wild beasts on the island. They say jackals, alligators, and crabs are numerous: the natives were anxious the sailors should return to the ship at night, and as they remained late, the Nicobars came down armed with a sort of spear; they were cautious of the strangers, but showed no fear, and told the men to come again the next day. It must be dangerous for strangers to sleep on shore at night, on account of the dense fog, so productive of fever.

The scene was beautiful at sunset; the bright tints in the sky contrasted with the deep hue of the trees; the shore covered with men and boats; the bee-hive village, and the novelty of the whole. Many of the savages adorned with European jackets, were strutting about the vainest of the vain, charmed with their new clothing; Lancour was also adorned with a cocked hat! The woman who appeared of the most consideration, perhaps the queen of the island, wore a red cap shaped like a sugar-loaf, a small square handkerchief tied over one shoulder, like a monkey mantle, and a piece of blue cloth round her hips; a necklace of silver wire, with bracelets, anklets, and rings on the fingers and toes without number. The pigs proved the most delicate food; they were very small, and fattened on cocoa-nuts: the poultry was excellent.

The natives make a liquor as intoxicating as gin from the cocoa-nut tree, by cutting a gash in the bark and collecting the juice in a cocoa-nut shell, which they suspend below the opening to receive it; it ferments and is very strong—the *taree* or toddy of India.

Little did I think it would ever have been my fate to visit such an uncivilized island, or to shake hands with such queer looking men; however, we agreed very well, and they were quite pleased to be noticed: one man, who made us understand he was called Lancour, sat down by my side, and smoked in my face by way of a compliment. They delight in tobacco, which they roll up in a leaf, and smoke in form of a cigar. I cannot refrain from writing about these people, being completely island struck.

It was of importance to the *Winchelsea*, in which there were a hundred and twenty on the sick list, to procure fruit and vegetables, as the scurvy had broken out amongst the crew.

We landed, Oct. 30th, and quitted the island, Nov. 2nd, with a fair wind: all the passengers on board were in good spirits, and the ship presented a perfect contrast to the time of the calm.

Nov. 3rd.—We passed the Andaman Islands, whose inhabitants are reported to have a fondness for strangers of a nature different to the Carnico barbarians—they are cannibals!

A steady, pleasant monsoon urged us bravely onwards: a passing squall caught us, which laid the vessel on her side, carried away the flying jib, and split the driver into shreds: the next moment it was quite calm.

Nov. 7th.—We fell in with the Pilot Schooner, off the Sand-heads, the pilot came on board, bringing Indian newspapers and fresh news.

Nov. 10th.—We anchored at Saugor.—Here we bade *adieu* to our fellow-passengers, and the old *Marchioness of Ely* perhaps a more agreeable voyage was never made, in spite of its duration, nearly five months.

Our neighbours, in the stern cabin, very excellent people, and ourselves, no less worthy, hired a decked vessel, and proceeded up the Hoogly; that night we anchored off Fulta, and enjoyed fine fresh new milk, &c.; the next tide took us to Budge-Budge by night, and the following morning we landed at Chandpaul Ghaut, Calcutta.

The Hoogly is a fine river, but the banks are very low; the most beautiful part, Garden Reach, we passed during the night. The first sight of the native fishermen in their little *dinghees* is very remarkable. In the cold of the early morning, they wrap themselves up in folds of linen, and have the appearance of men risen from the dead. Many boats passed us which looked as if

By skeleton forms the sails were furled,
And the hand that steered was not of this world.

Nov. 13th.—In the course of a few hours after our arrival, a good house was taken for us, which being sufficiently large to accommodate our companions, we set up our standards together in Park-street, Chowringhee, and thus opened our Indian campaign.

The four troops of the 16th Lancers, from the *Ely*, disembarked, and encamped on the glacis of Fort William; the *General Hewitt*, with the remainder of the regiment, did not arrive until six weeks afterwards, having watered at the Cape.

The Diary of an Officer of the 16th Lancers Part Two—In India

Arthur C. Lowe

Jan. 2, 1823.—A dinner was given in camp to Captain Kay, to present him our thanks for his obliging and gentleman-like conduct, and to beg his acceptance of a piece of plate. I never sat down to a worse dinner, and never formed one of a more noisy and disagreeable party.

Jan. 6.—The regiment embarked in boats, which had been for some time in readiness, and early on the morning of the 7th left Calcutta. I took half a *budgerow* with Harris. At Barrackpore the governor-general has a country residence. I could not go over the house; the grounds are extensive and tastefully laid out. In the park, there is a great variety of the deer species. In the menagerie were several tigers, lions, hyaenas, and a very beautiful collection of birds. The 38th Regiment were stationed at Berhampore, and gave a very pleasant ball as we passed through. I dined with old Trower Smith, a celebrated sportsman and hog-hunter, about the best among the old ones.

At Dinapore, General Gregory was very civil; he had married a namesake of mine rather late in life, and her son was his A. D. C. In his house I met a very odd man, General Stewart, known by the name of the Hindoo General, who is clever and affects singularity; he allows his hair to grow long, and turns it up after the fashion of a *sepoy*; he lives on rice and different sorts of grain, scarcely ever touches animal food, and abstains entirely from wine.

General Stewart who cannot be much less than 70, astonished me by his activity; after dinner he jumped over a very high chair with slight exertion. Lowe, the A. D. C., who accompanied Mrs. Enderby one day to her boat, had occasion to write a note to her; in a postscript he added he was afraid Mrs. Enderby had found him a stupid companion, as he had not learnt the art of talking nonsense. At Chaprah I remained a couple of days with Langford Kennedy, a brother of Arthur's, who was in the 18th. Colonel Newberry, Persse, and his wife, were staying here. I have not had such a lark since I have been in India.

Mr. Ward, who married a sister of Dashcomb's, sent me an invitation to his house at Allahabad. Major Persse and his missis and Luard-formed a party here for three days: our host is a gentleman-like man, and his wife an elegant and pleasing woman. Ward, who is collector at this station, which, by the Hindoos, is held in extreme veneration (from the junction of the Jumna with the Ganges,) told me that, in three days during the fair, a *lac* of *rupees* was collected from the pilgrims, who pay a fixed sum to be allowed to bathe in a particular spot.

April 23.—The regiment, after a tiresome passage up the Ganges of three months and three weeks, arrived at Cawnpore. I was particularly glad to get out of my *budgerow*. I was deceived in Harris. Sperling and I took a house together. Cawnpore is in lat. 26° 30' north, long. 80° 21' east. It is along straggling station stretching along the banks of the Ganges nearly seven miles, and may boast of the largest society in India excepting Calcutta. At the top of the tree are Mr. and Mrs. Grant, who have been resident for many years. Mrs. Grant says Grant is an extremely good old fellow, and does just whatever she thinks fit. Her husband has the reputation of being the veriest old rogue in India, not an enviable character anywhere, and particularly not so in a country where many virtues are made subservient to the love of accumulating wealth.

General Thomas, who commands the division, is a man not liked in his own service; he is married, but has separated from his wife who is in England, The general appears desirous to shew us attention; his nieces the two Misses Slators are ladylike and agreeable, and Irish; they dance well; and if the old adage of the nearer the bone the sweeter the flesh is true, they must be perfect syrup. Mr. Bird a civilian, although good-humoured, is pompous; his wife is very pretty. I am sorry to hear he is ordered from the station. Johnson, who has the charge of the *pashwah* at Bittoor is a quiet gentleman-like man, and Mrs. Johnson, although reserved, is pleasant, and may boast of a figure almost perfect. On becoming acquainted with the society of the place, I find it is divided into several parties. I shall be disappointed if the quarrelling is not productive of fun.

Nov., 1823.—The Assembly-Rooms, which have been very badly supported, are given up. Fowle, who is secretary, without consulting old Grant, has sent the whole of the furniture to auction, and it is disposed of to 50 different purchasers. The old couple are furious. Mrs. Grant says, an old window curtain, a warming pan, and some nameless utensils were her property; that she is determined to have her rights, and swears she will bring an action against Fowle. I told her that would be foul play. She looked as if she could have knocked me down. Poor Sperling is implicated, as we elected him steward.

March 25, 1824.—As Sperling is on leave, and will remain absent till June, I accepted McDowell's offer of chumming with him and Vincent. McDowell has got a perfect mania for cockfighting; a pit is formed in the compound, and meeting established every Saturday. The birds brought are good, and betting is very high—25 G. M's.=£50 is a common sum to have depending on a battle. A lieutenant of infantry had the other day 64 G.M.'s on one cock, and won his money. I heard an anecdote mentioned characteristic of the native character. A rich *baboo* in Bengal resolved to turn *fakir* and go on a pilgrimage to Gangoatri for the remission of his sins, leaving considerable wealth to his son. During his absence the son died, and I suppose he got tired of his pilgrimage; for, on the news reaching the *baboo*, he returned home, and claimed his money from his son's widow. But she refused to return it; and in this emergency the *baboo* applied to Mr. Oakley for justice, who decided the cause in favour of the plaintiff in the Zillah Court.

The widow now appealed to a higher court, the *Sudder Dewannee*; and through the exertion of Oakley against her, she was again cast. Oakley is a man very deeply involved in debt; to make him exert himself in his cause the *baboo* offered to pay off every *rupee*, and to advance him any sum of money that he might require; but these advances Oakley refused, although they would have been instantly complied with. Soon after the cause had been finally settled, Oakley was arrested for 10,000 *rupees*; and as he had a difficulty in paying the amount, he sent to the *baboo* for the sum, offering the same security and interest as be had given to the person who had arrested him. But the *baboo* said "It is very true I did offer to pay off all Mr. Oakley's debts, and would have done so had they amounted to 5 *lacs* of *rupees*; then I had something to gain. Now, what do I require from Mr. Oakley? He must be mad to make such a request."

Aug. 20.—I rode with Johnson to Bittoor to see a religious Mah-

BUDGEROW ON THE GANGES BY JOHN LUARD.

ratta festival. The *pashwah* was present with as many followers as he could muster, preceded by an image of the god Gunaise. When the procession arrived at the river the god was placed in a boat, which was rowed a short distance from the shore, and when passing the *pashwah*, Gunaise was pitched into the Ganges amongst the shouts of the Mahrattas; and the firing of two cannon, the whole of the *pashwah's* artillery. I thought the god was very scurvily used.

Sept. 15.—I went to Bittoor to be present at another Mahratta festival called the *Dessarah*, which takes place the beginning of the cold season, when the Mahrattas prepare to take the field. The *pashwah* appeared with the whole of his retinue, he rode on an elephant in the midst of his followers, who galloped about the country till they saw a jay, esteemed a bird of happy omen; when this bird was found a gun was fired, and the field from whence the jay got up was immediately entered and destroyed, every Mahratta taking a part of the produce home. A singular method in the beginning of a campaign to enforce discipline, but I never heard that the Mahrattas had any in their army.

Oct. 5.—I left Cawnpore with a large party consisting of Mordaunt Ricketts, the resident at the Court of the King of Oude, and Mrs. Ravenscroft, who he is taking to Lucknow, and to whom he is to be immediately married; the widow about nine months ago saw her husband murdered in her presence. Ricketts within a shorter period has become a widower, and was so inconsolable until he met Mrs. Ravenscroft, that good-natured people supposed his heart would break. The party was formed to be present at these nuptials, which are to be solemnised with unusual splendour. I fancy the consummation will not be on so grand a scale.

★★★★★★

The guests are Mr. and Mrs. Grant, Captain King and his wife, Garston, *et sa femme*, Mrs. Wilkinson and Mrs. Mack; Ellis, Lindsay, Hyde, Armstrong, and I are the bachelors. The first occurrence that happened to me on arrival on the Oude side of the Ganges was, finding my grey Arab 'A. D. C.' with his leg broken by a *sowar's* horse. I was unwillingly obliged to order poor 'A. D. C.' to be shot; he was particularly neat. On overtaking Mrs. Mack, she observed, I was riding Ellis's horse. I told her my horse had his leg dreadfully broken; she answered "*Oh La*, Mr. Lowe, can't you get it repaired!"

Woe worth the chase, woe worth the day,
That cost thy life my gallant grey.

The second day's march was scarcely finished at 7 o'clock a.m., when it began to rain. The tents had been pitched in a beautiful grove of trees, but unfortunately on the lowest spot in the neighbourhood. In a couple of hours, the encampment rose out of a fine piece of water. The wall which encompassed the ladies' tents fell in, at 12 o'clock the confusion was perfect. Scarcely a dry spot was visible and least so within the tents where the water was a foot deep. Although our situation was not enviable, to me there was something irresistibly comic in it. No regular breakfast could be prepared; everyone foraged for himself from the *khansama's* tent, which was abundantly supplied. Hyde was one of the very best figures I ever saw, looking like a piece of animated leather; he was indefatigable in his exertions for the ladies.

At one instant I saw him gallantly wading knee-deep through the water, carrying a round of beef almost as large as himself to Mrs. Mack; his *kitmagar*, allowing master to do all the work, followed him shivering, with a mustard pot in his hand. But I lost the best scene of the day. Mrs. Mack is sufficiently *embonpoint*, to weigh 15 stone; as all her cloaks had got wet, she borrowed Rickett's dressing-gown. How she in any way got into it I cannot imagine, as the resident is at most a 9-stone man. I am sure there must have been a space of two feet across her bosom uncovered. In this dress she was reclining on a couch with Hyde standing by her side, who ever and *anon* plied her with the round of beef. I told Mrs. Mack she was playing at hide-and-seek; she laughed and said I was pert.

The account of Lord Byron's death reached Cawnpore as we left it; Mrs. Wilkinson is so ardent an admirer of his writings that she has gone into mourning; Mr. Burchell would, I think, have said to this— Fudge! Mrs. Wilkinson, the wife of a civilian, is a singular character, without a heart or without what is deserving of the name, without the slightest propriety of feeling; she affects sensibility, walks by moonlight with men, quotes the most impassioned sentences from Lord Byron and Tommy Moore, and, when you talk of love, desires you will call it sentiment. She is seldom with her husband, for whom she entertains a sovereign contempt deservedly; if he were not contemptible he would not permit her to pursue her present line of conduct.

★★★★★★

The rain continued the whole day and night, and on the morning of the 7th, when Ricketts (who was far from being a bad figure, in his dressing gown and *pajamahs* wet through and through, his careful *cho-prasseh* still holding an umbrella over his oilskin hat,) told us we must make the best of our way into Lucknow, the view of our encampment was certainly a very dismal one. King writing to Hake emphatically said:

No tongue can tell, no pen can describe our condition.

As soon as the ladies were placed in their *palanquins*, King, Ellis, Armstrong, Lindsay, and myself mounted our horses and rode through the hardest rain I was ever out in to the Residency; the distance was about 30 miles, one-half of which was under water, in some places so deep that the nags were almost swimming. On our arrival Lockett, the assistant to Rickett, sent us an invitation to his house, lent us dry clothes, and gave us a very comfortable dinner.

Mrs. Lockett is a very fascinating woman; and if not perfectly handsome, she is nearly so, her bust exquisitely shaped. She possesses a softness of manner that is unusually met with in this country. Her two sisters, the Misses Dickey, very nice girls, but I wish they would not always speak in a whisper. The ladies of our party were out all night, they got thoroughly wet, and their dresses which were carried in *pitarrahs* were spoiled; but they soon recovered from their fatigue and bore the loss of their finery with good humour. The Grants took a day or two to come round; the old couple were so savage at being out all night, that they declared they would return to Cawnpore.

Oct. 12.—Ricketts presented us to the King of Oude, with whom we breakfasted; the palace in which we were entertained is scarcely superior to the house of a rich individual; the rooms are by no means splendidly furnished; the breakfast equipage was dirty, and the whole thing badly arranged. The king in his manner is easy and elegant, his countenance expresses benignity and openness of character, his person is tall, portly, and majestic. The Residency is built on an eminence and commands the several palaces of the king which are situated in Lucknow. No one palace is in itself magnificent. Several are erected in different parts of a large enclosed piece of ground.

Oct. 13.—Early in the morning I rode to the Imaum Bara, an extensive pile built in the form of a quadrangle. On entering I was much pleased with the mosque on the right-hand side; there is more than usual boldness in the design of the outward embellishments. In the part of the building, which is opposite to you on entering, is contained the tombs, formed of silver and inlaid with gold, or so coloured as to represent those metals, of Azuff-al-Dowlah and his wife; three other tombs are also erected, but untenanted. The walls of this aisle are covered with looking-glasses and mirrors, chandeliers hang in profusion from the ceiling, and dirty tinsel everywhere offends the eye. No attention whatever is paid to the cleanliness of the place.

The *Imaums* informed us that during the Mussulmaun *fête* of the Mahaurram, 500,000 lights blaze in the Imaum Bara. I did not believe him. On retiring, the Bomoh Durwanzah is distant about 100 yards on your left; this gate is copied from one of the same name at Constantinople; the style of architecture is singular, and the effect produced elegant. Immediately in the vicinity the Mosque with the Golden Dome rises. At one particular point the eye takes into its range the whole of these edifices. I have never seen the view equalled. Nothing can exceed the filth that abounds in this neighbourhood. I continued my ride to the Dowlah Khanna, a bad house, undeserving the name of palace; it was built by Azuff-al-Dowlah; in it is a curious picture of the *nawab* handling his bird at a cock fight. Colonel Mordaunt and General Martin are introduced in the painting; the warm baths appeared well constructed.

I heard an anecdote related of this Colonel Mordaunt: when a cadet, coming out to this country, he had delayed joining his ship so long that on his arrival at Deal she had just got under weigh. He had very little money: with all he had he endeavoured to bribe some boatmen to take him to the ship, but they were playing at "all-fours " and would not listen to his offer. Mordaunt looked over the game for some time; but soon called a sharp-looking fellow on one side, and promised if he would take him to the ship to learn him how to turn up Jack every time. Mordaunt shewed Jack the trick; he was taken to the ship, and by this was enabled to realise a fortune which he otherwise never could have gained.

In the evening I drove Rickett's team to Constantia, a palace built by General Martin, a Frenchman, who came to this country as a private soldier, and died enormously rich. It is situated two miles to the eastward of Lucknow; the architecture differs totally from any building I have seen; there is a mixture of all styles and orders, but so arranged as not materially to offend the eye. The base, or first storey, is considerably larger than the second, the second than the third in the same proportion, and the fourth is merely a tower. On the top of each of the three first storeys is a terrace, on the sides of which are erected figures, curiously carved, as large as life; enormous lions stand rampant at the corners of the first terrace.

No wood was employed in the construction of this curious place; the floors are formed of marble, the rooms are all arched, and the ceilings are elaborately carved and gilt; spiral staircases, dark and difficult of ascent, wind from the different corners of the hall, and iron doors fit into grooves at each landing place, so as entirely upon an emergency to cut off all communication with the lower storey. General Martin must have fancied an attack possible, and the building is well constructed to defeat assailants, as each terrace is completely commanded by the upper one. Any person is at liberty to take up his residency in Constantia for a month, but old Treves has remained here for a year. Underneath is a vault (to which you descend from the hall) where lie the remains of Martin.

At the head of the tomb is placed a fine bust of the general, and on a marble slab is an inscription in English which informs you his age, that his birthplace was Lyons and that he came to this country a private soldier. At the four corners of the vault stand four grenadiers resting on their arms; these figures are as large as life; the vault is constantly lighted. In front of the house is a lake, from the centre of which rises a handsome pillar, much smaller, but similar to that in the Place Vendome; the shaft is formed of one solid piece of marble.

The gardens are extensive and well laid out in the Dutch fashion. General Martin has left a sum, in itself a fortune, to be annually expended in repairs. General Garstin once asked Martin how he could have amassed such enormous wealth; he replied, "I will let you into the secret. I never received a *rupee*, without laying by eight *annas*." I shall again go over Constantia. I am by no means satisfied with the flying visit I have paid to it.

Oct. 16.—The king received us at one of his palaces on the banks of the Gumtee; we breakfasted in a tent, whilst the band of his bodyguard played in one direction, a set of half-caste fiddlers scraped away in another, and the king's favourite *nautch* woman, who looked like a large bloated toad, made such a noise as no one who has not heard her can fancy; I never heard any sound so discordant; a person learning to play on the bagpipes would be a fool to her. You may imagine the band playing the 16th's March, the fiddlers attempting a quadrille, and my friend the *nautch* woman drowning both with her voice, would not harmonise well together. When breakfast was finished, the king led the way into a veranda of the palace immediately overlooking the river.

On his appearing, elephants and ten rhinoceros were driven to the opposite bank, where the fun began with a fight between two elephants. I pitied the poor *mahouts*, who shifted from the neck to the back of the animal; notwithstanding all the shouting and goading the elephants shewed but tame sports; two rhinoceros showed capital fight—the rest afforded little amusement. At a short distance, tumblers displayed wonderful feats of activity. The space where all took place was not enclosed. The elephants' carriages were, after the beasts had been driven away, paraded; one was drawn by four, and two other carriages by two elephants each; these vehicles were gaudily painted and nearly covered with gilding. The bodyguard of "The Light of the World" dressed in humble imitation of the 16th Lancers were capering about in the distance. In the middle of the river two large boats were moored, in which *nautch* boys and girls performed and conjurors displayed their tricks.

A steam vessel constantly passed up and down the river in front of the palace. All this *tamaushau* was going forward at one and the same time, so that the eye could not rest sufficiently on any one object to become interested. On retiring the crown was exposed to our view; I was told it cost five *lacs* of *rupees*; it was not particularly handsome. The king wore a beautiful pearl necklace, each pearl as large as the very largest pea. On returning to the Residency we found the king had sent rams, antelopes, quail and partridges to fight for our amusement. The rams had their bodies painted and their horns, which were unusually large, gilt; the shock with which they met each other was quite tremendous, and how their heads escaped being broken was as surprising.

The battles between the antelopes were not so fierce, but from the elegance of their shapes more attractive; the condition of these animals was as fine as that of a well-trained horse. The partridges were dunghill, but the quails were very game, and shewed very good fun on the breakfast table. The usual drive of an evening is in the grounds of Dil Kushar, the "Delight of the Heart;" there is a palace here scarcely worth mentioning. All kinds of game, particularly the deer species, used to abound in this park; but the wall of late has been neglected, and much of the game has escaped or been destroyed. Driving a team through the "Delight of the Heart" is a great lounge, after a humble buggy on the dusty course of Cawnpore. At one extremity of these grounds Bibbypoor is situated; it was almost dark when I went over the house: but the rooms were large, and appeared well furnished. In Lucknow it is unusual to meet a man unarmed; most men carry a sword and dagger.

Oct. 19.—The king sent breakfast and *tiffin* to Beirone, a favourite palace about two miles to the west of the city and four from the Residency. Beirone is better deserving the name of palace than any one I have seen in Lucknow. The principal room in which we ate was about 70 feet long by 46 feet. On the walls were hung prints of different views in this country, executed in London. In every department of the king's affairs a radical reform is necessary, but in none more than the cuisine. I fancied I now had an opportunity of tasting oriental cookery in perfection; but if this was the best display of the art, defend me from ever partaking of the worst.

The *pilaus* covered with gold and silver leaf were execrable, contaminated with *assafoetida*; the fish and rice very bad, and the stews worse. Hyde, who is a man of considerable fortune at home, left Piccadilly on the top of a stage coach six years ago to visit Paris; he has continued his travels through Egypt, Syria, Persia, and is now making a tour through Indostan. He has picked up a good deal of information, but certainly not as much as he might have done; he can scarcely make himself understood in any language except English: of Hindoostanee he has not the slightest knowledge. Treves, shaking his head, said, when he first became acquainted with Hyde, he thought him a prosing good sort of man, till he told him he had 6,000 a year at home. "By Gad, sir, since then I have never been able to speak to the man; I have thought him such a damned fool for broiling in this country instead of spending his money in England."

Hyde at this meal partook of each dish, and ate like a traveller. After breakfast tumblers exhibited in front of the house and performed wonderful feats of activity. A woman stood on a square frame of separate pieces of wood, but slightly attached; this was placed on a piece of bamboo 1½ foot long, which was poised, the woman standing on the frame, on the head of a man, who ran round a circle with great speed. Another woman had her legs tied to a high pair of stilts, with which she stood on a long piece of bamboo, the size of a man's arm, placed on the ground: this was taken up and put on the shoulders of two men who carried her standing on the bamboo over a tight rope 10 feet from the ground; the ascent and descent were the most difficult part.

A third woman leant back supporting herself on her hands, and picked up with her mouth a silver ring which was placed in a hole dug for the purpose, and which was filled with water; the whole of her head and neck were under water. Mrs. Wilkinson sat great part of the day under a tree in the garden reading *Lalla Rookh* in the most sentimental attitudes; her trowsers were so oriental that that princess herself might have worn them.

At *tiffin* I tasted a stewed cucumber which created a nausea for the remainder of the day; I sent the dish to Hyde as a curiosity, and he ate the whole of its contents. When *tiffin* was over, some fun was excited by a letter being brought into Ricketts as if coming from the king's nephew to propose for Mrs. Mack and offering to place her at the head of his *seraglio*; this word was not at all to Mrs. Mack's mind. The joke was carried rather too far, as it made the fattest and best-natured creature in the world cry. Ellis and I rode races. I deserved for this folly, what I was fortunate in escaping, a fever.

Oct. 20.—Breakfasted with Agger Meere, the prime minister, who has had the title of *Mootim-ood-Dowlat*, the "Pillar of the State," conferred on him. The room in which he entertained us was handsome, and the breakfast and equipage generally better than the king's. The number of attendants in waiting and standing round the table, were numerous, and several of their dresses were splendid. During the time of breakfast, separate parties of *nautch* girls danced, some of whom might boast of beauty; the king's own especial fool appeared, as a *beastye*, and made us laugh almost as much as Grimaldi was used to do. We afterwards went into a veranda, in which men exhibited various modes of attack and defence with the sword and shield, and shewed great agility as well in the offensive as in avoiding the blow of their opponent.

Another exercise was shewn by two men who were sitting down armed with daggers; they surprised us by the great quickness with which they parried the weapon of their adversary, and by a peculiar method of pinioning him with the leg. A man who called forth the repeated plaudits of the natives flourished a great double-handed sword, six or eight feet long, and managed this unwieldy weapon admirably. Cock fighting succeeded; as the birds were not spurred, the sport was insipid.

We were now conducted into another veranda where shawls were spread out; the ladies had each a pearl necklace presented to them, the gentlemen each a pair of shawls, *deckhna ka waustee*; these presents were no sooner received than they were returned into the treasury of our government. The minister is one of the worst countenanced men I ever saw; there is scarcely an atrocity which he could not commit and few that he has not been guilty of. On leaving the minister's house he placed a tinsel silver necklace round each of our necks.

By-the-bye, the king always performs this ceremony on leaving his presence. I called on Holmes, who is miniature painter to the king and a tolerable artist; he had a good picture of Lord Hastings and a strong likeness of Sir Edward Paget, but his best painting was one of his first wife, who must have been lovely if it is a likeness. Mr. Holmes's son has something to do in the management of the king's horses, and he shewed us some of the favourites. Tanjan, an old grey Arab, is a very clever horse; he was the pet of Sidet Ali, the present king's father. Some of the home-bred colts are very promising.

In the evening I rode to the menagerie, where several tigers, lions, bears and hyaenas are kept; a great variety of the deer species are here; and a very beautiful collection of birds, particularly of pheasants; and a princely establishment of falconers and hawks were paraded. A wild man adorns this menagerie, of which he is not the least curiosity; he was caught in the jungles; he speaks no language, but makes a noise and looks like an idiot: I suspect this wild man is a humbug.

Oct. 21.—I went to a palace situated at one end of a canal about 150 yards long, on one side of which was standing the palace where we first breakfasted, and through which I now passed; my object was to see the throne, over which a sentinel was placed; the throne is elevated three steps, the edges of which are studded with precious stones and covered with crimson velvet; it has no canopy, and although covered with crimson velvet and profusely studded with diamonds, rubies, and emeralds, it is not handsome. It looked dirty and tawdry. The *chattah* which is carried before the king on State occasions was exhibited; it is also covered with crimson velvet, and so studded with diamonds as almost to act like a mirror.

When I had satisfied my curiosity, I walked to another palace at the other end of the canal, and passed through a garden laid out in the Dutch style. I was much amused with seeing the hair of the different statues which were miserable casts, with their hair and eyes painted brown; the Venus di Medici was lavishly adorned in this way. Charles Grant and I mounted an elephant to visit the tombs of Sidir Ali and his wife, each contained in buildings of similar architecture crowned with domes. The exteriors are most elaborately carved; the interiors consist of one large octagonal apartment. At the head of the *nawaub's* tomb is placed his sword, part of his *hookar* apparatus, and articles of even smaller value. These buildings form a handsome object wherever they are visible; but they are falling as fast into decay as negligence will permit. This may be said of all the edifices erected by Sidir Ali, some of which are really splendid.

No Mussulmaun will repair the work of his predecessor; he fancies he gets no credit by so doing. The principal street in Lucknow runs nearly east and west; three handsome gateways are built at unequal distances through which you pass to go to Dil Kushar; on the north side of the street runs the wall which encloses the ground where the king's palaces are situated; on the south side are the tombs of Sidir Ali and his wife, the treasury, and, at a short distance, a princely range of stabling. I have omitted mentioning that a gun fires when the king rises in the morning and another when he retires to rest at night.

Oct. 22.—I visited the Chuta Imaum Bara of very recent structure, and much smaller than the building of that name which I have already described. I had a short argument with the *Imaums* as to gaining admittance without taking off my boots, but the point was ceded as I was *sepoy loge*. Nothing can be more tawdry than the interior decorations, I mean those independent of the building, which I think light and elegant. In the centre is placed a large silver tomb, intended, I believe, as the final resting place of his present Majesty. At the corners stand four large tigers of green glass, three feet high, and large awkward silver fish (the crest of the king) prance at the sides. The walls are covered with large looking-glasses and mirrors, which are intersected with quantities of tinsel, and handsome chandeliers of divers colours hang in crowds from the ceiling.

The streets in the city are very narrow and dirty beyond the powers of exaggeration; every species of abomination abounds: how the inhabitants escape the plague is miraculous; what saves them from that curse must be the ablutions which from their religion they are so constantly obliged to make. I spent a day with Smallpage in the cantonments, distant about five miles to the north; I had to pass the only bridge over the Gumtee, which is of considerable extent, but the numerous arches are of small span. No money appears to be laid out in the repairs which are absolutely necessary, and this bridge like all the public buildings must soon fall into a very dilapidated state.

Here I had a very fine view, the best of the city; the number of domes and minarets, several of which were gilded, glittering in the morning sun, gave it a very magnificent appearance. Smallpage is Brigade-Major at this station; we resumed our favourite amusement of sparring; since he has become a major, he has turned a regular ruffian.

Mrs. Smallpage is as pleasing and good-natured as ever.

Oct. 23.—As I was obliged to be present to muster with my regiment on the 24th, I could not remain to see the nuptials celebrated, which were deferred till the first of November, that the Bishop of Calcutta might tie the knot superlatively tight. I scarcely regretted my absence. Ricketts who had the whole of the party staying with him lived 'en-prince'—the most costly wines were handed about profusely; Lindsay counted the number of glasses of champagne one lively lady drank; when they amounted to ten he held up both hands, and discontinued the score. Madam was decidedly screwed: I think this was not a singular instance. I fancied I had seen more than one bright eye look funny. In the evening I got into my *palanquin* and travelled *dawk* to Cawnpore, where I arrived at sunrise on the morning of the 24th; I found Roche staying in my house.

Dec. 6.—The Cawnpore Races commenced and continued alternate days for a fortnight; the horses were not very good, but were pretty well matched; a well-contested race was run between "Red Gauntlet" and "Osmond," Johnson's horse winning from superior jockeyship. Havelock can't ride.

There was another capital race between "Red Gauntlet," "Charley," "Osmond" and "Magistrate" for the 50 *G.Ms.* for all Arabs," Magistrate" so dark a horse that he was never even thought of winning both heats cleverly. He belonged to my old school-fellow Worrall. Jenkins of the 11th Dragoons came down from Meerut and took away a little money; he recognised having met me in France. I should not have recollected him; he now looks like the coachman of a heavy drag. Jenkins married a plain half-caste daughter of Colonel Paton; she resembles a turkey's egg, all black and yellow, or rather yellow with black spots. Such as she is, Colonel Sleigh, who commands the 11th, pays her a good deal of attention. Jenkins one day seeing the colonel talking to his wife, said I cannot think what the colonel sees in Soph to be so much with her.

During this fortnight, if parties and ball constitute gaiety, no place could be gayer than Cawnpore. I never was in my own house except to sleep; the time passed away too rapidly. The Johnsons took the house formerly inhabited by Ravenscroft, and made it the pleasantest lounge in the station. Mrs. Johnson improves wonderfully on acquaintance; her conversation, I think, somehow enhances the symmetry of her person. Mr. Cowell, the circuit judge, has brought his two daughters;

one is reckoned pretty. Sperling, writing me an account of her, allowed her this attraction, but added, with simplicity, he did not think she had a warm heart. Jane Cowell has a silly way of saying: "Oh Dear, Yes," to everything. Baron Osten, sitting by her, observed in the course of conversation that the great drawback to marriage in this country was the having annually to send to England the pledge of mutual affection. Jane drawled out: "Oh Dear, Yes."

This was a hazardous remark for the baron to have made. *Mademoiselle* must have learnt this from her mother, who pretends to be passionately fond of children; she is constantly talking of them, and always calls them: "*Oh, the sweet little things.*" In a large party the conversation had turned to the Blue Devils. Mrs. Enderby remarked: "They are *such* a bore; don't you think so, Mrs. Cowell?" She, fancying Mrs. Enderby must have been speaking of children, replied; "Oh Dear, no, the sweet little things."

Jan. 1, 1825.—At 3 o'clock a.m. I was awoke by the orderly corporal of the troop, who told me the right squadron were instantly ordered for duty. On galloping down to the barracks, I found our destination was Calpee, 50 miles distant. On the Grand Parade the 15th N. I., who had the previous day completed a march of three months from Nagpore, were turned out, but we were not to proceed till a detachment of guns arrived. I never began a New Year in so warlike a manner. As the squadron was not allowed to leave the guns and infantry our march was very tiresome. At Bara we halted for four hours; but as the *syces* had not come up, so dependent is a soldier in India, the utmost confusion prevailed, and some men could not dismount from their horses.

At 4 o'clock on the morning of the 2nd we arrived at the River Jumna; some of the horses were so leg-weary that they fell down with exhaustion, and all were sadly knocked up. Had an enemy now appeared we should have made but a sorry figure; the last of the squadron did not cross the river before 3 o'clock p.m. Colonel Burgh commanded the detachment, and Major Persse our squadron. In the fort, which is situated on the south-west bank of the Jumna (on this side impregnable from its elevation, on all others the surrounding country is intersected with deep ravines,) I met my old shipmate, Sir Harry Darrell, who had been frightened out of his wits. The fort, which in some places is so weak that it might be scaled without the assistance of a ladder, had been attacked at 7 o'clock a.m., on the morning of the

31st December, by 300 or 400 irregular followers of Nanhoo Pundit, an insignificant person who held a *jagheer* of land, and possessed a mud fort on the River Betwah, about 18 miles south of Calpee.

But the magnanimous Nanhoo disdaining to take advantage of the weakness of the place, made his attack at just the strongest point, and failed in his object of carrying off the treasure, which amounted to three *lacs* of *rupees*. Only a company of the 41st N. I. were in the fort at the time; a *havildar's* party sallied out, and were sufficient to drive the contemptible assailants with the loss of 13 killed from the ravines: 5 *sepoys* were wounded. Poor Sir Harry was walking from his house at the time the firing commenced. He ran at his best pace to the collector's house, seized a piece of paper lying on Calvert's table, and scrawled in every direction a few lines to Sir Gabriel Martindale commanding at Cawnpore, saying the fort is attacked, and at all hazards he estimated the enemy at 7,000 men, hourly increasing.

A similar note he despatched to the officer commanding at Keitah, another to the judge of the district, Ainslie, and a fourth to Banda; in consequence of these despatches, written with all the agitation and exaggeration of fear, a force was collected sufficient to have subdued the whole of Bundlecund. There were collected a squadron of the 16th Lancers, 3 troops of the 5th N. Cavalry, the 15th N. I., 2 companies from Keitah, and 2 six-pounders. The first question on meeting a man you knew was: "And what are you come here, too?" When Sir Harry had despatched these notes by his own account, trembling with fear, he begged of Calvert to cross the river with him in a boat which he had taken the precaution to procure; Calvert begged sufficient time to load his gun. Sir Harry stammered: "Come along, come along, we shall be sacrificed."

"Do, Sir Harry, allow me one moment to load my gun."

"I'll wait for nothing, Sir, I have a wife and children at home, Sir, Dear Lady Darrell, Sir. What, you will load your gun? Then I abandon you to your fate; your blood be on your own head."

As he was flying out of the room, he had the good nature to turn back and articulate, "May God preserve you." Yet Sir Harry Darrell is one of the best men I ever knew. At an advanced period of life, he has returned to this country to procure by his exertion an independent fortune for his children, and his appointment of Commercial Resident at Calpee is so lucrative a one, that by his own account he yearly sends home a provision for a child. The baronet would not return to his own house, but took up his quarters in the fort with Captain Ramsay who commanded: here he provided breakfast and dinner for the whole of the officers, and the campaign at the table was, at all events, a hard one. During the 3rd no party was sent out to reconnoitre, and the most contradictory accounts were brought in of the strength of the fort.

Ainslie arrived from Humerapore, and gave orders to Burgh to destroy or take the fort at Porassan, and to seize Nanhoo Pundit. Burgh asked how he was to take the fort. Ainslie answered he could not presume as a civilian to give instructions to a military man. Our chief took the precaution of writing for a battering train. On the 4th accounts arrived that Nanhoo had fled; he might, to use Sir Alexander Campbell's expression in his despatch from Rangoon, have mistaken system for timidity. Ainslie mentioned an instance of the duplicity of Nanhoo; he had represented to him the impropriety of his raising a force. Pundit said he was at enmity with the Rajah of Jalaun to whom he was feudatory, and that he expected to be attacked. Ainslie, who was this man's only friend, assured him of the protection of the British Government, and as an earnest sent two *darogahs* and two dragoons to his house.

The first act of the perfidious native was to confine these men, and instead of disbanding his force which he had solemnly promised, he attacked the fort of Calpee. On the 5th we began our march back to Cawnpore, rather an illustration of the King of France with 20,000 men marched up a hill, and then marched down again. On the 6th Persse allowed me to ride into Cawnpore to a ball that Barton gave. People were quite surprised when I told them one horse did the forty miles in six hours.

Jan. 12, 1825.—Having obtained 6 months' leave of absence McDowell and I left Cawnpore. McNair a friend of McDowell's accompanied us on some marches. When marching from Nagpore, passing through the Cota *rajah's* territory, a part of McNair's regiment was ordered to attack Bulwunt Sing, the Rajah of Boundee, a man who had frequently signalised himself for courage: he was then absent from his fort attending a marriage. When he saw our troops advancing, he blockaded the house which, like the generality of any consequence, had loop-holes, and made a vigorous defence till guns were brought up and rendered the place untenable. Bulwunt Sing had now only to cut his way through the *sepoys* who guarded the gate, and he effected it; but soon received a gunshot wound and fell. He got up and endeavoured to effect his retreat, he was a second time shot and fell, he again

110

rose and tried to force his way: he received a third ball which so disabled him that he could not rise, but supporting himself he continued fighting till he was cut to pieces.

This native had not more than thirty Rajputs with him at the time he was attacked. Scarce one of these escaped or wished to do so; they sold their lives as dearly as they could. When the news of Bulwunt Sing's death reached his wife, she first stabbed her two infants, and then herself: on its being related to his sister she threw herself from a tower; the event was fatal—the family are extinct. Mr. Mills in his *History of India* would persuade that courage is a virtue unknown amongst the Hindoos, and that the Rajputs are a cowardly race of men. He depresses them to a lower standard than they deserve, in very many instances. From never having been in the country that author does not, and cannot form, a just conception of their characters, manners, or customs.

At Kurrah we overtook the 15th N.I., McNair's regiment, in the course of one evening. At their Mess I exchanged four horses. At Dleilgunge, Thomas and Turton dined with us, and there was rather a good scene in the evening; the merit of wines got from Mr. Crump, a wine merchant at Cawnpore, was under discussion. McDowell said he knew nothing about his wines, but that there were three women in his house who he should like to kiss.

Turton with lively anxiety asked, "What, like to kiss them all?"

"Yes; by heavens, all," was McDowell's reply.

I shall never forget Turton when he said, "Why one of them is my wife:" he had married Miss Crump. McDowell literally thrust his *hooka* into the husband's mouth, and to turn the conversation asked him if he was a judge of a *chillum*.

Feb. 15.—Arrived at Agra; on the following morning ordered the tents to be removed and pitched in an outer court of the Taje. In my life I have never been so much delighted with the sight of anything inanimate as with this mausoleum, which was erected by the Emperor Shah Jehan over his favourite, Sultana Arjemund Banu, who he dignified by the title of *Mumtaza Zemani*, the most exalted of the age. She was the daughter of Asiph Jah, who was brother to Nour Mahal or Noor Jehan, the favourite of Jehangire, the preceding emperor. *Mumtaza* had been twenty years married to Shah Jehan, and bore him a child almost every year; she died 1041, *Hijri* (1631 *A.D.*)

According to Dow the expense of this mausoleum was £750,000;

The Taj Mahal by John Luard.

considering the price of labour, now only 3 *annas* a day, or 6*d*. of our money, this sum is enormous. The gardens and space on which the Taje stands is about ten of our acres in extent. You enter them through a gateway of red freestone inlaid with white and a dark-coloured marble; over the arch is a pattern of flowers in mosaic on white marble; the outer arch is, I should guess, 50 feet high, over it are eleven small domes of white marble, and at the angles are four cupolas of the same. From this gateway you look on the Taje, which itself is built entirely of white marble, through an avenue of cypress trees; between them a shallow canal runs from which twenty-five fountains spout, the canal is supplied from a basin in the centre of the avenue, a similar canal runs from the basin to the Taje, so that from the gateway fifty fountains play, besides those in the basin.

A bed of flowers is on either side, then a broad pavement, and another avenue of trees, so that you look through a double row. From the garden you ascend to a terrace, the pavement of which is inlaid; on each side of the building is a beautiful gateway, but through the eastern one only is there an entrance. The height of these gateways from the terrace is 92 feet, that of the dome, I think, 180; it is surmounted with a cullis, and the crescent, and is surrounded by four cupolas. Minarets rise in such proportions of height as perfectly to harmonise. The minarets erected at right angles are 130 feet: to the top are 159 steps. Each of these four pillars is crowned with a cupola: in my opinion they are the perfection of elegance. You descend to the tombs of Shah Jehan and the Taje Bibby.

The cenotaph is on a level with you on entrance, placed in the centre of a large octagonal apartment, which I made 66 yards round. It is surrounded by a screen which is also octagonal, and tastefully carved into filigree from large slabs of marble; in every eighth there are three compartments, each bordered with flowers in mosaic. Each of the eight arches in this apartment forms a recess, and every alternate one is latticed so as freely to admit, but at the same time to soften, the light. On the square of each arch is inlaid in black a scroll in Persian. The roof is about 80 feet high, it is concave, and the carving is so managed as to give the marble the appearance of spa.

The cenotaph of Shah Jehan is five yards in length and three in breadth; the Taje Bibby is somewhat less. The emperor is covered with different patterns of flowers in mosaic, with the cornelian, agate and blood-stones, so exquisitely worked as to give the appearance of painting; no division is perceptible. In one small flower I was informed sixty stones were inlaid; the flowers are shaded with darker cornelian so as to produce a very beautiful effect. On the cenotaph as well as tomb of *Moomtaza* her name and titles are inlaid in the Persian. At the base of the wall slabs of marble, of equal size, about five feet high, have each three flowers, boldly and finely carved in relief on them, and each is surrounded with a border in mosaic. On the exterior flowers and mosaic are executed similar to this. I have heard the dome of this mausoleum found fault with on account of the bulge not being sufficient.

I think the whole defies criticism, and should favour the opinion of those men who having seen most of the admired edifices in Europe, declare the Taje eminently unrivalled. General Blair wrote verses in a small room which has obtained the name of the Poet's Corner. Several other poetical effusions are written on the walls of this small room. I could not avoid at the moment writing underneath one of affected smartness, and decided vulgarity, alluding to Shah Jehan and *Moomtaza*—

> *Oh what a theme! how totally unfit*
> *To cause the vain attempt of blockhead's wit.*

Mrs. Jack Hawker gave an evening party to which I went, and soon found I was booked in a very slow coach. Barnett who has had the title of Lady Betty Barnett conferred on him, took, or rather chaperoned, me. My chaperone is one of the most singular-looking persons I ever saw, and equally remarkable in the style of his dress. He is the most weaselly-looking fellow, his waist uncommonly small, and his shoulders scarcely broader, a very thin face, and a very long nose; he is an amateur in performing women's characters on the stage; just that sort of man.

After supper Lady Betty was requested to sing, and he commenced a song of Moore's in a voice like a cracked penny trumpet, but he soon broke down, and I thought he was foundered; he, however, was again brought to the post, and after a false start, he went off briskly; by looking steadfastly on the table I was enabled to restrain a fit of laughter till the last verse when, unfortunately, I raised my eyes, and saw the figure who was squeaking. The combined effect was too much. In endeavouring to smother a violent fit of laughter, I was thrown into an equally violent one of coughing, which saved me from being guilty of boisterous rudeness.

Feb. 17.—Went over the fort—the foundation was laid by Akbar 972 *Hijri* (*A. D.* 1563). The curtain is 60, probably 80 feet high, and the circumference I should guess at mile or 2 miles; it is built of red freestone; the gates are curiously inlaid. This great and magnificent work was finished in four years. Although I have seen many stronger forts, I never saw one that had so imposing an appearance. It surrendered to Lord Lake in 1803, after a short and vigorous siege. One battery was erected near the river to the eastward, and another after the Tripolia was taken, where we sustained the principal loss, on the Jumma Musjid to the westward. The exterior of the palace of Akbar forms a portion of the N. E. curtain, and immediately overlooks the Jumna. The principal rooms are composed of white marble, inlaid with coloured stones.

The private audience chamber, having a recess at either end, is particularly deserving of attention, both on account of the proportion and the surprising beauty of the mosaic. The baths in their way are equally beautiful, and the pattern of the floor is the most elegant in Agra. These are in a sad dilapidated state, and one has been entirely destroyed by Lord Hastings who sent the mosaic to England. The Ina Khanna is quite the admiration of the natives; it forms part of the *zenana*, and contains two rooms gaudily painted, which have small pieces of looking-glass so arranged in the walls and roof which is arched as to have the light reflected in almost innumerable rays. The centre of each room forms a basin from which small fountains play; these are supplied by a waterfall which is conducted through the wall. The public audience chamber of Akbar is now converted into an armoury.

In the fort is the *Mootee Musjid*, "Mosque of Pearl," where the Court of Akbar attended the service of Mahommed. I imagine this building cannot be surpassed in elegance. You ascend to it by fifty steps, and pass through a gate of white marble, simply and chastely carved. On the top are three cupolas surmounted with a cullis (roof channel to carry away rain water). This leads you into a quadrangle, at each side of which is a corridor divided in the centre by a gateway, similar to the one described, the pavement is slightly inlaid; in the centre of the quadrangle a basin is formed where fountains used to play. The *musjid* occupies the S. W. side, the front is composed of seven arches, the span of each about seven yards, and over each arch is placed a cupola. It is crowned with three domes, and at each angle a cupola rises, double the size of those which are placed in front over the seven arches.

In the interior there are three equal corridors of arches; the roof of each alternate arch in the centre corridor is concave. I made the *musjid* forty-eight steps, equal to fifty yards. The pavement is simply inlaid with a yellow stone, and the walls are chastely decorated with sculpture. In the centre of the S. W. wall is a recess; at one side a plain slab of marble is elevated by four steps, and on this the priest stood when performing his duty. This edifice is composed entirely of white marble, with the exception of the stone that is employed in inlaying the pavement. When the sun is up the glare of light is horridly offensive to the eye. The "Mosque of Pearl" I consider the acme of chasteness and good taste.

On the night of the 18th a Subscription Ball was given in the fort, in the rooms where Shah Jehan was confined by his son Aurungzebe, and we supped in the apartment in which he died; the Ina Khauna was lighted upon the occasion, and looked much better than it had by daylight—very much like the concluding scene in a Christmas pantomime. This evening quadrilles (only think) were attempted, and a kind of Spanish dance, where the gentleman and lady turn back to back, was exhibited ludicrously enough. On the whole, I have seldom seen a more perfect piece of tomfoolery.

Feb. 20.—Barnett sent breakfast to Ram Baugh, a garden and retreat of the celebrated Nour Mahal, the favourite Sultana of Jehangire. A romantic story of this princess is translated by Dow from the Persian. About the year 1590 *A. D.*, Chaja Aiass, a native of the Western Tartary, left that country to push his fortune in Hindoostan, his wife accompanied him, and on the road was taken in labour and brought forth a daughter. As they were unable to carry the infant with them, they agreed to expose her on the highway, she was partly covered with leaves, and left under a tree. Aiass had proceeded some way when his wife fell into a paroxysm of grief at the loss of her daughter, and the husband agreed to return and bring her. He arrived at the place, but no sooner had his eyes reached the child than he was almost struck dead with horror. A black snake was coiled round it, and Aiass beheld the serpent extending his jaws to devour the infant.

The father rushed forward, and the serpent alarmed at his vociferations retired into the hollow tree. He took up his daughter unhurt and returned to the mother. Some travellers appeared and relieved them of their wants. They proceeded gradually to Lahore where Akbar was then keeping his Court. Chaja Aiass in process of time became Master of the Household; and, his genius being still greater than his good fortune, he raised himself to the office and title of *Achemad-ul-Dowlah*, or High Treasurer of the empire. The daughter who had been so miraculously saved, received the name of *Mher-ul-Nissa*, or the "Sun of Women." She had some right to the appellation, for in beauty she excelled all the women of the East.

Jehangire became enamoured of her, but she had been betrothed to Shere Afkan, a Turkomanian nobleman of great renown, and Akbar would not be guilty of an act of injustice to favour his son's passion. Soon after Jehangire ascended the throne he caused Shere Afkan, one of the bravest of his nobles to be assassinated. *Mher-ul-Nissa* was brought into the *zenana*, and a magnificent festival was prepared for the celebration of his nuptials. Her name was changed into *Noor Mahal*, the "Light of the *Haram*," and seven years afterwards it was again altered to *Noor Jahan*, or the "Light of the World."

Shah Jehan, the son of Jehangire, married Kudsia, the daughter of Asiph Jah, who was brother to Noor Jehan. Kudsia had the title of *Moomtaza Zenani* conferred on her, and is the *Taje Bibby*. The residence in the Ram Baugh is by no means deserving the name of palace. There are two separate dwellings on either side of a paved court, which has a basin in the middle of it; a small bow room terminates each of these buildings on the river side which is immediately underneath, and from them you have a fine view up and down the Jumna. The gardens are pretty and extensive, most of the walls are paved, on each side of which small canals of water run; *chaboatas* are built every fifty yards; many are placed in the middle of a basin, so that fountains would play all round you. Several fine trees are in this garden and one tamarind tree is remarkable.

After breakfast we dropped down the river, and immediately passed the gardens and palace of Jehanara, the daughter of Shah Jehan, who shared his confinement with him. We soon came to the China Ke Rhosa, a building quite unique. The exterior is entirely mosaic, formed of China tile of various colours which have still retained their brightness; the pattern in which it is inlaid, from its boldness, considerably augments the beauty of this edifice, which it is to be regretted is fast falling to decay, but the pillars of the brightest purple and gold are still in a tolerable state of preservation. The interior corresponds with the outward appearance, but is more elaborately inlaid: the cornice in the octagonal apartment is well designed and the concave roof is beautiful. This splendid place is now converted into a stable for bullocks who pollute the tomb of the unknown builder.

From hence we passed further down to the tomb of *Achemad-ul-Dowlah* erected by Noor Mahal over her father; her mother is also buried here. At a little distance this building does not promise well from its appearance. When you arrive at it you are agreeably surprised to find it composed of white marble exquisitely sculptured in relief, and most elaborately inlaid. The interior does not correspond, being chunaramed and painted. The cenotaph above is the most beautiful part, the tombs are formed of a yellow stone very scarce, the pavement is of mosaic, the pattern of flowers boldly designed and well executed. The trellice which forms the sides of this apartment is delightfully carved out of the marble into a variety of forms. Here we had a fine view of the fort and Taje which are on the S. W. side of the Jumna, opposite to the places I this this day have visited.

Achemad-ul-Dowlah's tomb has got into the possession of a native who is so negligent as to allow sad depredations to be committed on the mosaic, and so indifferent as to permit the refuse of the garden to be thrown into some of the rooms. We again got into our boat and passed underneath the fort and palace of Akbar. By the side of the river is an immense cannon which Government intended to have sent home. It almost instantly sunk the boat that was to have conveyed it to Calcutta, but was recovered, and has since remained by the side of the river. Dow mentions that Akbar had two guns which were employed at the siege of Rintinpoor capable of carrying a stone ball of 6 or 7 *maunds*, or an iron one of 30—a *maund* is equal to 80 of our pounds. I conclude this to be one of them. We continued floating down the stream till we passed the Taje, which certainly should be seen from the river.

Feb. 21.—Drove to Secundra, 7 miles to the west of the city. The entrance is through a splendid gateway of red stone inlaid with white and dark-coloured marble. The heights of the arch I should guess at 60 feet, and the top of the gateway is probably 15 feet higher. From each angle four large white marble pillars appear so as to rise from the roof: these may be 100 feet high. Part of the shaft is fluted, the summit is decayed, so that the pillars are now of unequal height. From hence a broad pavement of a quarter of a mile leads straight to the tomb; half way down this path is a basin where fountains used to play. Secundra is a square building of 110 yards by my steps, and so composed of red stone and marble as to have a grand and, at the same time, pleasing effect. On each of the four sides, in the centre is a gateway of red stone inlaid with black, white, and yellow marble, having a corridor of five arches of handsome span on either side; over the gateway is a cupola of white marble and at each angle of the square one of red stone.

The only entrance is through the eastern gateway.You pass through a vaulted passage to a large lofty apartment where Akbar was laid in a perfectly plain white marble tomb in 1014 *Hijri*, A.D. 1605. On the top of the base of Secundra is a fine terrace, the pavement inlaid. At the base of the second storey at each side is a corridor of twenty-four small arches of red stone, surmounted with five cupolas of the same, but the dome is of white marble. The base of the third storey has a corridor of eleven arches in the same style. Each side is surmounted with three cupolas, those at the angles composed of blue and gold China tile which gives the effect of porcelain.

This mausoleum is crowned with the cenotaph formed wholly of white marble minutely carved in relief, several Persian characters are inscribed on it in the same style; it stands on an elevated pavement, and would be exposed to the weather were it not for a rude frame of wood which supports a thatched covering. The cenotaph, or place where it stands, is twenty-eight yards square, the corridor on the sides is elegant, and the lattice, as usual, is exquisitely worked. The country near the road from the Delhi Derwassah to Secundra is thickly interspersed with the ruins of former magnificence. On the left-hand side of the road there is a curious statue of a horse rather rudely executed in red stone. The artist must have been a bad judge of the points of that animal.

Feb. 23. Arrived at Futteypoor Sicri, twenty-four miles to the west and south of Agra. Akbar when passing through the village of Sicri was foretold by Shaick Selim Chistee, a man of renowned holiness in these parts, that he would shortly be blessed with a son, an event much desired by the emperor, who was persuaded to send some of his most beautiful *sultanas* to Sicri that they might profit by the prayers and intercessions of Selim. It may be imagined that the Saint prayed with greater fervour than devotion, and addressed his supplications more to the lovely princesses of the monarch than to the Prophet. However, that may be, Selim prayed with so much earnestness and so much to the purpose, that shortly three sons were born. The eldest was named Selim, and afterwards reigned by the title of Jehangire. I fancy Akbar must have had more faith than good works: there may be a blot in the escutcheon even of the House of Timur.

The emperor esteeming the village of Sicri fortunate from these events, founded a city here, 1570 *A.D.*, and, after the conquest of

Guzerat, called it the "City of Victory." It was built on a bank or small ridge of hill, and now only presents a heap of ruins. On the death of Selim, a splendid mausoleum was erected by Akbar over his ashes. I entered the quadrangle of 130 yards from corridor to corridor, through the eastern gateway which is built of red stone and inlaid with white and dark-coloured marble; on the top are cupolas. There is another gateway to the south, which is the largest I have seen; there are three arches in it of considerable span, and the height of the centre one must he near 80 feet, and the cupola on the summit I should guess at 120. From it you have an extensive view over a flat country. This gateway is built on the side of a bank; you ascend from the south up a large flight of steps; from the bottom the structure is prodigiously fine.

A corridor of red stone, the arches handsome, is on each side of the quadrangle; cupolas are thickly placed on the top. The *musjid* fronts the east; it is 80 yards long. The effect produced, when at one end you look through six arches, between each, two double pillars rise on either side to the other extremity, is very good. The part where the service was performed is a square apartment having the angles above cut off by an arch, the walls, and roof, which is concave, are elaborately inlaid with stone, and different coloured China tile. An inscription in Arabic from the *Koran* is in relief on the square of a recess which is sunk in the centre of the west wall; by the side of it a slab of marble is elevated by three steps; from this the priest performed. The *musjid* is a handsome building; it is built of red stone, of not so dark a colour as the fort at Agra, or the mausoleum at Secundra.

The tomb of Selim is on the north side, and I think not happily situated. Had it been in the centre, or quite at the side, it would have been better. Now, it detracts from the appearance of the quadrangle and has not the advantage of being well seen till you nearly approach it. The mausoleum is formed wholly of white marble beautifully carved in relief; the columns which support the portico are singular, elegant and well carved. The tomb is placed in an apartment eight yards square, the pavement inlaid with different coloured stones, and the walls have flowers in mosaic on them, I thought not so well executed as at Secundra or the Taje. The door has the panels carved into lattice; and there is a similar figure on each side to admit the light. The tomb is of white marble, elegantly sculptured into trellis; it is covered by a canopy of scarce wood overspread with mother-of-pearl.

A passage runs on each side of this apartment having the outer wall latticed. The whole building is a square of 15 feet, and is crowned with a dome. On the east side of this mausoleum is a large edifice of red stone surmounted with a dome which contains several tombs, particularly of women. I was very much gratified with this place on first entrance. The quadrangle, the *musjid* fronting you, the magnificent gate on your left, and the last, not least, the mausoleum on your right, produce altogether an effect I have never seen surpassed. The palace of Akbar is adjoining, towards the north. The extensive ruins give a great idea of its ancient magnificence. It was built with the red stone. The residence of a favourite *sultana* remains perfect, and is curious for the minuteness with which the walls and ceilings have been carved all over.

There are four rooms in this house, about 15 feet square, with an arched door on each side so large as to occupy one-half of the wall. The ceilings are arched. Another residence, the Ecumba, is perfect and singular. A handsome pillar is erected in the centre and rises half-way up to the roof. It is sufficiently large on the top to allow six or eight persons to sit down with ease. A narrow pathway of stone crosses from each corner to the top of the column. Akbar delighted in sitting on this, to look at the beautiful girls of the *haram* playing underneath, I believe at blindman's buff or some similar game. The Di Dookna is close to this. It consists of a large room with many arches and a narrow passage on each side. Hide-and-seek was performed here for the emperor's diversion. The *catcherree*, the gate from whence the elephant fights were viewed, the different tanks and the baths, as well as hospital are all separately deserving of attention. Agra and its environs give a vast idea of the prodigious resources of the Mogul sovereigns.

Feb. 26.—Halted at Muttra, a city on the Jumna. The 3rd Cavalry and regiment of native infantry were stationed here. I met with Captain Festing who mentioned a very narrow escape he had for his life about a twelve month ago whilst shooting in the Tirhoot country. He had just passed a small wild rose-bush, when he heard a roar. He cocked his gun and instantly turned round, but too late; his knee was already in the mouth of tiger; his bearer on perceiving his situation ran forward, and seizing him by the other leg, endeavoured to extricate his master from the grasp. Fortunately, at this instant, Festing had sufficient recollection to pull the trigger. The flash and report frightening the tiger, he relinquished his prey, retreating to a short distance.

The elephant came up, and Festing had just strength to get into the *howdah*, whilst reloading his gun to have a shot at the tiger which remained looking at him twenty yards off. He fainted. He has since been a cripple, and I doubt if he will perfectly recover the use of his leg. He showed the marks of the tiger's claws on his arm. McDowell and I had intended to have visited Burtpoor and Deeg from Agra, but the *vakeel* who offered to give us a firman, (official permit), recommended our not accepting it, urging as a reason, that during the festival of the Hooly, the *rajah* himself has scarcely sufficient authority to quell the excesses which annually take place.

As I was anxious to visit Burtpoor, the fort having repulsed three attacks made on it during Lord Lake's war, and the *rajah* having always maintained his independence; and also the palace at Deeg which amply repays the visit. I was very much disappointed at not being able with prudence to extend the route to those places. The Hindoo festivals of the Hooly resembles the Saturnalia of the Romans. During its continuance every species of debauchery is abundant. Preparatory to it, the natives, particularly on the approach of women, sing the most indecent songs, which their language has the facility of expressing with peculiar grossness. The men besmear themselves with red and yellow, and throw powder of the same colours on those they meet.

This holiday is by no means kept up with the same brutality as formerly. *Sepoys* had the liberty, and still retain it in some decree, of abusing their officers, and servants indulged in the same liberty towards their masters. Barnett told me he remembered twenty men, in the costume of Adam and Eve in Paradise, performing a dance in the Chandee Choke at Delhi. I have not witnessed anything so offensive since I have been in the country. Between Bominy, Kherha, and Sicri a range of hills in the distance broke the unvaried expanse of plain that I had looked over for two years. The variety was as refreshing as the sight of verdure after having been long at sea.

At Sicri I met with an old woman so infirm from age and so emaciated by disease that I have seldom seen a more pitiable object. I stopped and told her to go to the tents, and my *sirdar* would give her some *pice*. I could not persuade her to venture, she fancied, God bless her, that I was captivated by her charms and had an intent on her honour. For the sake of my character, I endeavoured to convince her of my innocence with regard to her, but the more I asserted it the more she doubted my veracity. So, we parted company—the old Hindoo preferred going without alms. I thought her a fool, and the old woman believed me a "Perfidy Man."

March 6.—I arrived at Delhi, and stayed with Lowis This city was founded by Shah Jehan, and is called by the Mussulmauns Shah Jehanabad; ancient Delhi is a heap of ruins. The wall encircles a space of about seven miles, the bastions and curtain have been of late, and still are much improving, and when the glacis is completed Delhi will be a place of considerable strength. The streets are wider, better constructed, and cleaner than those of any city I have visited. A canal is conducted from the Jumna where it falls into the plains from the hills; and empties itself again into the same river at Delhi, having passed through, and irrigated a large extent of country. A branch of this canal runs through the centre of the Chandee Choke, the principal street of the city, and another branch is opening through the Delhi street. In the evening Lowis and I visited the palace, entering the fort by the Delhi gate. Both the palace and fort were built by Shah Jehan. After passing the gate, I drove through a street with miserable shops and hovels on each side.

A canal, which from being out of repair allows the dirty water to remain stagnant, is in the centre, and the pavement is as much out of order as it can be: this leads into a square where such a gun is placed, to fire when the king goes to bed (between 10 and 11 o'clock), as I never saw. The carriage is only kept together by pieces of rope, and the cannon itself is almost in as dilapidated a state. On the N. E or right-hand side of the square, is the Knobut Khanna, a gateway of red stone, over which the drum of State is kept. The exterior of this building is in different compartments carved in relief with flowers, and the studded door of bronze is massive and handsome.

Opposite to the Knobut Khanna is the Aum Dewan. Here the king gave audience to the inferior class of his subjects. The front forms, *I think,* seven arches, and the interior consists of three arcades, the whole of white marble. The mosaic in the Hkooshee where the king sat is more than usually elaborate and beautiful. A figure of Orpheus is very curious, the flowers are well executed, and the *lapis lazulae* inlaid in the figures of birds had a very brilliant effect. The private entrance for the monarch is coarsely stopped up with brick, presenting a rude contrast to the other parts, and pigeons are allowed to defile what could only have been completed by infinite toil and expense. This building is now disused, and no place can well be more dirty, or more neglected.

From hence I passed through the Loll Purdah ke Derhsasseh, a bronze gate having flowers elegantly relieved on it, to the Dewau Khass or Audience Chamber. The length of this magnificent edifice is 28 yards, its breadth 21. It is composed of white marble, the front formed by five arches. The interior consists of one apartment formed by three arches on each side, which occupies three-fourths of the building, and a veranda. The *musnud* is placed in the centre, underneath which a small canal of water is conducted. The decorations are splendid without being gaudy. The flowers on the arches are alternately gilded and worked in mosaic, and the four corners of this apartment are inscribed and gilded in the Persian style. If there be an Elysium on earth, it is this. The ceiling is beautifully carved and gilded.

From the tulip, a flower unknown in Hindoostan, being frequently represented here, as well as at the Taje at Agra, a supposition has been expressed that an European artist was employed in the superintendence of the decorations of these buildings, and as it is known that several Italians were present at the Court of Shah Jehan, it is not an unfair conclusion to come to. From the Diwan-i-Khas, which I could scarcely sufficiently admire, I went to the Humaums. The mosaic on the pavement is excellent, but sad depredations have been committed on it; the *chobdar* taxed the Mahrattas with the crime. A small *musjid* was built by Aurungzebe of white marble. The front forms three arches, the centre one considerably the largest. On the top are three gilt domes, which appear too large to be in proportion. The walls of the court are elegantly carved in relief; in the centre of it is a fountain.

The erection of this mosque was began after the murder of Dara by his brother Aurungzebe. It will never atone for the crimes that paved the way to the *musnud* for that hypocritical devotee, for that crafty and profound politician. I now visited the Motee Mahal. A canal, the bottom and sides of which are mosaic, runs through this building. In the middle of the principal apartment a large shell carved from one piece of marble receives a fountain, the overflowing of which are conducted into a basin about four yards square, cut out of one mass of marble. I looked minutely to detect a joining, but I could not.

From hence I went to the Shah Boorj, the northern bastion of the palace and fort. It is well-deserving of notice on account of the mosaic; water is conducted into every part of this building, fountains play in several places, a bath is so constructed that by sitting in the centre four fountains play on you at the same time.

A reservoir of marble coloured, if not naturally a light green, had a very pretty effect, from the dark green of the blood-stone, and the red-shaded flowers in mosaic. The arched ceiling of this apartment is gaudily painted, and glass is so inlaid as to reflect the light in a number of rays. The time to visit this place, like the Ina Khannah at Agra, should be by candlelight. The gardens of the palace would be pretty if properly attended to, but the poverty of the king is everywhere apparent; no one place is properly kept, with the exception of the Diwan-i-Khas.

Water is abundantly supplied, and canals would conduct it to every part of the palace, its courts, and gardens, if the descendant of the Great Moguls were not too poor to put them in order. The air in the gardens is pleasantly perfumed from the orange, citron, and pomegranate trees.

I returned through a fine lofty arcade to the Lahore gate, from which you look up the Chandee Choke, incomparably the finest street I have seen in India. It cannot boast of the number of fine buildings which adorn the principal street in Lucknow, but there is a gaiety and bustle that makes more than amends. The houses are irregular but good; on the left-hand side, half-way up the street, is the mosque where Nadir Shah, the Persian invader, sat to behold the massacre of the inhabitants. The Chandee Choke is terminated at one end by the fort, at the other by a *musjid* with handsome *minars*. In the cool of the evening this is the principal resort. Crowds of different natives of the East are lounging about. All native processions are obliged to keep on the left-hand side of the canal which prevents annoyance.

The police is admirable; a *berkaandoss* runs before your buggy to clear the way; he is relieved every 100 yards by a comrade. Mr. Metcalfe mentioned a story of Mirza Baba, the second son of the king. He saw the prince one evening driving a pair of horses in his carriage, himself postilion, a man rode on the left side with the *hookah* which Mirza smoked, as he was riding and driving; this occurred in a court of the palace. Whenever Mirza is driven out in his carriage, his *hookabadar* rides on the right hand, the snake is passed through the window, and he incessantly smokes; I have never seen him morning or evening without this attendant.

March 10.—Went to the Jumai or Jumna Musjid. The flight of steps by which you ascend is handsome, the terrace is almost a perfect quadrangle, the colonnade on three of the sides is light and elegant, the and *musjid* forms the fourth side.

In the centre of the building is a fine and bold gateway of red stone, inlaid with white or greyish marble. On either side is an arcade of five arches, principally composed of marble. Over each on a large slab of marble is inscribed in Arabic passages from the *Koran*: the *mus-*

jid is crowned with three domes of white marble striped with black from the cullis to the base; the centre dome is the largest. The front of the building is flanked by two splendid *minars* 180 feet high. They are built of red stone, and striped longitudinally with white. Each is surmounted with a cupola of white marble. The view of the city from these pillars is fine, and of the country extensive, and interesting; as far as the eye can reach the country is covered with ruins.

Flying pigeons are a great amusement among the natives. Numbers of houses had a place constructed on the top for the purpose. Since I have been in Delhi, I saw a man flying pigeons from an elephant. A large bamboo cage was placed as the *howdah*, the man sat behind, and the birds appear to pitch without fear when called. The *mahout* had the worst of the amusement, the cage extended so far forwards as to prevent his sitting upright. From the Jumai Musjid I went to the ruins of the palace of Feroz Shah, an Afghan, who ascended the throne 1235. These ruins are situated about half a mile to the south-east of the city, and are chiefly remarkable on account of a pillar about 50 feet high hewn from one piece of stone.

It rises from a building which was, I imagine, purposely erected for its support to give sufficient to such a weight; this pillar must be sunk some depth in the building. A part of the top is broken off apparently by lightning; on the shaft are inscriptions in three or four different characters, not one of which is now decipherable, so that this pillar must belong to a period much anterior to the reign of Feroz Shah. A pig and an elephant endeavouring to tear up a tree with his trunk are rudely engraved on it. A similar, though not so large a pillar, lies in the Fort of Allahabad, and the characters on it are as unintelligible.

March 14. I drove in the morning to the tomb of Humaion, the father of Akbar: it is situated 4 miles to south-east of the city. It is a fine building of red stone, inlaid with white, grey and yellow marbles. The style of the embellishments is bold and unusually plain, and over each of the four archways are two small cupolas, their domes composed of China tile, blue and gold. The terrace on which this building is erected is extensive. I was not so much pleased here, as with many, indeed most of the mausoleums I have seen: the dome appeared to me not well proportioned. From hence I proceeded a short distance to the Chousut Cumba, and passed a curious old Patan *musjid*, the walls of which are sloping, and the roof is quite covered with a number of small black domes.

I forgot to mention that in the compound of Humaion's tomb are contained an elegant tomb for that monarch's *sirdar*, and another, the dome of which is composed of China tile, where lies his barber. The Chousut Cumba is a very elegant square building of white marble; the interior is composed of a square arcade of five arches, the roof over each concave and beautifully carved. Azim Khan's tomb is well-deserving attention on account of its elaborate and perfect sculpture. The Bowlee, which is close at hand, presented an extraordinary scene; it is a square pond of water, very deep; its sides are bricked. There is a descent to it on one side by a number of steps, on the other three sides, buildings rise from the water to the height of 50 feet; the square may be about twenty or twenty-five yards.

Several men and boys were in attendance to jump from the top of the buildings into the Bowlee, and a few of the most expert leaped from a dome which increased the height 10 feet. I observed that the leapers always closed their legs when near touching the water; many performed this feat, and some exhibited several times; these people were also very expert divers. They begged of me to throw a *rupee* into the water. I obliged them all to remain at the sides to give the *rupee* fair play. The instant the money touched the water they dashed at it like so many sharks at their prey, and invariably secured it before it reached the bottom.

Nizamau-din appears to have more respect paid to his memory than the Mogul Emperors. I fancy he claimed descent from the Prophet. The *Imaums* would not allow me to enter the apartment where his tomb is contained, nor would they take the cloth covering from it, for my inspection. The interior of this marble sepulchre is so gaudily painted as to offend the eye; this fault does not attach to the ceiling of the veranda; the pattern is well chosen, and the colours blue, red, and gold harmonise well together: the trellis work is light and elegant. At a few yards distance is Mahmed Shah's tomb, purely formed of white marble. The solid marble door at the entrance is very elegantly carved in relief, as are also the pillars which support it.

Next to Mahmed Shah's is the tomb of Jehanara, the favourite daughter of Shah Jehan, who shared his prison, and was with him at his death. Her resting-place is extremely plain and simple. Instead of the usual covering the tomb is filled up with earth; at the head of it stands a detached slab of marble, with an inscription in Persian, the literal translation of which is:—

On Jehanara'a silent tomb
Let nought but sacred earth be laid;
There may the early floweret bloom,
Best emblem of a virtuous maid.

March 15.—Lowis and I left Delhi, for Gourgawan, *via* the Cuttub Minar, and on the road passed the beautiful tomb of Sufter Jung. This splendid pillar is generally supposed to have been erected by Cuttub-ud-deen, who took possession of Delhi from the Hindoo princes *A.D.* 1193, and commenced the series of Afghan Sovereigns, which reigned until the invasion of Baber, the great-grandson of Timour. The inscriptions confirm this opinion, but the Hindoos lay claim to the *minar*. They deny that Cuttub was the founder, but admit that he cased it with stone, and gave to it its present form and appearance. The Cuttub is about 12 miles south-west from Delhi, the present height is 238 feet; it originally was surmounted with a cupola of 26 feet, which made its former height 264. Its base is a polygon of 27 sides, and rises in a circular form. The exterior part is fluted into 27 divisions, which are alternately semi-circular and triangular.

At the height of 95 feet a kind of balcony surrounds the pillar. On this first storey there are two belts of engraving in the Arabic, the capital of it is deeply engraved, and the cornice underneath the balcony is charmingly carved in the style of the florid Gothic. A second balcony is at the height of 145 feet, the pillars of this portion are all semi-circular. They are surrounded with two belts of Arabic engraving, the cornice corresponds with the pillars, and differs from that on the summit of the base or first storey. The stone of this part is of a lighter colour than the others. There is a third balcony at the height of 186 feet. The pillars of this portion are all triangular, and belted with engraving similar to the second storey. The cornice harmonises with the columns and differs from each of the others.

At the height of 212 feet there is a fourth balcony. This portion has no pillars, the lower half is of red stone, and the upper of white marble, intersected with a belt of red stone; the capital of this storey is deeply carved. The fifth storey is composed of semi-circular pillars in white marble, which are terminated half-way up, by a slight cornice; the capital is of red stone ornamented with white. At each balcony there is a door to the westward, but the entrance to the *minar* is to the north; the circumference of the base is 144 feet. A spiral stair leads you to the summit, but towards the top large blocks of stone have fallen in, so as to render the ascent difficult.

The bird's-eye view is very extensive. Towards Delhi the country is scattered over with ruins, and the remains of ancient tombs and *mosques* rise thickly as far as the eye can reach. I believe this to have been the site of ancient Delhi. This monument appears to have been intended for a *minar* to a *mosque* which never was completed. One hundred and forty-two yards to the northward the base of a similar pillar which rises about 50 feet, and which appears never to have been further completed, favours this supposition. The tomb of Cuttub stands a short distance to the westward. In this direction there is a line of archways which have occupied a space equal to that between the two pillars. Most of these arches are in ruins, but the gateway is still perfect and admirable for its symmetry and deep and masterly carving. I have never seen the art carried to such perfection—the sculpture even now retains its sharpness.

The gateway is 47 feet, the arch being 43½. The architecture is Hindoo. In a court between these archways and the *kelaat*, a curious pillar 23 feet high rises. It is composed of several different kinds of metals, and has characters engraved on it, apparently similar to the inscriptions on the stone pillar at Feroz Shah's palace. There are several beautiful as well as curious specimens of Hindoo architecture immediately in this neighbourhood. Some colonnades are very singular, the pillars are each formed by three stones; two long square stones each about 6 feet in length are divided in the centre by a square stone probably 9 inches in thickness. These pillars are connected by one stone which goes from the top of one pillar to the other, and another stone placed diagonally gives strength to the colonnade. No cement appears to have been employed in these buildings.

The Arabic inscriptions on the Cuttub have been, with infinite trouble, transcribed and translated by Mr. Ewar. I was fortunate in getting a copy from Colonel Childers. It runs thus:—

Kutteeb ud din Ibek, on whom be the mercy of God, constructed this *mosque*.
In the name of the most merciful God—the Lord has invited to Paradise and brings into the way of righteousness him who wills it. In the year 592 this building was commenced by the high command of Moez-ud-dunya-uddin-Mahomed Beni Sam-Nasir Amir-ul Mominin.
The Sultan Shems-ul-Hak-wa-ud-din Altamsh erected this

building.

In the year 907 this *minar* having been injured by lightning; by the aid of, and favour of God, Firozmund Yamini restored whatever was needed by the building; may the Lord preserve this lofty edifice from future mischance.

The erection of this building was commanded in the glorious time of the great Sultan, the mighty King of Kings, the Master of Mankind, the Lord of the Monarchs of Turkestan, Arabia, and Persia; the Son of the World and Religion, of the Faith and the Faithful, the Lord of Safety and Protection, the heir of the Kingdom of Suliman Abul Muzeffer Altamsh Nasir Amir-ul Mominin.

The Prophet, on whom be the mercy and peace of God, has declared, 'Whoever erects a temple to the true God on earth, shall receive six such dwellings in Paradise.' The *minar*, the dwelling of the King of Kings, Shems-ud-dunyawa-ud-din now in peace and pardon, be his tomb protected, and his place be assigned in heaven—was injured by lightning in the reign of the exalted monarch Secunder, the son of Behlol (may his power and empire last for ever, and his reign be glorious), and therefore his slave Futteh Khan, the son of Musnud Ali, the liberal of the liberals, and the meritorious servant of the King, repaired it according to command the 13th of Rabi-ul-Akbar in the year 909.

March 16.—I rode with Lewis to Tughlikabad, the ruins of a fort and city 5 miles to the east of the Cuttub. Tughlik was seated on the throne 1821. These ruins are very extensive. I had not time minutely to inspect them, but I was surprised at the enormous masses of stone which were employed in the architecture. A pass between two small hills is strongly fortified for those times. We returned to our tents at the Cuttub, and I spent the greater part of the day in admiration of that splendid pillar. The following morning, we drove to Gourgawan over as bad a road as a buggy can be fancied to get over.

Whilst staying with Hawkes and his irregular hussars, I heard a story told of Colonel Skinner, an eminently brave and good officer, and Fraser, a civilian, who imitates in dress and some other points the native character, and who is a great friend of the colonel's. They were out lion shooting together, when a lion or tiger got into a very small bush jungle, and they could not get him out. Fraser dismounted from his elephant, and taking a sword and shield, invited Skinner to do the same and to attack him on foot, but Skinner would not be persuaded. At last Fraser said, "you are a coward, *Secunder*."

The colonel replied, "I will fight with man as long as you like, but let beast fight with beast; go you in, and kill him, Fraser."

These friends are now out in the neighbourhood of Hansi, lion hunting on horseback, a service of considerable danger, and requiring extreme skill. Fraser as well as Skinner have frequently killed tigers from horseback.

March 20.—As we were leaving Gourgawan Mr. Inlay, the adjutant of Lowis' regiment, came running after us, to say that during the night an express had arrived, desiring the regiment to hold itself in readiness for service at a moment's warning. On arriving at Delhi, we found this force was to be directed against Bhurtpoor.

A few months ago, Sir David Aucterlony had placed the eldest son, the legitimate heir, on the throne, or rather guaranteed the succession on the death of the *rajah* his father, which took place about the end of February. The son is now only seven years old, his guardians have quarrelled for the regency, and have fought a battle near the fort, in which the brother of the late *rajah* has proved victorious, and slain his colleague. The young *rajah* is deposed, and the uncle has seated himself on the *musnud*. On the 21st McDowell and I quitted Delhi for Meerut. We crossed the Jumna just above the palace, and having done so, re-entered the Dooab.

March 23.—Arrived at Meerut, and learnt that the 16th were not ordered on this expedition. I could not have visited this pleasant station at a more unfavourable opportunity. The orders had been received for the troops to hold themselves in readiness, the officers were all hustle and preparation, their wives all tears and lamentations. My old acquaintance Miss Slator who is just married to Tuckett of the 11th Dragoons, proposes, I hear, to spend the latter end of the honeymoon in camp with her husband; it would be charitable to recommend a tattied petticoat, though even that would scarcely keep her cool.

I think the bride is rather improved by matrimony, but she has not yet had time to thicken on it. Mr. Fisher in preaching a farewell sermon to the troops was so pathetic and touching in his discourse, that he set all the ladies a weeping when he informed them that the Lord of Hosts was on our side. Mrs. Jenkins was quite overcome, but when he recommended them to sing the 46th Psalm, little Soph was

OFFICERS OF THE 14TH FOOT.

nearly dissolved; 6 o'clock a.m. is not a sufficiently sentimental hour to make such a display. The person, though a man of exemplary devotion, was formerly a keen sportsman. Cooper, calling at McConchys', entered a room unobserved, where Fraser, with evident satisfaction, was contemplating some hunting prints. Not aware that anyone was present, he said, "Well that's the *true thing after all!!*"

Cooper quite floored him by answering, "So it is, Sir."

H. M.'s 14th Foot marched on the morning of the 28th, the 11th Dragoons were to follow on the 30th, and the artillery the day after.

March 29.—Quitted Meerut. On the 2nd April saw the first commencement of harvesting. In the evening at Lundhoura I went out shooting, and had very bad sport, but some fun from coming unexpectedly on two hyenas; one passed close by me, but I could not obtain another glimpse of him till he had got 25 yards off, when he received the contents of both barrels loaded with shot *en arriere*; he turned round, shewed his teeth, but was afraid to bite. The other hyena had run by my mate bearer. In my life I never saw a man so terrified. He screeched with fright, and tottering up to me swore he had seen a tiger with a mouth, "*etna burrah, Sahib,*" measuring about two feet of his *lattee.*

The ride from Lundhoura to Hardwar, where I arrived on the 3rd April, is extremely picturesque and beautiful; the last 8 miles is through a jungle not so disagreeably thick as to intercept the view which is terminated from the north to the eastward by the hills. Vast numbers of people were going to the fair of Hardwar: the variegated dresses of the natives, the gaudy trowsers and apparel of the women, the constant succession of horsemen, who had generally a very picturesque seat on their nags, occasionally seeing amongst them an irregular trooper clothed in his long scarlet vest, and carrying a lance 14 feet long, the groups that were seated under those trees which afforded the most abundant shade, the bullock-hackeries, and the long strings of horses winding through the wood, each horse led by a *syce*, altogether gave a pleasing gaiety to the scene, and added materially to the colouring of the picture, which, divested of these figures, is in itself particularly striking from the fine features of the landscape.

The fair is annually held at this season, and is the greatest mart in this part of the world for horses, as well as shawls from Cashmere, and different merchandises, fruits and spices which are brought from all parts of the East. The concourse of people is greatly increased by the numbers of pilgrims and devotees who perform great distances to bathe in the Ganges at this season. The period of ablution is that of the sun's entering Aries, which, according to the Hindoo computation, happens twenty days later than the vernal equinox.

Every 12th year at the *Cuma* (the Hindostannee term for the watercarrier or Aquarius) when Jupiter is in Aquarius at the time of the sun's entering Aries, the number of pilgrims is greatly augmented, and has at some *Cumas* been computed at a million. Hardwar is a small town, and one of the few that has increased in consequence during late years; many of the houses here are covered with designs, and indeed it is a general custom in this part of the country to have the exterior of the houses covered with paintings of gods, men horses, elephants, tiger hunts, &c., &c.

Sometimes a representation of an Englishman appears dressed in scarlet, but never without the accompaniment of a bottle of beer or some potent liquor. Hardwar is a place held in extreme veneration by the Hindoos, and being translated is rendered, the Gate of God, or rather of Hurrhee, one of their favourite divinities. The *ghaut* frequented by the devotees has been greatly enlarged and improved by our government, in consequence of a dreadful accident which occurred six years ago; great numbers were hurrying down the steps which were then very steep and narrow to bathe, and these were met by numbers who were returning, neither sect would give way, a crush ensued, some fell, others quickly tumbled over them, and the passage became soon stopped up by a bank of dead bodies, which amounted almost to 400.

This accident commenced at about 2 o'clock a.m. Grindell the judge of the district, hastened to the spot between 7 and 8: the mischief was then completed, and the horror scarcely to be surpassed. Grindell told me the bodies were so jammed, that it was with much difficulty, and only by great strength, they could be extracted from the heap. By the late improvements, executed by Debundee an engineer officer, a recurrence of such a catastrophe is effectually prevented. This *ghaut* is called by the Hindoos Hur ke purrhee (the steps of Hurrhee), and the spot is shewn by the Brahmins from whence the god jumped into the Ganges. A constant succession in considerable numbers of each sex repair to this sacred spot to perform their ablutions, and to throw into the river the ashes of their relatives. They have an idea that if the bones are consigned to the Ganges at the particular time of the transit of the planets, whatever may have been the crimes of the deceased, even if he had killed a Brahmin, no question will be asked of him, but at that instant he will be admitted into Paradise.

At all times, performing ablution at this spot, and committing the ashes of a departed relation to the Ganges, are supposed to be efficacious, but not in an equal degree to this short period. The men and women bathe promiscuously, the latter with just a thin sheet wrapped round them, so that, only for the honour of the thing, they might as well be naked; many are of this opinion and dispense with it altogether. Numbers of *fakirs* are always present, and they are the most grotesque figures, some paint their faces white, some cover their face, hair and bodies with ashes and cow-dung, some paint their bodies in streaks of white as well as their faces, some wear a little linen which is dyed a tawny orange colour, others dispense entirely with clothing.

I saw one fellow who had tied a long piece of cloth to his penis, the opposite end of the linen was fastened to the covering of a booth, and kept his *qui vive* at an angle of about 45 degrees; he remained in this exposed situation singing, accompanied by some other right devout men, who beat a sort of tune on sticks. The number of *fakirs* who frequent the fair is prodigious one of the brotherhood calculated them at 5,000 and I should think he far from overrated the number: a line of five or six frequently arrive together, and go through the Fair successively shouting "*Alla-a-a*." At dusk the scene at the Hur ke purrhee is even more extraordinary than during the day, though the bathers are not so numerous as in the morning.

At this time the temples are lighted up, amidst a surprising noise made by the Brahmins with their shells and drums, and the river is strongly illuminated by lights which are turned adrift on a small raft of straw, as propitiatory offerings to the Goddess Ganga. If these lights quickly disappear it is deemed unlucky to the offerer; whereas if they long continue ignited, the omen is good.

I passed my time very pleasantly at this place where I had the good fortune to meet a very pleasant party consisting of Persse and his wife, a fine woman, and pleasant companion; my fat friend Mrs. Mack who is in love, talks sentiment, and reads the *Man of Feeling*, and *The Whole Duty of Man*. I never saw a woman make a greater simpleton of herself; Captain Barclay and his little wife; Colonel Skinner, a distinguished officer, who commands a regiment of Irregular Horse, and his friend Fraser, who dresses like a native and allows his beard to grow; McDowell's uncle, Captain Sissmore; Grindell, the judge at Seharanpore; Shore who also dresses like a native, but in the style of a

NATHANIEL WALLICH, (1786–1854)

A renowned Danish surgeon and botanist who was involved in the development of the Calcutta Botanical Garden. He described many new plant species, several of which were named after him. His huge herbarium collections are recognised as a significant contribution to his subject and have been distributed internationally. One of them, 'The Wallich Collection', is held at Kew Gardens, London.

kitmagar, Dr. Wallich, the Superintendent of the Botanical Garden at Calcutta; Satchwell and Hearsey The greater part of this party used to meet every evening at dinner, and excepting the glorious campaign at Calpee, I have not met with more jollity since I have been in India.

April 12.—The Hur ke Purrhee pass, which leads from Hardwar into the Valley of the Doone, has been so improved under the superintendence of Debundee by cutting away the rock in some places, by embankments in others, and by throwing a bridge over the ravine, as to be now rendered passable for carriages. Till very lately the path was so narrow, and so steep, and so rugged, that more than two people could not pass each other on it. This work is not yet completed, but sufficiently so, to give an idea of the great labour and talent that was necessary to forward it to its present state, which is quite the admiration of those who remember what it originally was. The sun just appeared over the mountains as I rode through the pass, and gladdened the most splendid scenery I ever beheld. To the westward the hill through which the road is cut rises boldly and abruptly on your left-hand, being, where the rocks will permit, covered with dwarfish wood and long grass: the Ganges, in a clear and rapid stream which is almost fordable, winds under the pass on your right.

The descent to the river is considerable, and in some places almost perpendicular. The view to the eastward is bounded by a fine range of mountains, and fronting you appears the Valley of the Doone beautifully wooded, and watered by the Ganges. At Kanuck I found Dr. Wallich, Hearsey and Satchwell I accepted their invitation to breakfast, and found they proposed going in the evening to Rickeecase. As I intended to visit that place, I gladly availed myself of the opportunity of joining their party, especially as the Danish doctor is an excellent companion, and Hearsey who speaks the language like a native, is also a very pleasant fellow, and possesses an unusual share of information of the manners and habits of the country.

At 5 p.m. we got on our elephants, and on the road at Bibby wallah had most capital deer shooting. The situation of Rickeecase is extremely romantic and is about 3 miles from Tuppoobund where the Ganges descends from the mountains. In a temple of the village stands Ram Chunda or Bhart Gee, and numbers repair to pay their adorations to this idol, than which no figure can be more grim. The god is black, and his eyes which are very large are white; to add to the solemnity the sanctum is only dimly lighted; the Brahmins made some slight objection to showing the god whose face was only visible, his body being screened by a purdah of white cloth. This they would not remove till a Brahmin having first washed his hands, dressed the divinity in a red *kummarbund*.

The Hindus have a story that in early days the evil spirits dammed up the Ganges in the mountains, to prevent the inhabitants of the lower country from participating in the benefits derived from ablution in the river; when Bhurt Gee, with Hurrhee and other good spirits commiserating the miserable situation of the people, opened a course through the mountains, when the sacred stream flowed with such rapidity that the evil spirits were never able to stop its progress.

April 16.—Arrived at Deyrah; on the last 8 miles an excellent road has been made, which will be carried on to Hardwar; Persse his wife and Mrs. Mack, Barclay and his wife, the doctor's party and ourselves pitched our tents in Young's compound, who commands the Goorkah Battalion. On the following day, excepting the ladies, we all went to Sunshur or Shasteradhara (the thousand drops). The descent for the last mile and half is so steep that we were obliged to leave our horses on the brow of the hill and to proceed on foot up a narrow valley to the dripping rock which stands on the base of a mountain thickly wooded, and washed by a rapid little stream of the clearest water in which are both trout and grayling; the landscape is perfected by the brilliant tints of the petrifactions.

It is impossible to describe the charming sensations produced by such scenery after having been for a length of time accustomed to the dusty monotony of the plains: the day was not long enough to enjoy this retreat. In the evening we ascended the hill, and mounting our elephants proceeded to Kalanga where Gillespie rashly sacrificed his valuable life.

The fort is now completely demolished, but with the assistance of a guide you easily trace its former extent. It stood on an eminence commanding the surrounding country, and is surrounded with jungle which, at all events, would have afforded shelter to assailants. The supply of water might have been effectually cut off, so that the fort must have surrendered: the attack was at the least as ill-judged as fatal; the besieged evacuated it two days after our failure.

We returned late to dinner, when Fisher mentioned an instance of great bravery and discipline displayed by one of the Goorkah *sepoys* who had accompanied Young and Childers tiger shooting. The stout little Goorkah whilst walking by the side of the elephants suddenly dropped on one knee, and presenting his musket called to Young that he was close on a tiger. Neither of the sportsmen being able to see the beast, Young ordered the man to recover arms; he instantly obeyed his commanding officer, but kept his eye steadfastly fixed on one point.

Young now ordered the soldier to present arms, who did so, evidently aiming at an object close to him. Young delighted at such steadiness exclaimed; "Childers that's a brave fellow, I must stand by him," and quickly getting from his elephant, went directly up to the Goorkah; standing close to him he could not see the tiger, he looked along the musket, still he could not see him: afraid the man was after all playing a trick he told him to fire; the tiger rolled over, within four feet of the muzzle of the musket, dead. Young promoted the steady little fellow the first opportunity that occurred.

April 18.—A party was made for an excursion of three days up the hills to a place called the Potatoe Garden. At the end of the second day our tents did not come up; Wallich fearing rain threw cold water on the trip. We returned, much to my mortification, without accomplishing our object. The Danish botanist was transported in finding on this day's march the ilex, the wild cherry, the raspberry, the larkspur, cowslip, primrose, buttercup, dandelion, the paper plant, mint, thyme, rue, and a variety of plants with interminable names. On the 19th I, in advance, returned to Deyrah by breakfast-time, and found nobody at our host's, everyone having gone to the dripping rock.

Today I saw some of the Goorkahs at exercise; they wear a green uniform and are drilled as Light Infantry. I should say many more men are under 5' 3" than above it, and a great number do not appear higher than 5 feet. The face of a real Goorkah is very broad, the eyes are small, and the nose flat; he is as ugly a little fellow as you can imagine, but what he loses in beauty he amply makes up in activity joined to prodigious strength of limb. The more feeble and enervated inhabitants of the plains have a great opinion of their power and bravery.

My bearer acquainted me on arriving at Deyrah that they were *haram zaadars*—(bastards)—to fight, and my tailor, backing his opinion, said that one of their women could beat three such men as he was. On the evening of the 20th we were all again assembled at Young's, and as this was my last evening with the party, so was it the pleasantest. The relating all the events that had occurred produced capital fun. Parsons on the road found a flower which he gallantly presented to his wife as a primrose, who, by no means persuaded of its identity, pronounced it a cowslip. Wallich had informed the Parsons that it was impossible to mistake the primrose, and pointed out a nerve as the test. Parsons endeavoured to make the primrose nervous, but his wife would not be humbugged. He could not come botanist over her.

After breakfast Mrs. Mack would bathe. I should wickedly have liked to have witnessed this scene, as the Dane said, just for the curiosity of the thing. At night the ladies slept in one covered shed, which has been erected for the accommodation of visitors, the gentlemen in another one of the same description which is close by. The ladies did take the precaution to surround their apartment with *kurnauts*. How Young's finger got into Mrs. Mack's mouth when she was in bed, I don't know, but there it did get, or Mrs. Mack could not have bit it. In galloping over to Lucheewallah on the following morning I tried to make a laugh for the party who did not leave till the evening, by making some doggerel verses which I sent over to them at dinner.

Wallich when asked the name of a plant which he did not know amused me by his invariable answer in a foreign accent, "My good fellow, am I God Almighty? Can I know everything?"

April 23.—Crossed the Jumna at Rajghaut, the river runs like a sluice, with a greater body of water than there is in the Ganges at Rickeecase. On the following day's march, I met a colony of *saump wallahs*, who produced three snakes 10 or 12 feet long, which they allowed to crawl over themselves, and to convolve round their children, who showed no symptoms of fear. The tents were pitched in a low situation. I never saw the firefly so numerous; in the evening it is scarcely an exaggeration to say that the spot was illuminated by them.

April 26.—Climbed up the hill to Nahan, where the *ranee* had ordered a small bungalow to be prepared for our reception: her son, the *rajah*, had made an excursion to solemnise a marriage, adding one to his numerous wives. The queen-mother provided coolies to convey our tents and baggage, and sent the chief men of her court to pay their respects, who were neither so well-dressed or so well-locking as our servants. Nahan is situated on the summit of a hill, and built on separate flats: you ascend from one to the other by steps, and the palace of the *rajah* commands the town; the *bazaar* is clean and orderly, and the houses are neater, and have a greater appearance of comfort than those generally met with in the plains.

I was amused by my *sirdar* endeavouring to explain a very long story to a P'harrhee, who either did not, or would not, understand him, exclaiming in the most contemptuous manner—"these *haramzadaaar loge* know nothing." I was dissuaded by the queen's people from taking my horses across the hills, and foolishly following their advice, sent them back into the plains with orders to meet me at Baar. On the morning of the 27th McDowell and I mustered our *coolies* amounting to between 30 and 40 and started for Subathoo; the road in the most deceiving and provoking manner winds round the mountains, so that after considerable fatigue, on looking back, the distance you have come appears trifling. About two *coss* from Nahan the road becomes so good that horses could have no difficulty in travelling it.

More than once during this day's walk when thoroughly blown, I repented of having separated myself from my horses; how I could be so young as to follow the opinion of a black fellow surprises me. The scenery through which we pass is particularly bold and magnificent, the Scotch fir grows in considerable numbers and flourishes, the wild rose and jasmine I frequently detected by their delicious perfume, and the raspberry and strawberry are constantly met with, the flavour of the former when quite ripe is very fine. Twice or thrice during today's journey I got distinct views of the snowy range, which, if I had been gifted with a pair of seven-leagued boots, I could have reached in a hop, skip and a jump; the country people told me they were distant three days' short journey.

Our tent was pitched about 10 o'clock on very high ground at Penattee, from whence the view across the Doone is extensive. There is a perceptible change for the better in the climate; a strong breeze from the north-west perfectly cool and refreshing has blown all day, and the night is so cold that one blanket is scarcely sufficient to afford warmth. On the 28th we continued our march and encamped at Surang. On the 29th my *kitmagar* directed my attention to a small shed by the roadside in which two children were watching an infant who was covered up in a rug and asleep. I crawled into the hovel and found the top of the child's head was uncovered, and placed under a small fall of water which constantly dropped on the brain of the infant.

My servants told me they had already seen several instances of this method of bringing up children hardy, and a man in the service of the Rajah who was passing at the time, said it was a constant practice in the hills to keep children in this state for the four or five hot months during the daytime, until they were six years old, and that in after-life they were less liable to fevers, and were rendered remarkably strong;

certainly, they should be very cool-headed.

April 30—After a long march we arrived at Subathoo, on an elevation of rather more than 4,000 feet above the level of the sea. In the evening we dined with Nicholson the adjutant to the Goorkah Battalion, who is the very best drill I have seen in the country, and by all accounts the very worst husband; he is unfortunately married to a poor half-caste girl who he locks up and guards so closely that his most intimate friends have never had a glimpse of her for the last four years.

In consequence of the charming description given of Simla where Captain Roberts his wife, and Mrs. Ainslie, and Mr. and Mrs. Warde were living, we resolved to visit the place, and on the following morning, having had *gooles* lent us, started at 4 o'clock. On the road I met Kennedy who commands the Goorkhas, returning to Subathoo; he endeavoured to persuade me to return with him, urging the impossibility of my reaching Simla before midday: notwithstanding, I got there half an hour before Roberts's breakfast hour, 9 o'clock. Simla is distant a long 23 miles from Subathoo at an elevation of 7,800 feet, and the thermometer at a mean may be said to be through the year 11° lower than at the latter place. The scenery between Subathoo and Simla is excessively beautiful and superior in point of grandeur and variety to the country between Subathoo and Nahan. Roberts's house, built with fir in the Chinese style, is situated on a mountain clothed with the oak, cedar, and a variety of the fir species, all of which flourish. I perceived the holly and more than one kind of ivy.

At breakfast our host appeared in a cloth coat and trowsers, and the ladies wore cloth dresses. The salutary effects of the climate were very perceptible in this party, who are more improved in appearance than I could have thought possible. Their residence in the hills has changed in the complexions of the ladies, the tint of the daffadowndilly for the hue of the rose. At 1 o'clock the thermometer was 60°. In the evening the ladies ascended Jackoo, 9,300 feet above the level of the sea. They were carried in *jampaans*, a conveyance constructed with a seat placed between two firm bamboos about 8 feet long, which are fastened at either end with rope; in the centre of these lashings another bamboo is attached 4 feet long, which the bearers place on their shoulders.

The *jampaan* is carried by four men, two go between the shafts, and it requires occasionally, in very steep places, one or two extra bearers to steady it, and with this assistance there is scarcely any place however difficult that you may not be safely taken over. From having consider-able play, it requires some steadiness to sit in the *jampaan*; it is the only kind of carriage used in the hills; the *palanquin* is quite useless.

From the top of the mountain we had a distinct view of the River Sutlej, and a near and very favourable one of the snowy range. I re-turned with Mrs. Ainslie more pleased than ever with hill scenery, and found a fire which was lighted in no way uncomfortable.

May 2.—Returned to Subathoo, and spent a very pleasant day with Kennedy. By the roadside I frequently passed small huts which are inhabited by Brahmins for a part of the year, that they may sup-ply travellers with water. A small piece of hollow bamboo, supported slantingly on four pieces of stick, is placed outside these huts, and from this little conductor all castes of Hindoos and even the Mussulmauns may allay their thirst. Every spot of land that there is a probability of yielding produce is snatched from waste, and the earth which is washed down, and propelled into projections by the rains, after be-ing embanked by buttresses of loose stones into successive terraces, is brought with indefatigable labour into cultivation, and produces wheat, barley, and a variety of small grains.

Kennedy has introduced the potato, which he told me thrives well, and I think the P'harrees may anticipate very great benefit from the introduction of this root into their regions. The natives of the hills differ materially from the inhabitants of the plains, their complexions are lighter and more of an olive colour, and men are shorter, broader-faced, and much more stoutly-limbed. Instead of the turban they wear a small woollen or linen skull cap; they also dispense with the regular *dootee*, having merely a small strip of cloth passed between their legs and fastened round the waist with a string.

In the winter they wear a kind of woollen shirt, not very much unlike a London drayman's jacket. The women are well-shaped, and occasionally you may see a tint of red in their complexions; their manners are under less restraint than in the plains; they have the char-acter of great immorality, and in some parts a plurality of husbands is customary. Both men and women constantly are seen with a chain of flowers (usually the lotus) suspended from their ears. I saw many of each sex with the swelled throat, and so frequently that the disease must be very common.

The houses are invariably flat-roofed, and are usually of two sto-reys, the upper one being of far less dimensions than the base. There is

143

an air of neatness and comfort about these cottages, that may in vain be searched after in the plains; the exterior is frequently whitewashed, but a white border surrounding the doors and windows is almost always to be seen. In the adjoining ground the apple, apricot, or cherry, and often all these fruits are found, and, the strawberry and raspberry grow everywhere wild in the greatest abundance; the walnut tree, though met with, is not common.

May 3. —Left Subathoo most unwillingly, scarcely anything would have afforded me more pleasure than to have made an excursion far into the interior of the Himalaya. The climate is delicious, and after two years' broiling residence at Cawnpore appears heavenly. The scenery is always grand and frequently enchanting, and must have as beneficial an effect on the spirits as the climate has on the health. At Baar we entered the Singh or Seik country which commences as soon as you have descended from the hills. The founder of the Seik sect was Nanac or Nanuk Sah who, before his apostasy, was a Hindoo; he lived about the year 1,400 *A.D.* He was a man sprung from a low origin, but of a strong mind and of austere virtue. Nanac endeavoured to form a religion by uniting the purest and most unexceptionable parts of the Hindoo and Mussulmaun, rejecting the idolatry of the one and the intolerance of the other.

He, at his death, left a book highly revered among the sect, which teaches that there is but one God omnipotent and omnipresent; filling all space and pervading all matter, and that He alone is to be worshipped and invoked; that there will be a day of retribution when virtue will be rewarded and vice punished. It not only commands universal toleration, but forbids disputes with those of another persuasion. Theft, murder and such other deeds as are by the majority of mankind esteemed crimes against society are forbidden. The practice of all the virtues is inculcated, but particularly an universal philanthropy and a general hospitality to travellers and strangers. Nanac did not allow his followers to carry the sword; he preached to them peace and good-will among men.

But the Seiks assumed a totally different character under Goroo Govind, a priest in no way less revered than Nanac and a leader of acknowledged valour and abilities: now they always appeared armed, or carried steel about their persons. The Seiks in these respects differ from the Hindoos; they eat all meats, excepting that of the cow; they reject the worship of images, admit proselytes, and have no distinction

of caste. The shape of their turban is different from the other inhabitants of the plains, and the *dootee* is usually made of blue striped cloth.
Found our tent pitched according to order at Moonymagery, and suffered excessively from the heat.

May 4.— Rode to Umballah, where we met with much civility
from Mr. Murray

May 5.—Made a very long and forced march into Kurnaul. I met
with a very hospitable reception from Barclay; here I again met Mrs.
Mack making love and pleasantly burlesquing the passion. During
my stay a farewell ball was given to the widow. I could not avoid the
remembrance of the scene in Tom and Jerry, and suggested the propriety, or rather applicability, of having had a transparent representation
of the lady at one end of the room, with 'Welcome to Almack's in the
East' written underneath. Left Kurnaul on the 12th.

May 13.—Got to Meerut before Neville's breakfast hour. Whilst
at this place I was witness of a most tremendous hailstorm which fell
on the 17th; it came on about 6 o'clock p.m. with the appearance of a
north-wester and lasted about half an hour. Several hailstones, or rather masses of ice, were picked up twelve inches in circumference, and I
heard Sandham declare he saw one which measured fifteen inches. At
Delhi the stones fell with such violence that Garstin's *palanquin* which
was exposed to it, was perforated by one. I left Meerut on the 19th,
and arrived at my boat at Gurmetesur Ghaut; the following day got
under weigh.

The Ganges here is no longer the clear rapid river as at Hardwar,
but assumes its characteristic muddiness. Stopped on the 24th with
Labouche at Futteyghur, which appears a desirable station. Arrived on
the 27th at Bittoor, and remained with the Johnson's till the expiration
of my leave on the 31st May.

Aug. 25.—Left the mess early with Douglas that we might be present at the procession of the *tazziahs* at the Mussulmaunee fast of the
Mohurrum. These *tazziahs* are fanciful representations of the tombs
of Hussein and Hoossain, the grandsons of Mahommed. They are
formed of a frame-work of slight bamboo, covered with gaudy paper
and tinsel, and are carried on the shoulders of men. Their appearance
at a distance is very singular, being sometimes 20 or even 30 feet high.
In front of these *tazziahs* women are employed with *chowries* fanning
the air, and men fantastically dressed, dance before it, and beating their

145

breasts rapidly, they repeat the words: "Hussein," "Hoossain."

Great numbers of these paper constructions of a variety of shapes and sizes were about midnight to be seen moving about the parade ground. Some were surmounted by a magnificent peacock, others by a terrible-looking tiger, and others of a meaner kind, had things stuck about them which I imagine represented nothing on the earth, or the waters under the earth. The artist must have had a fearful dread of breaking the second Commandment.

The whole parade ground, which is of considerable extent, was one blaze of light from the number of torches and lamps which were carried. The multitude of people assembled on this occasion, both Mussulmauns and Hindus, is always very great; the buzz of voices, the appearance of the *tazziahs* moving through the crowd, the discharge of firearms, parties displaying their skill with the sword and shield, whilst others are exhibiting the most extraordinary activity by twirling about a stick with a quantity of tow lighted at each end; the shrill sound of the native instruments and the incessant beating of the tom-toms, formed altogether such a scene as you might in vain travel over Europe to witness. My head, which is not easily put out of the way, ached the whole day after this *tumashau*.

August 28.—The society at Cawnpore was now more disunited than ever, and the Grant's house, certainly the pleasantest in the place, was now visited by only a few of our officers. A Bagatelle Club was endeavoured to be established, but broke down after two balls. Mrs. Nation the wife of a colonel, at the first ball flew into a violent passion because she was not handed to supper by the proper person. The company officers sided with the colonel's lady, and were very national. Fame spoke but slightingly of the fair in question, and no one doubted her being very gay. I, who was frequently at the house, liked her as an amusing companion. I wrote some verses, taking especial care that Mrs. Nation should not see them, as the loss of an eye would have been the least that I could have expected.

Sept. 16.—The weather was dreadfully oppressive, and a kind of epidemic disorder which had passed all up the country from Calcutta now attacked almost every European in the station, and though we did not lose any men, we had a greater number in hospital than at any former period. The attack generally lasted from four to seven days, and in that short space the patient became so debilitated, as to be in the last stage of weakness. I have not heard of any one instance in which the epidemic has proved fatal. After coming home from my ride this morning, as usual I laid down on the couch, and was awoke by my servants to witness a phenomenon which I shall never forget.

A large cloud appeared, approaching from the south-west, with a kind of buzzing noise unlike anything I had ever heard. I could not understand from my servants what it was, but as the cloud neared, I perceived that it was a flight of locusts. As they passed over to the eastward the sun was obscured as much as it would be by a dense cloud, and these millions and hundred of millions of insects were passing over the station for about an hour. The gardeners and servants with *tom-toms*, and everything they could collect to make a noise, endeavoured to prevent their settling in a body. Where they did alight for a short time there was not an appearance of verdure; some settled on a tree near my house, and so covered it that you would have imagined it had been stripped of its foliage; a detachment fell in the adjutant's grounds, and when it again took wing, the spot where they had settled was entirely discoloured with black excrement.

The natives caught them, and said they were excellent in a curry. I had no inclination to try their virtue in this way. I should imagine that wherever this flight were to settle in a body, the whole produce of the spot would be consumed, and thinking at breakfast, what ruin it would bring on the poor *ryots* or husbandmen, I took up my Bible and turning to the 10th chapter of Exodus found this description, verse 5th:

> They shall cover the face of the earth, that one cannot be able to see the earth, and they shall eat the residue of that which is escaped, which remaineth unto you from the hail, and shall eat every tree which groweth for you out of the field. And they shall fill your houses, and the houses of thy servants, and the houses of all the Egyptians, which neither thy fathers, nor thy father's fathers, have seen since the day that they were upon the earth unto this day.

And again, verse 13th:

> And Moses stretched forth his rod over the land of Egypt, and the Lord brought an east wind upon the land, all that day and all that night, and when it was morning the east wind brought the locusts. And the locusts went up over all the land of Egypt, and rested in all the coasts of Egypt, very grievous were they; before them there were no such locusts as they, neither after them shall be such. For they covered the face of the whole earth, so that the land was darkened; and they did eat every herb of the land, and all the fruit of the trees which the hail had left, and there remained not any green thing in the trees or in the herbs of the field through all the land of Egypt.

I had for some time been very intimate at Mr. Nation's house and spent a great portion of my time there; the little woman improved surprisingly on acquaintance, and few people had greater power of making themselves agreeable. Mrs. Nation could not boast of much beauty, but, on a small scale, her figure was very pretty, and she was not a little proud of a very small waist and a very neat foot. One day she asked me to write something for her scrap-book, and I scribbled some, which I read to, but did not give, her, tearing them out.

Oct. 15.—A report was current and generally believed that an army would take the field in the beginning of November to attack the Fort of Bhurtpoor; and as everybody was very anxious to march against this place, which from having repulsed Lord Lake was considered by the natives impregnable, of course everyone was desirous to have these rumours confirmed.

Nov. 5.—In the evening I was going to Johnston's at Bittoor, and as there had been a report that the *rajah* had acceded to the terms proposed by our Government, I had made no preparation for the march. Accidentally I met Manners of the 59th, who halloed out as I passed him: "You're off tomorrow morning."

I did not at all like the thoughts of giving up a visit, from which I anticipated a good deal of pleasure, and still less the idea of being unprepared for the march. In this emergency I met Colonel Murray who told me, we should not march till the 10th, so I resolved to drive to Bittoor, and seeing Palmer requested him to procure three camels from Maloch, at his own price. On my return home the following night I found my *sirdar* bearer crying, or rather blubbering like a child; I asked him rather anxiously what was the matter, expecting no good. He fell at my feet and, putting his hands up to his forehead, said that whilst I was absent, some *haram zaadar* had taken the keys from his side and had stolen all my money, which amounted to *Rs*, 140 that he himself was a beggar having sold everything he had in the world to make up the loss, but that there was a deficiency of *Rs*. 30.

From the manner of the man, though he had lived with me unsuspected for three years, I fancied that he was the culprit, and sent for my *chokedar* to ask (as he was responsible for any robbery that might be committed on me) how a thief unperceived by him could get into the house. The *chokedar* immediately told me that it was all a humbug, that the day before my *sirdar* had lent out *Rs*. 400 at interest in the *bazaar*, and rather forcibly asked me, how he could make that money honestly in my service as he had only acted as *sirdar* for a short time. Whilst he was carrying on this conversation with me, the *sirdar* came into the room, and almost flying at the *chokedar* said: "You rascal, since I have been in the *sahib's* service, I have saved *Rs.* 500, and expect with the blessing of God to make as much more, if he permits it. Scoundrel, what right have you to interfere?"

This rather opened my eyes, and seeing the necessity of preventing my *sirdar* (who had been my *factotum*) making with the blessing of God so good a thing of me, I parted with him, though he never could have proved himself a rogue at a more inconvenient time. However, I got a particularly active man in his place, and I soon found everything ready for marching.

Nov. 8.—Paying a visit, I met Mrs. Wilkinson as highly rouged and as sentimental as ever. She was having her likeness taken by Loll Gee, a native miniature painter, and was flirting away with half a dozen young men who were living on her smiles. She showed me a small kaleidoscope which was attached to her watch, and shrewdly remarked to me that the changes were so frequent that it was scarcely possible to catch the same figure twice. I, intending to do a "little bit of pretty," fully acquiesced in her observation; adding that I had never seen anything (excepting the endless variety of expression which she gave to her features) so variable.

Mrs. Wilkinson said, "Why Mr. Lowe I do declare that's a compliment. I do declare it is so pretty that you must put it into verse for me."

There was no help, and as she produced pen and paper, I gave her some lines.

Nov. 10.—At 7 o'clock a.m. the regiment marched from the cantonments. As the men were mounting their horses, a dragoon of Captain, The Baron Osten's troop, without any apparent cause drew his pistol from the holster and blew his brains out. This is the fourth or fifth instance of suicide that has occurred in the regiment since it has been stationed at Cawnpore. We halted at Cockadoo where the 1st Extra Light Cavalry, H. M.'s 59th, the 82nd Native Infantry, a troop of horse artillery, and some foot artillery were already encamped. As I had two tents and Douglas only one, we agreed to breakfast in my tent, I was glad to find my camels carried their loads well.

Nov. 11.—Marched to Choubeepoor.

Nov. 12.—Marched to Poorah.

Nov. 13.—Marched to Noroul.

Nov. 14.—Marched to Meran ke Serai.

Nov. 15.—Jellalabad, within about a mile of the encampment were the ancient ruins of Kanoge, a city of great antiquity and former celebrity. At present it consists of one street, but for an extent of six miles the mixture of small pieces of brick and the occasional vestiges of a building point out the site of this ancient capital of Hindoostan. Here are the tombs of two Mohammedan saints who lie in state under two mausoleums on an elevation covered with trees. From the terrace which surrounds them is a pleasant view of the plain, covered with ruined temples and tombs. Small broken images are constantly seen. No buildings of any consequence now remain.

Nov. 16.—Secunderpoor.

Nov. 17.—Nubbeegunge.

Nov. 18.—Baogong.

Nov. 19 and *20.*—Mynpoorie.

We were encamped in separate enclosures, each forming an orchard of mango trees; dismissed my *hackerie*, got two more camels.

Nov. 21.—Bickeree.

Nov. 22.—Beraul.

Nov. 23.—Shekoabad.

Nov. 24.—Ferozabad.

Nov. 25.—Etimadpoor. We were encamped close to a tank called by the natives Bourise ke Talou; my servants told me it derived its name from an old woman, who, a great many years ago, sat on the banks all day and night to seduce the unwary traveller, who no sooner halted, than he was robbed and thrown into the tank. In the centre of this piece of water is the burial-place of some Mussalmaun of consequence, and a bridge of several small arches conducts you to this building, from the top of which you have a distinct view of the Taje at Agra. Whilst halting at this place we had some good fun with bagged foxes, and I got some fair shooting amongst the ravines towards the Jumma.

Nov. 30. —The troops were turned out at midnight to greet the arrival of Lord Combermere who passed by our camp.

Dec. 3.—Made a long march into Agra; the last six miles of the road is through ravines, which are so narrow that only in places can two carriages of any description pass each other. As we were winding through these ravines with a high bank on either side, I could not help thinking what execution a few riflemen would commit amongst us. We crossed over a bridge of boats which had been constructed across the Jumna by Barton. After passing by the fort, and through the town, we found Lord Combermere, who had stationed himself on the right-hand side of the road that he might inspect the troops as they passed.

Dec. 4.—Our brigade, consisting of 16th Lancers, the 6th, 8th and the 1st Extra Cavalry, were reviewed by Lord Combermere, who was introduced to each officer when the review was over. I rode a beast of a horse that I got from Bishop who assured me he was an excellent charger. Notwithstanding, he was so unsteady that I must have fallen out, if Persse had not lent me a spare horse of his own. After breakfast, Douglas and I got into my buggy and drove to the Mootee Musjid, and afterwards to the Taje. I received as much pleasure from this my second visit to these exquisitely chaste and beautiful buildings, as when I first saw them a year ago with McDowell

In the gardens were some officers of the 59th, and we walked with them to a paper manufactory, immediately in the neighbourhood. Nothing can be more simple than the process employed to make this article. Old rope and the coarsest canvass are first placed in a sort of well, and beat with a log of wood of considerable weight, which is attached to a beam, and worked by the pressure of six men who stand at the other extremity. When sufficiently beaten the hemp is placed in small pans, and mixed with lime and water.

After it has been dried it undergoes a similar process. When the hemp is sufficiently cleansed, a quantity is thrown into a square well or vat which is filled with water. The manufacturer sits at one end, and with a bamboo stirs the water till it becomes of a proper consistency; he then dips a sieve, simply formed of grass, or slight reed, as often into it as is required to form the proper texture. From this it is taken to another apartment and stuck on the wall. When the sheets fall off, they are sufficiently dry; and the process is completed. The paper I saw made was coarse, but sufficiently fine to write upon.

Dec. 6.—Mrs. Persse sent breakfast to the Taje, and I spent great part of the day there with a very pleasant party. Byron drove me to the Mootee Musjid, which I should never tire looking at; we then went to

LORD COMBERMERE.

Stapleton Cotton, (1773-1865), first met Arthur Wellesley, the future Duke of Wellington, in 1799 in India during the Anglo-Mysore War. He became commanding officer of the 16th Light Dragoons in 1800 and shortly thereafter became the regiment's colonel. He is best known as a major-general commanding cavalry under Wellington during the Peninsular War.

Although Wellington did not hold him in particularly high regard, he endorsed Combermere's appointment as commander in the operations against Bhurtpore.

the banks of the Jumna to see the great gun of Agra which lies partly buried in the sand, by the north-west curtain of the fort. The calibre of this gun is 2 feet, depth of metal at the muzzle 1 foot; length 14 feet, weight 1,207½ *maunds*, or 96,600 lbs. Lord Lake after the capture of Agra endeavoured to remove this enormous engine of destruction to England, and constructed a raft for the purpose of taking it to Calcutta; but the raft had proceeded a very few yards when it sunk.

The gun was with difficulty afterwards got ashore; it has remained on the banks ever since, without further attempts having been made for its removal. I got into the gun without difficulty, and turned from one side to the other. Byron now drove me across the Tripolia to the Burrah Bazaar which is very extensive. The natives of this place are excellent workmen in gold and silver laces, and also in all kinds of brass work.

Dec. 8.—At 3 a.m. the turn-out sounded, and we marched from Agra, and encamped about two *coss* from Futteypoor-Sicri; as I had a perfect recollection of the ruins of Akbar's palace, I did not regret my being unable again to visit this celebrated place.

Dec. 9.—On the march an alarm was given that the enemy's troops were in sight. We were formed in half squadrons and orders given for the balls to be taken off the points of the lances. We were then briskly trotted forwards, and arrived quite in time to ascertain that the report was like the old one of the mountain and mouse. The advanced guard had seen about thirty scouts, who, on being discovered, disappeared among the jungle. We were encamped at a small village called Agapoor, about six miles to the southward of Bhurtpoor; close to our encampment was a bank or slight elevation of ground which commanded the surrounding country; this was a complete lounge to walk up to; everyone anxious to get a view of the place which was to be attacked, and speculating on the probability of the spot where we should make our approaches.

Dec. 10.—The brigade turned out at 4 o'clock as a brigade of reconnaissance; the object was to ascertain if the bund of a lake which could supply the ditches of the fort with water had been cut so as to fill them. We were to take and keep possession of this embankment, and to dam up the embankment if it were cut. On the march Carpenter, a man in Enderby's troop, fell into a well when it was dark, and wonderful to say neither the man or his horse were in the least hurt. At daybreak the skirmishers commanded by Luard surprised a party

NATIVE CAVALRYMAN.

of the enemy's horse that were encamped near the village of Seewah and were soon partially engaged with them. These troops belonged to a *rajah* who had come to Bhurtpoor to pay a visit to Dourjan Sal; they were completely taken by surprise and endeavoured to get into the fort through the jungle.

Our skirmishers and Skinner's Horse cut off about fifty, who with the *rajah* were killed. We did not lose a single man, and had only one wounded. Armstrong was struck by a spent ball. Fraser who was with Skinner's Horse, had a scratch from a spear. Our left squadron and the left squadron of the 6th Cavalry were sent forward to reinforce the skirmishers, but their support was unnecessary, for the enemy had fled in all directions. I never heard of greater proofs of passive courage than were displayed by some of the enemy; four were surrounded by our men, and desired to give up their arms, and surrender themselves prisoners. This they refused, and when told that resistance was in vain, and that if they did not give up their arms, they would be killed, an old man turned round to his son, who seemed disposed to give up his arms and said to him; "If you don't fight to the last, I will kill you myself."

The remainder of our brigade were drawn up in front of a jungle, which, in the imperfect light of the morning, hid the fort from us. However, we had not been five minutes in line when the guns from the fort opened on us; at first the shot fell short of us; four or five balls in quick succession, bounded through our squadron interval, and as the spent balls were bounding through our ranks in all directions, it is wonderful how our men and horses escaped. Douglas' *syce* had his arm broken, and a horse of the artillery was struck; these are the only accidents I heard of. It was now thought prudent to change our position, as the enemy were getting the range of us.

When we were safe the men were dismounted by alternate squadrons, whilst Colonel Murray our brigadier, reconnoitred the *bund* which he found had been cut but very lately. No resistance whatever was met with, and it was a most extraordinary oversight of the enemy to allow us quietly to get possession of a post which was of vital importance to them. When we were dismounted, Hamilton amused us all by remarking: "Only let us have remained one other quarter of an hour where we were, and we should have had some fun by the immortal God. Jintleraen, I never saw balls getting a prettier direction." Hamilton had been in the Peninsula, and was speaking to young soldiers. I forgot to mention that our skirmishers lost two horses and had two wounded; we returned to our old encampment at Agapoor.

Dec. 11.—The infantry were sent into the jungle to drive out any of the enemy that might be found in it, and we skirted it to attack those who might appear on the plain. General Nichol with two engineer officers reconnoitred the fort; eight or ten men of his escort were killed. We did not see any of the enemy and were encamped at Noh on the eastern face of the fort.

Dec. 12.—Moved off our ground at 8 o'clock; the road for the greater part of the march passed through a jungle. At 12 we pitched our tents on the spot where Lord Lake formerly encamped, about a mile and a half from the spot where our skirmishers fell in with the enemy on the 10th. At 4 p.m. a cry of "turn-out" was heard, "the enemy are collecting in our front!" the troops were particularly alert. We had scarcely galloped off our troop when we discovered that it was a false report, and we returned laughing to our tents. A report was circulated that Madho Sing, the Deeg Rajah, intended to throw into the fort during the night a body of troops for the relief of his brother Dourjan Sal.

Dec. 13.—In the evening walked with Douglas and Walker to a mud hut, the residence of an old *fakir*, which was situated at the extremity of a ridge of hill which ran in the rear of our encampment. The *fakir* informed us he had inhabited the same spot for forty years and was present during the storming of Bhurtpoor by Lord Lake. We asked him if he thought we should take the place; he answered we might, or we might not. "*Kodaar ke khoosi*," (just as it is God's pleasure). I had heard from some officers who had seen the *fakir* in the morning, that his beard was so long that it touched his knees when he stood upright. I had a curiosity to see if it was true, so asked the old devotee to let me see how long his beard was.

When he loosened it, for he had twisted it twice round his head, it reached nearer to his ankles than his knees, and from never being combed was all matted together. After having loosened his beard and his hair which was wound round and round his head like a turban, supposing we had a curiosity to see his whole figure, he untied the small piece of linen which passed round his loins, and stood up before us perfectly naked and perfectly unconcerned. From the top of this *fakir's* hut an excellent view of the fort is obtained, and with a glass the troops on the ramparts were clearly discernible.

Dec. 15.—Turned out at 6 o'clock; everyone said we were to march to Kombeer, a town fortified, about six miles to the north-west of Bhurtpoor, and from which several marauding parties had issued, annoying our foragers and taking off cattle. It was, however, soon evident that we could not be intended for that service, as we moved off in an opposite direction towards the *bund* of the lake. When near the bund we were formed in close column of squadrons, and our position was masked by an embankment which rose in our front. We had not been long here, before General Nichol and afterwards Lord Combermere and his staff, passed by us. I asked what was to be done, and was answered, "Oh, yours is merely a diverting party."

When we moved from this position in alternate squadrons in echelon, across the plain, we were exposed to a sharp fire from the western face of the fort. We did not lose a man or horse, but everyone had a story, how very near different balls had passed to him. The native cavalry and *sepoys* met with a very trifling loss on this diverting party. The object of this manoeuvre I now found, was to distract the attention of the enemy towards the western side of the fort, whilst the engineer officers were making a reconnaissance on the others, unmolested.

Dec. 17.—On piquet with Hake. During the day several small parties of *ryots* and *coolies*, who were endeavouring to get from the Fort into the country, were taken by our videttes and brought to our tents. They were just searched and dismissed. About 7 o'clock, just as we had finished our dinner, Colonel Badderly, the field officer of the day, galloped up and required a party from our piquet. He said that the piquet of the 6th Cavalry had been forced and three or four *gooles* of about 100 horsemen each had got into the fort. We saw nothing of them.

Dec. 23.—Orderly officer; the brigade turned out for the purpose of attracting the attention of the fort; during the night our sappers and miners broke ground.

Dec. 25.—During the greater part of the day our batteries were throwing shells into the town. About 3 o'clock a party of horse from Kombeer appeared in the rear of our camp and captured some camels. Harris with twelve men went in pursuit, but failed in recovering the camels. He had considerable difficulty in effecting his retreat, as he was almost surrounded by the enemy, who sallied from the fort of Kombeer in great numbers. Fisher, a private in Luard's troop, was taken prisoner from his horse falling. In the evening we assembled a large party at the Mess, where there was an excellent dinner. Grapes, apples, and walnuts were laid out for dessert; these fruits are brought

PLAN OF BHURTPOOR.

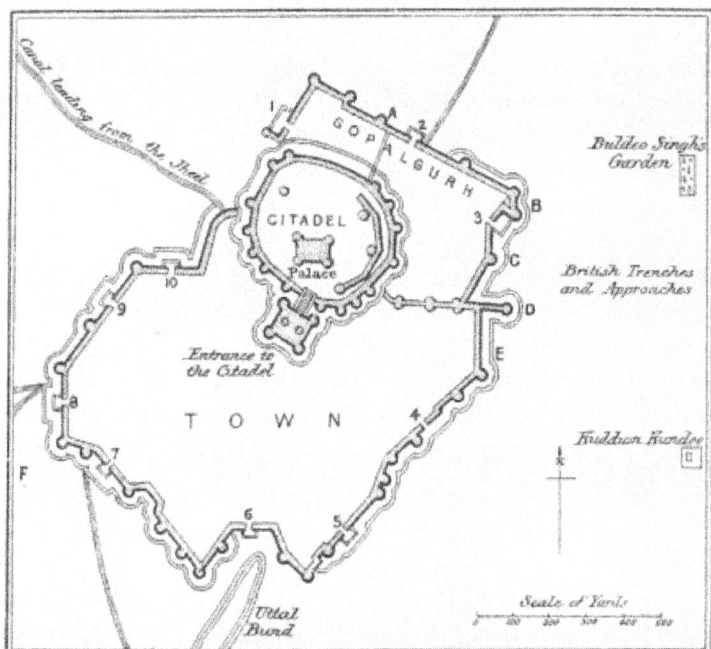

1 GOPALGURH GATE
2 JUNGEENAH GATE
3 SOORAJPORE GATE
4 MUTTRA GATE
5 BEERNARAIN GATE
6 UTTAL-BUND GATE
7 NEEMDAH GATE
8 ANAH GATE
9 KOMBHEER GATE
10 BANSOO GATE

A   Breach assaulted by Lt.-Col. Delamain.
B   General Reynell's Main Attack.
C   Colonel Wilson's Attack.
D   General Nicholls' Main Attack.
E   Extreme Left Breach.
F   Site of Lord Lake's Batteries (1804-5).

BHURTPORE.

FORT OF BHARATPUR.

from Cabul and Persia.

Dec. 26. —A heavy discharge of artillery was heard all day from our batteries. Not a bad remark was made by an officer of ours who visited the trenches "that the breaching batteries had the appearance of a common *bazaar,* but the grand mortar battery in which general officers and their staff were lounging about, resembled more a coffee house."

The engineer officers have very properly represented the annoyance and delay that must ensue from the batteries being constantly crowded with so many idlers and amateurs, and in future no one except he who is on duty is to be admitted into them. Just as I had got into bed, and was comfortably falling to sleep, I heard the old cry: "Turn out, the right-centre squadron!" We were ordered quickly to proceed to a pass on the hill in the rear of our encampment, to intercept a party of the enemy who had escaped from the fort, and were endeavouring to get to Kombeer. Enderby took us to the pass at a quick gallop. We found they had forced a piquet of Skinner's Horse, and had made their escape. We endeavoured to overtake them, but the night was so dark that pursuit was unavailing.

Dec. 27.—The 1st Extra Light Cavalry dined with us. After dinner there was some good singing, and the party had the appearance of being a jovial one. About 11 o'clock, whilst Palmer was singing a very good song, and McConchy in his mincing brogue was asking, "Lowe do you think now, there'll be anything to do tonight?"

"No," I answered.

"Well, then, faith," said McConchy "I believe I'll take another glass of claret."

The words were scarcely uttered, when a sergeant came into the tent to inform us we were ordered to turn out instantly. In a moment the Mess tent was deserted, and everyone was quickly on horseback. Firing was now distinctly heard in different directions. The left squadron was on duty, and I requested Enderby to allow me to join it. There was a good deal of confusion, and from the darkness of the night nobody appeared to know where we had best go to—to use a slang expression *we were all abroad*. At last the firing was heard to increase on our right; when we got to the spot, we found the 1st Extra's blazing away like furies, and no enemy appeared in sight. It was soon discovered by us that we were in far greater danger from our friends than foes, as the balls from the cavalry's pistols were whirling in all directions among our men.

When we got up it was all over or nearly so. Out of the party who had been sitting so jovially at the Mess a few minutes before three were wounded, all belonging to the 1st Extra's. Captain Chambers had his fore-finger cut off, and another nearly severed from his hand; Captain Palmer had a deep sabre wound in his thigh, and another severe wound on his arm; Brooke was very slightly touched on the wrist; Bishop's horse was shot in two places. We had three men wounded. Returned to our camp (this took place immediately in front of it) at 1 o'clock. As we were dismounting a horseman was seen galloping towards our guard with two native troopers after him. The sergeant of our guard with the greatest coolness took up his lance, and as the fellow was passing ran him through; the man fell; besides the lance wound he had two or three cruel sabre cuts. I got up to him two or three minutes after he fell, and in that short space the *syces* and grass-cutters of the guard, had contrived to strip the unfortunate wretch to the skin; they left him nothing. I abused them with all my heart and soul, made some of them run to the hospital for a *dhoolie*, into which I had the wounded man placed and carried to the hospital.

Dec. 28.—Rode early to the ground where we had been drawn up last night; several bodies were lying on the field, but I did not see the corpse of an European or a *sepoy*. Pratt the quartermaster of the 16th, was busy in getting the bodies buried. About fifty of the enemy must have been killed; several wounded were brought to our hospital, and some prisoners were taken. These gave an account that they had sallied out of the fort, headed by Dourjan Sal's brother-in-law with 150 picked men; that the attack in our front was merely a feint, and that the *rajah's* brother had accomplished his object of making his escape with valuable property in jewels. If this account is correct, one-third of the party were killed and another third wounded and taken prisoners.

After an event of this kind there is always some fun in listening to the wonderful stories of different men; at breakfast one declared, and without hesitation swore to it, that he had seen a man the night before twice as big as Kelly who is 6 feet 4 inches and stout in proportion. Another had seen a similar giant with the interesting addition of carrying an infant in one arm, whilst he dealt death and destruction to all that opposed him with the other. I put a cocked hat on the child's head, and started the story afresh; about noon this imaginary infant became very ludicrously apparelled.

Yesterday a man of the artillery, who had been a sergeant, deserted

JAT NOBLES.

to the enemy; this man's name is Herbert.

A very material alteration for the better was perceived today in the firing from the fort, and double the number of guns were brought to play on our trenches, and they were directed with much greater precision.

Lord Combermere was in the habit of retiring to a small house, close to our first parapet, to eat his breakfast in. He had today scarcely sat down to this meal when three shots came spinning through the walls; a *kitmagar* who was waiting at table had his leg carried away. Herbert, I think, runs every chance of coming to an untimely end. I had scarcely sat down to dinner when Enderby's troop were ordered on duty; we had to bivouac during the night; the enemy made no attempt to sally from the fort, as was expected.

Dec. 29.—Returned from this advanced piquet at sunrise; our encampment was this day removed about 500 yards to the front; it was quite time to get away from the filth that had accumulated on our old ground.

Dec. 30.—Rode with Walker and Douglas to the trenches which were now carried to the very counterscarp of the ditch; as yet our breaching batteries had effected little; our shot appeared to do but slight damage to the bastion against which they were directed; the balls buried themselves in the mud walls, and just a little earth crumbled away from the spot where they struck. I had certainly expected to have seen an almost practicable breach effected. Whilst standing with Colonel Bowyer, Cox, and two or three more, we had foolishly got out of the trenches, and were standing opposite an embrasure in our mortar battery, a matchlock ball passed so immediately through our party that each with one accord clapped his hand up to his ear. An old artillery man who was cutting fuses in the battery where he was quite safe, coolly turned round and said: "Well, I'm sure, I thought it must have hit some on ye."

Jan. 4. 1826.—Was on outlying piquet.

Jan. 5.—A meeting of the officers was held in Persse's tent to ascertain who would volunteer for a dismounted party, who were to escalade, if the European Regiment did not arrive in time. This detachment was to consist of 1 captain, 2 subalterns, 80 men and a proportion of non-commissioned officers. Luard, McConchy and Walker volunteered for this service, and there was a great competition amongst the men. The party was paraded in the evening, all in admirable spirits: the men were ordered to strip the flag from their lances, and to carry a sword and pistol which was stuck through their girdle.

Jan. 6.—On the main piquet with Byron about 3 o'clock our volunteers passed on their way to the camp of the 11th Dragoons. We fancied that the storm would take place the following morning. The night was beautifully clear and starlight; occasionally you could hear the beating of a drum and the hum of voices from the fort. Byron and I sat outside our tents nearly the whole night watching the direction of the shells which were being thrown into the town from Whish's battery. He had seven mortars, and kept up a continued fire during the night. The scene to me was a very beautiful one. I could distinctly follow the course of the shells, and as Whish fired his mortars in the quickest succession, seven shells were to be seen at one moment in the air, an occasional one ineffectually bursting too high up for execution.

In the course of the night I could distinctly perceive four or five fires kindled in different parts of the town by these infernal engines of destruction. I have called this scene a beautiful one: it was so; but whilst viewing it, and listening to the jokes and stories of our men on piquet, I could not avoid occasionally thinking of the miserable and pitiable state of the inhabitants of Bhurtpoor, and of the death, ruin and destruction, that I was coolly viewing as a splendid picture.

Jan. 7.—About 4 o'clock a.m., before I had been relieved from piquet, a mine was sprung under the north-east bastion, but the effect did not quite answer expectation. During the day it was confidently reported that we were to storm tomorrow: in the evening I dined with Sleigh who commanded the cavalry. We were kept waiting a long time for dinner, Sleigh had been sent for in a hurry to headquarters, where he had been detained by Lord Combermere. Our host said the commander-in-chief had been particularly anxious to have stormed the fort on the following morning, but that a council of engineer officers had decided unanimously against the measure, declaring the breach was impracticable for a body. Sleigh mentioned an instance of great intrepidity in a Gourkah who scrambled up the breach and brought down from the ramparts a glove and leathern jacket.

Jan. 9—At 2 a.m. a tremendous fire was discovered which we all supposed was raging in the fort, but it proceeded from our own batteries. It was said a shot had struck an ammunition tumbril (open cart) and caused it to explode. However, the accident happened, about eighty hackeries were burnt, and several ammunition tumbrils blew up. The light was so great that even our side of the fort became perfectly illuminated.

Jan. 10.—The right wing were ordered at 3 a.m. to proceed to the Attub bund gate, as it was supposed that Dourjan Sal with a few chosen horse would endeavour to escape about daybreak by that passage. No enemy appearing, we returned about 9 o'clock.

Jan. 11.—On outlying piquet with Enderby .

Jan. 17.—At the mess it was known for certain that the fort was to be stormed on the following morning. At midnight the order was circulated for the right wing of the regiment to proceed towards the Attub bund gate so as to arrive there by 7 a.m.

Jan. 18.—Left the camp with the right-centre squadron; we arrived on our ground at the appointed time. A squadron of the 3rd Cavalry and 3 squadrons of Skinner's Horse were on our left. The 10th Cavalry were posted on our right so as to prevent the possibility of escape between us and Malaye, a village on a rising ground to the southward of the fort. At this village a battery had been erected under the command of Colonel Childers supported by the squadron of the 11th Dragoons. The face of the fort, where we were posted, was so closely invested as to render any attempt at escape hopeless. We knew that the blowing up of a grand mine (the largest I believe ever charged) was to be the signal of attack, and it was believed that the explosion would take place at 8 o'clock. The explosion was anxiously expected, but could not be heard on our side.

About half-past eight a heavy discharge of artillery was heard, and shortly afterwards a brisk fire of musketry, rapidly increasing till it became unremitting. Our guns were now silent; and as we were five or six miles from the breaches, and could know nothing of what was going on, nothing could exceed our anxiety as to the cause. Presently the fire of musketry became slacker, now it was only heard at intervals, and we fancied we could distinguish its approach to us as each succeeding bastion was carried. Soon after 10 o'clock Corporal Derbyshire and a private who had been sent to patrol a short way into the jungle in our front, galloped back to us, and said they had seen a party of horse, who had come close up to them in the wood. Persse imagined that possibly these men might have mistaken Skinner's Irregular Horse for the enemy.

I told the major I would return with the men and ascertain who they were. When I had proceeded a short distance into the jungle, I perceived a few straggling horsemen, who retired on seeing us; not knowing their numbers, I did not think it would be safe with only two men to follow them far into the wood, so contented myself with being able to report that some of the *rajah's* horse were in our front. I was now about a quarter of a mile in front of our two squadrons. I thought I heard a murmur from the fort which was concealed from me by the wood; I stopped my horse and listened; I could distinctly hear the buzz of voices. I proceeded a little further, after a volley of musketry I distinguished the British hurrah, another, and another, and another followed. I was confident of the sound and returned in high spirits to our squadrons, convinced that the fort was ours, or shortly would be so.

About 12 o'clock some of the enemy's horse appeared on the plain and endeavoured to make their point good, but failed, being stopped by the 8th Cavalry. Our brigadier Murray ordered Hodgson to pour grape into them from his two 6-pound guns, and Enderby who was sent after them with our squadron, led at such a pace to cut them off before they could recover the wood, that we nearly felt the effects of the grape. We did not succeed in preventing the *rajah's* troops from reaching the jungle, but had gone so fast to effect this that by the time we got into the wood we formed a perfectly irregular body of horse. I with six men went headlong in pursuit, and soon found myself with this small detachment completely separated from the squadron.

As the enemy were scattered through the jungle, I found it impossible to keep even the six men together, and every one acted for himself. I got on the near side of a horseman, and being within the parry of his spear tumbled him off his horse: another passed and had the speed of me, and as he appeared to be preparing his matchlock for a shot at me, I thought it as well to be beforehand with him. I fired my pistol at him and missed him; he instantly threw away his matchlock, and finding I was now gaining on him, he threw himself from his horse on the offside, put up his hands and asked for mercy. I desired him to give up his sword to McCaw, an old servant of mine, who now came up; the man did so immediately.

McCaw was not satisfied with this, so suiting the action to the word brought his lance down, saying: "Sure Mr. Lowe wouldn't it be better just to give him a poke."

I would by no means comply with this cruel desire, and the horse was led away, and the man, made prisoner. I could not even at the time well refrain from laughter at seeing Griffiths, Enderby's lanceman, riding after a fellow whose shield was slung at his back so as completely to defend it; (by the bye, a shield slung in this manner appears the most useful part of the armour of these troops). Whenever Griffiths got in position to give point the lance rattled off the shield, without doing the man any injury, and poor Griffiths was quite in despair. I galloped up to this man and foolishly got on his right side. He made a cut at me, which I parried, but the point glancing off slightly grazed my left arm. I changed my position to his near side and then had him at my command. His turban fell off, and the rolls of linen which fasten it, by being rolled over the head and underneath the chin, being now unloosened, I cut him across the neck, and he fell, but was not killed.

I was now very near the fort, and being out of the jungle I had a distinct view of it. On the bastion the British flag was waving, but underneath the walls, and close to the ditch I perceived not quite so agreeable an object, *viz.*, a *goole* or troop of the *rajah's* horse drawn up, who, I fancied, on seeing us showed a disposition to cut off our retreat; however Enderby and his squadron came up with them, charged, and completely routed them, killing a great portion and making prisoners of the rest. It was a complete success.

The 59th who were on the ramparts of the fort cheered our men. We returned to our former position, and it was imagined that all was over, and that never was a fort, supposed to be impregnable, so very easily taken; cold meat, wine and water, and *segars* were produced, and we all made a very hearty meal; the camp-followers were continually passing us laden with all kinds of arms, many of them mounted on horses which they had caught in the jungle.

At 2 o'clock we moved off our ground towards our camp. In passing through Ghoolpara an officer informed us that a body of the enemy commanded by some person of distinction were in the jungle opposite to the village. We were irresolutely halted here some time. Some of our officers who had dismounted and were standing on some rising ground could perceive a dust flying across the plain we had occupied all the morning. We were now ordered to scour the jungle, the right squadron taking one direction, whilst the right-centre took another; we, however, saw nothing. On coming to the Anah gate the squadron was halted, and several of us went into the fort, passing through numbers of wounded, the dying, and the dead.

On the ramparts we found the 59th in high spirits, looking like so many devils, their faces were so blackened with powder, the officers

167

THE TAKING OF DOURJAN SAL BY LIEUTENANT BARBER.

just as bad as the men. Amongst these I recognised several acquaint-ances, and was sorry to hear from them of the death of poor Pitman who fell covered with wounds whilst cheering on the grenadiers; his younger brother was also mentioned as mortally wounded, since dead. The citadel as yet had not fallen, and occasional shots were sent at the men on the ramparts. The town appeared to be deserted, not a soul appearing in it. I could not remain here long; nothing was known of the *rajah*, or what going forward with regard to the citadel; I rejoined the squadron and marched with it across salt-pits towards our camp.

By the roadside under a tree a poor wretch was stretched out cov-ered by his *gudthee* or quilt, and apparently in the last stage of life. Sev-eral of the men had their joke in passing him, but one created a roar of laughter in the troop by saying he has just chosen that sturdy tree for a tombstone. "Arrah, well done, Pat," was heard in all directions. When we had nearly arrived at our camp, I perceived a detachment of Native Cavalry who were guarding a native. I rode up to it, and found that Dourjan Sal was the prisoner. The *rajah* rode a large bay Persian horse overloaded with flesh, on which he sat well considering his weight, which must be 18 stone (all fat): he looked dejected, as well he might, but still dignified and important; he had even now the appearance of a man used to command. He had endeavoured to make his escape over the ground where we had been posted all the morning, and was taken after little resistance by an out piquet of the 8th Cavalry commanded by Lieutenant Barber, who now rode in advance of the prisoner with the splendid sword he had taken from the *rajah*, stuck in his girdle.

The piquet had in the most shameful manner plundered and stripped Dourjan Sal, whose dress now consisted of the slightest *dootee*, a pink *kummeerbund* was thrown over his shoulders and could only partially cover his naked body and thighs, and a dirty pink turban was on his head, such as only your lowest caste servants would wear. In this plight he was conducted to the tent of Lord Combermere. His favourite wife followed him, sitting behind her brother on a fine horse; Dourjan's son was also taken prisoner and formed one of this party. The poor boy had been shot through the hand, but he bore his wound bravely. Major Barlow rode on one side of Dourjan Sal, Capt. Fouchard on the other; escape was impossible.

Jan. 19.—I was anxious to visit the town, but Enderby and Childers both wished to go, so I, the junior, was obliged to remain with the troop: during the day numbers of horses, matchlocks, swords, shields and curious spears were brought into camp.

Jan. 20.—The regiment shifted its ground about two miles in the rear, towards Kombeer; Persse allowed me to be absent to visit the Lions, and King and I rode together into the fort through the Kombeer gate. The town differs but little from the generality of native towns, the *bazaars* are narrow, and the shops and houses, with very few exceptions, constructed of mud. Nothing could well be more horrible or disgusting than the scene through which we had to pass before we could get to the citadel. Corpses were lying in all directions through the streets; their countenances and attitudes expressing the agony in which they expired, many of them half burnt.

The Jaats were usually dressed in a linen jacket and trowsers of either a dark green, or very dark yellow colour; and these dresses are so thickly stuffed with cotton as to afford almost a protection against the cut of a sabre, and in this way they are extremely serviceable; but against shot, if the wounded man is near to the musket which is fired at him, his death becomes doubly shocking, his stuffed clothes catch fire, and he is literally roasted alive, his ammunition of which he has usually a good supply about his person at length blows up, and puts an end to his sufferings. Here a dead camel nearly blocked up the road, and in another place the carcasses of bullocks, horses, and pigs were mixed with the corpses of natives which were being devoured by dogs. Every now and then a wounded horse might be seen stalking through this scene of desolation.

The *banians* and natives of the *bazaar* appeared to be recovering from their terror, and were beginning to re-open and cleanse their shops. More than once King and I were overtaken by people crying in the name of the company for justice and protection against plunder from the rascally *sepoys*, who at this work are inconceivably active. The ditch which surrounds the citadel is very wide and exceedingly deep, though now only half filled with water.

After crossing the bridge at the principal gate, a guard of the 14th were placed, the officer, Ormsby was busily employed in searching passengers for concealed treasure, and he appeared perfectly to understand his duty; cloths, *rasais*, arms and articles of small value were scattered all about this spot, and loose horses were galloping about in all directions, to the immediate peril of those who were mounted, as I happened to be, on a vicious horse. Never was there a greater libertine than 'Don Juan,' a beast of a mare would keep just before him, and wound him up to such a pitch, that I had great difficulty in pacifying him. At the Mint we found Captain Rochfort of the 14th, who during the night had discovered six *lacs* of *rupees* which were piled up outside the building. The palace is raised on a terrace, on entering, the Diwan-i-Khas is opposite to you, on either side of which is a corresponding building; that on the left hand was now appropriated by the 14th to a mess-room; the opposite building appeared to have been made a kind of lumber room of. In it were several boxes filled with toys (many of them indecent), English stationery, plated pencil cases with glass seals at the top, and such articles as you would find in a paltry shop in a small country town.

A splendid *palanquin*, covered with scarlet cloth, richly embroidered and fringed with gold, was standing in this building: Lord Combermere, who now came in with all his staff, said he would send it home to the king. From this apartment a passage led to the baths, which were well constructed, and so newly repaired that the scaffolding was not removed from the walls: the pavement was inlaid with different coloured stones, plundered, I imagine, by the Jaats either from Delhi or Agra. The Diwan-i-Khas is a large apartment; a table, after the European fashion, was placed in the room; on three sides of this apartment were recesses in the walls, used, I fancy, as sleeping rooms. There appeared to me nothing particularly deserving of notice about these buildings.

Whilst lounging about, I found my old friend James Grant of the 14th, who had gone up the breach with the grenadiers, and who, I was happy to perceive, had escaped unhurt. King and I now tried very hard for a breakfast, and cast in every direction among the staff; but we could not make one out, and were obliged to return to our own camp. We left the town by the Agra gate, where there must have been a dreadful slaughter; numbers of bodies were being dragged out of the town to be consumed by fire; the stench arising from this burning was perfectly sickening. In the ditch many bodies were lying, and several, who had during the storm been thrown over the ramparts with the bayonet, were to be seen in the most distorted attitudes half-way up the curtain.

At the breach, where the 14th ascended, several bodies half buried from the explosion of our mine were visible, —here and there just a leg or an arm sticking out. At the Delhi gate several hundred bodies were collected for burning. At each of the gateways the principal slaughter took place: I had never witnessed such a scene as this morning exhibited, King and I returned to a late breakfast in my tent.

Jan. 21.—Smyth and I went out shooting. I killed two very fine wild hogs; and had a long shot at a *nylgai*, but missed him. Some matchlock men joined us; and as the country was of course unsettled, I can't say I much liked their company: one of the horsemen offered to shew us some hogs, which he did; he asked us for some powder and shot, with which he went away quite delighted. A man with a matchlock joined us and offered to show us game; he had no turban on, and was, with the exception of the *dootee*, naked. Since I have been in India, I have seen nothing so savage as this man; the wild man at Lucknow is a fool to him. He called himself a *Bileiah Wallah*; by this time some of his companions joined him, and he now showed me what he meant by the term, and how, by the management of a bullock most admirably trained, he contrived to get near his game.

A string passed through the bullock's nose, and by this was guided in any way that was wished, the *Bileiah Wallah* creeping by his side so as to be completely concealed himself; he got by this means near enough to his object, when the bullock's back served as a rest for his matchlock.

Jan. 22.—Rode with Douglas and Enderby into the fort and again went over the palace and were conducted by a *chuprasseh*, who was, though black, an image of Sancho Panza, into an outer court of the *zenanah*, situated a short distance to the left of the palace. We asked to see the young *rajah,* who is a miserable child, but he would not shew. Douglas and I walked up to the high double-necked bastion; the atmosphere was so cloudy that I was disappointed in the view I had expected. At the base of this bastion the cavalry had been stationed during the siege; now several carcasses of horses were lying about, and a few poor horses that had lingered till this time were now to be seen dying from their wounds and thirst. It would be a mercy to send some soldiers to destroy these animals.

Jan. 23.—Lord Combermere and the staff of the army dined at our mess. Two single-poled tents were pitched at the ends of our mess-tent. Everything was admirably arranged and the dinner was excellent. The commander-in-chief ate like a trooper and his staff were in no way behind him. His Lordship's table is not very well supplied. The A. D. C.'s say his beef is white, the veal brown, the mutton lean, and everything sour but the vinegar. Lord Combermere appeared to enjoy himself much, and staid till a late hour with his old regiment. Many stories were told of the witticisms of the men during the storm. One of the 59th, whilst mounting the breach, hallooed out, "We'll give 'em a stick with His Majesty's darning needle," meaning the bayonet.

Another story was told of two men of the 14th who met after the fort fell. Mick says one, "have you fired away all your ammunition?"

"Yes, I did Daniel, did you?"

"No, I did not," says Mick, "I have 8 rounds remaining."

"Well, however, did you manage that?"

"Why; sure, those black beggars would not fight any longer, how could I help it."

In the early formation of the Jaat States, oracles were consulted as to the duration of Bhurtpoor; and they answered, that the place should never fall till a crocodile had ascended the ramparts. As there is no river of consequence within a considerable distance, the prophecy was confidently interpreted into the perfect security of the fort for ever; and well might they, for it would not be a whit more impossible for a crocodile to trot up the dome of St. Paul's. When the place fell, the men of wisdom were regarded as little better than humbugs; but they, in no way dismayed, exclaimed the prophecy was fulfilled, a crocodile had walked over the ramparts, and that all human efforts to have saved the place must have proved unavailing.

Lord Combermere is the crocodile; the natives pronounce the name Combere, and Kombeer is the Hindustanee name for a crocodile. Thus, the wise men have preserved their character; the natives reconcile themselves to the change as they do to everything else, by saying:

It's God's pleasure, what use is there in contending against our fate? The Company are now our masters, and we must bow our neck to obedience towards them.

Jan. 25.—Lord Combermere had a grand *battue*, and everyone was allowed to join it: 20 elephants entered the jungle in line, and some of them were handsomely caparisoned, 100 of Skinner's horse were on our flanks prancing about and showing their skill in horsemanship and dexterity with the lance. The dress of these troops is very gaudy, but still looks well, and is strictly in character; they wear a bright steel cap, a long yellow coat, green trowsers, and long boots; the covering to their saddles is red and yellow cloth cut in lozenges.

As we advanced through the wood the scenery was magnificent, almost sufficiently so to make amends for our very bad sport. A herd of hogs were found. Persse, Luard, Spence, Newbery, Archer, and I mounted our horses and followed them; one, about three-quarters grown, gave an excellent run. I was fortunate in getting the spear, and killing him.

Jan. 26.—Walker and I went out shooting over the ground we had beat yesterday, and again had a bad day's sport: between us we killed a *nylgai,*—sent a camel out to bring him home.

Jan. 28.—Drove Lucius Smyth in my buggy to the headquarter camp. Whilst there, Madhoo Sing, the Deeg Rajah, and brother to Bhurtpoor, came to make his submission to Lord Combermere and to hear the determination of our government concerning him. He was dressed quite plainly, but rode the handsomest elephant I ever saw; the *mahout* with a great deal of state fanned the air with a *chowrie,* and halloed out the titles of the *rajah*; an elephant was ridden quite close to the *rajah's* on either side; on these were men employed in a similar way, fanning the air. Some of Madhoo Sing's followers were well appointed, and carried a musket; these were well dressed in a dark-green turban, and a quilted cotton jacket and trowsers. His cavalry followers were miserably mounted and were in every respect despicable. Whilst looking at this parade my old friend, Lady Betty Barnett came up and got into the buggy, and began a very long story about his having been unjustly suspended the service, for neglect which he was in no way blameable for.

"But only think," squeaked Lady Betty, "of the barbarity of that revengeful wretch, General Nichol, who on meeting Cunliffe the other day asked him if he had yet hung that commissariat officer, meaning me. Did you ever, Lowe hear of anything so barbarous?"

I could not very well tell my friend he had mistaken his profession, but such is the case. In the evening dined with Lord Combermere. On the table were placed two very large candelabras of filigree silver most delicately worked; they were part of the plunder of Bhurtpoor. Returned home with Harris, Enderby and Walker on the greatest beast of an elephant I ever rode.

Jan. 29.—The whole army were ordered out to attend the execution of Herbert, the artilleryman who deserted from the trenches to the enemy. To the last he solemnly protested that he did not desert, but was taken prisoner, and was forced at the risk of his life to work and point their guns. Herbert was hanged on the cavalier of the N. E. Bastion, (where the 14th stormed); he was for some time dreadfully convulsed. Two other artillerymen named O'Brien and Hennessy were also taken in the fort, and were at the same time tried for desertion; the court sentenced each to 14 years' transportation; this verdict justly produced a very severe animadversion from the commander-in-chief.

Jan. 31.—The regiment and several of the staff dined with us; the party was so heavy that I went to bed at 9 o'clock; it is ungrateful in me to complain of this party, for I sold an elephant to Cureton for 860 *rupees*, which I purchased in the morning at auction for 430.

Feb. 1.—Brigadier-General Sleigh inspected the regiment. I was on piquet.

Feb. 5.—As the regiment were ordered to march towards Alwah on the following day, I obtained permission to visit Deeg, and to join on the march. I left our camp early and arrived at the tents of the 9th Cavalry before breakfast-time, after having had several battles with my libertine Arab 'Don Juan,' who got nothing by his obstinacy except having to do the 18 miles in less than an hour and half including stoppages.

After breakfast Palmer, King and I rode to the palace, where we found Bishop and his wife, and Duffin had taken up their quarters. Brook also formed one of the party. On entering the gardens, the Diwan-i-Khas is immediately on your right hand, and is a building of singular beauty; the stone of the exterior is simply and elegantly carved, and a double cornice which is on each side of this edifice is much to be admired. The corridor in the interior is handsome, and the ceiling of a dark-coloured wood is elaborately carved. I cannot remember having seen a similar one in India. The arches which support this massive roof and ceiling are so light as to have been incapable of affording to them a sufficient prop.

To afford this it has been found necessary, and I should think recently, to erect four pillars, and they have been built, and in such miserable taste plastered and painted with gods and goddesses, crocodiles elephants, peacocks, and numbers of things which are totally indescribable, so as greatly to disfigure this otherwise beautiful building. The Diwan-i-Khas and the Aum Dewan, which is situated on the right side of the gardens, are both Moorish or Musselmannee buildings; and though materially differing from each other, are in the same style of architecture. The residence of Madhoo Sing is on the opposite side of the gardens to the Diwan-i-Khas, and in the Hindooee style; on the top of the palace is a large reservoir of water which supplies the

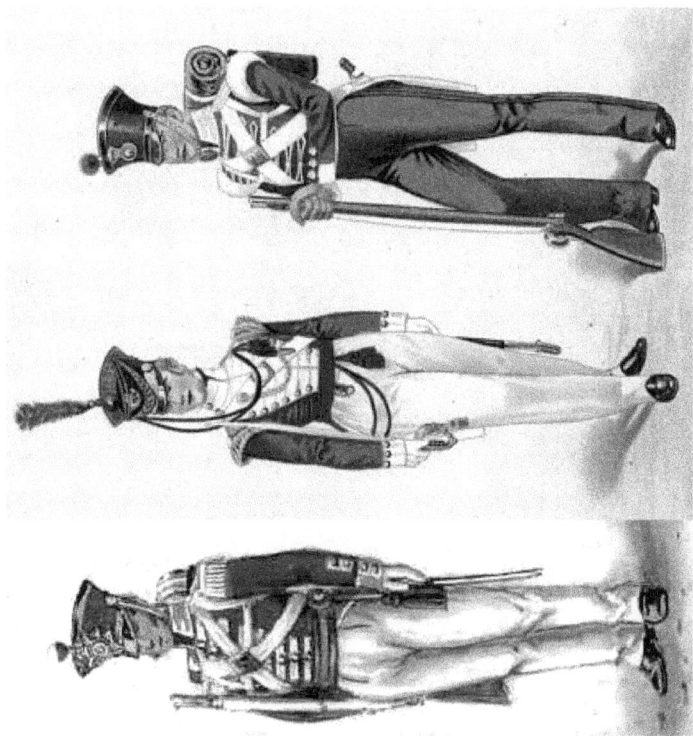

BRITISH INFANTRY.

numerous fountains in the gardens.

Opposite to the Aum Dewan is an open building overlooking a tank to which you descend by 30 steps. In a verandah are fountains which would force the water to the height of the roof; under the pavement of the apartment water is conducted so as to supply smaller fountains which are placed at the edges of the pavement. No place by art could be rendered more cool. The garden is a perfectly enchanting place; in the centre is a large basin from which canals run at right angles so as to quarter the garden; in each of these fountains play at equal distances; and opposite to each of the buildings, I have endeavoured to describe, is a canal equal to the length of the buildings. The air in this delicious spot is fragrant from the orange, lemon, and pomegranate trees, and the jasmin, which grows luxuriantly, adds considerably to the perfume.

In the shade of a magnificent tamarind tree, which is of all trees the most elegant, is placed the Beithue Bahar, or "Seat of Delight." It is cut out of one block of black marble, and is rather a couch than a seat. In the evening Mrs. Bishop and I very sentimentally walked down to the tank for the purpose of fishing. There is always something interesting in a woman who shortly expects to produce the first sweet pledge of mutual affection, as she expressed herself. As we had only one chair, I sat down at her feet, baited her hook, placed the float at a proper distance, and then threw it into a likely spot to ensnare some unfortunate fish. What I should have done next I don't know; an accident determined me: the Bishop's wife should remember that it is not fair upon her acquaintance, particularly if they have to sit at her feet, to wear very dirty cotton stockings in an extremely hot climate. I changed my position. We returned together, but there was an end to all sentiment.

Before we sat down to dinner nothing would please Bishop but he must spar with me. I told him that I did not like it; but he would take no denial, and to please him I stood up. Key and Brook saying: "Take care of Westminster, Bishop." I saw Bishop was bent on a shew off, and unfortunately, he got a flush hit which tapped his claret; at first, he was exceedingly savage with me, but soon left me to attack Key and Brook.

The former was roaring with laughter and screaming: "Why, Bishop, I never knew the way to tap your claret before" (my antagonist keeps an awfully bad table). Brook in a corner was hiding his face, and making his laughter ten times more mortifying by pretending to smother it. All this together, was quite too much for Bishop, who

Bhurtpore, 1826, assault on the north-east bastion

wanted immediately to fight Brook for £200 in a 12-foot ring; but I would in no way consent to this as dinner was coming on table. Good humour was shortly restored, and everyone was merry excepting Bishop could not enjoy his snuff because his nose was sore; he was sulky the whole evening.

Feb. 6.—Breakfasted and passed the day in the gardens, and the evening rode with Colonel Pepper into the citadel: the ditch which surrounds it is broad and deep, and the curtain which is built of stone is of great height, and now bears the mark of shot which struck it, when besieged by Lord Lake, or rather by General Fraser, who took the place without much loss; the fortifications are not reckoned strong. In one of the magazines was a contrivance which was new to me; ten or a dozen barrels were let into a frame, and a fuse running along the touch-holes one match would fire them at the same instant. The town of Deeg is not remarkable; the bazaar appeared to be well furnished.

Feb. 7.—Left Deeg, and after a long ride overtook the Dragoons. My horse was so completely done up that I gladly accepted Colonel Childer's invitation to stay the day with them. I put up with my old friend Neville. The 11th are in a most uncomfortable state, and divided into separate parties. Jenkins, who has been tried by a court-martial and acquitted, sat at one end of the table, and nobody spoke to him. Hare was under arrest and to be tried, and some other officers would not join the mess.

Feb. 8.—Joined my regiment at Mugger, a village or rather small town situated on rising ground, on the height of which there is a strong little mud fort lately repaired. Our encampment is in a beautiful plain, exceedingly well cultivated, and partly surrounded to the westward by an amphitheatre of hills; the country itself in some ways reminds me of France.

Feb. 9.—Heard that the differences between our government and the Alwah Rajah were settled by his acceding to the terms proposed to him; we are now on the border of his territories.

Feb. 10.—Went out shooting with Smythe, and had three hours' good sport. I bagged two brace of hares, three brace of partridges and five couple of quail.

Feb. 12.—Lord Combermere reviewed us first in brigade and then inspected us separately by regiments. The dust was so thick as to prevent our manoeuvres being distinctly seen, and it was fortunate for us that it was so. The 6th Cavalry made a very respectable exhibition. Persse gave breakfast to the commander-in-chief and a large party.

Feb. 17.—The whole cavalry were reviewed by Lord Combermere, the movements in brigade were tolerably performed, but the dust again befriended us.

Feb. 22.—Commenced our march towards Meerut, everyone delighted at being sent to that station, which is reckoned the most desirable one in India: we encamped under a hill, not more than three miles from our old ground. In the evening rode my curiously-spotted pony 'The Cheetah' up this hill, and had a fine view over a well-cultivated country, bounded towards the westward by a belt of hills in the territory of the Alwah Rajah,

Feb. 23.—Marched to Deeg; at evening stables, Enderby and I had a regular blow up; after dinner Walker acted as peace-maker between us: this will not be forgotten by either party. I rode into Deeg, and walked about the delightful gardens till it was dark. The fortifications were being dismantled; one bastion had been blown up.

Feb. 24.—Continued our march. I had occasion to tell Rowe, an old soldier, who was not drunk absolutely, but as a non-commissioned officer would say, "had been a-drinking," to sit steady on his horse, and to keep in his place.

The man replied "Yes, I will, Lieutenant Lowe, for you're a good soldier, by God!" and turning round to his comrades said: "I saw him at Bhurtpoor run three black fellows through the body."

I gave Rowe a devil of a rowing for talking in the ranks, but own I never was so much flattered in my life.

Feb. 25.—Crossed the Jumna at Muttra on a bridge of boats; I had not breakfasted long, when I received a note from Clarkson, an old Westminster school-fellow, to spend the day with him. I would not remain to '*tiff*' with him, and he promised to come down to our encampment in the evening. After having bought a buggy and horse from me, he accompanied me over the old Hindoo city of Muttra, which I had neglected to see, when passing by last year with McDowell. The *bazaars* are very narrow, and excessively dirty; but many of the shops appeared to be well-furnished with merchandise, and the *mhanjhan loge* or merchants looked fat and opulent. A great proportion of the buildings are built of brick or stone; numbers of monkeys are seen skipping about the houses; these animals are here regarded with superstitious reverence; and were you to kill one, you could scarcely expect to escape from the fury that such an act would occasion amongst the Hindoos.

I visited a temple lately erected, indeed not yet completed, by a wealthy Hindoo named Pooruck, and I rather think this place of worship is dedicated to Krishna. The building is of stone, and covers a considerable space of ground: the balcony over each corridor is coarsely and gaudily painted. I forget the number of *lacs* a Brahmin told me this building had cost. I certainly would not again take the trouble to visit it, but can easily imagine, that no Hindoo could look at it without exclaiming in admiration: "*Wah! Wah! Wah.*"

The city is abundantly populous, and is much celebrated, and venerated, as the scene of the birth and early adventures of their favorite deity Krishna. Dined with Clarkson; and after partaking rather freely of his good cheer, we resolved to go into the town to a *nautch*. As we were riding down on this exhibition, I was much amused by young Brownlow, a remarkably fine lad, exclaiming: "Well, then, bad luck to you Martin for giving me a pair of breeches with holes in the pockets; sure I've lost my bunch of patent keys, and will have to send to England for a new set."

The *nautch* was like all other *nautches*, and ended just in the same way; one girl was very pretty. We returned very late, and rode home by the banks of the Jumna: the night was moonlight; the river silently flowing on our left hand, gave a calmness to the picture, which strongly contrasted itself to the debauchery we had just left. Hindooee temples of curious structure are crowded on this bank of the Jumna, as well as *ghauts* for the convenience of bathers. When I got to our camp, it was almost time to turn out for the march.

March 6.—Arrived with my regiment at our cantonments in Meerut. As I had determined on applying for leave of absence to return to England, I gladly availed myself of Douglas' offer to live with him, as my doing so prevented the necessity of purchasing a bungalow.

March 12.—I was paying a morning visit at Garstin's, where a large assemblage of ladies were collected. Paddy Stack of the 14th called, and was asked by Mrs. Garstin if he had seen the newly-arrived spinster. Stack answered. Indeed, he had, and "without flattery she was just the ugliest girl in India." There was a laugh at the richness of brogue with which this was uttered, and this induced Paddy to suppose that, as usual, he had committed some blunder; to extricate himself, he added, "present company of course excepted." I thought some of the party would have gone into fits from laughter.

March 27.—Dined at Enderby's. The conversation turned on the conviction of some very brave soldiers, that they should be killed, when about to go into action; I mentioned an instance that I had heard, when in the 18th, of an officer who was so convinced that he should not escape that before going into action, he said "I am quite confident I shall be killed;" and putting on a clean shirt remarked, "now I shall be found in clean linen, as a gentleman should he." The presentiment was just, for the officer fell. The little woman said, she thought it was a very proper feeling; and that if she knew for certain that she was about to die, she should put on her very prettiest satin shoe—that when dead her foot might appear to the best possible advantage. I never saw any person so vain as Mrs. Enderby of a pretty foot. I wrote some verses, and sent them to her.

I now spent much of my time at Crighton's house, who had come to Meerut for the purpose of conducting his wife to Cawnpore; she is a particularly pleasing woman, with the advantage of being of a good family. As the captain's leave of absence had now nearly expired, he began to think of his march, and asked me to accompany them for the first two or three days. I accepted this invitation.

April 4.—Left Meerut with the Crightons and accompanied them as far as Haupper. Wyatt has here the superintendent of the company's stud, and I think that shortly under his management this establishment, which is now in its infancy, will rival that at Ghazeepoor. The colts were in excellent condition; greater attention could scarcely be paid them. The weather was now getting hot to be under canvass; after two days I returned to Meerut, having received great marks of kindness. The society in this station is more sociable and united than at Cawnpore, and I now passed my time agreeably and gaily; musical parties, balls, and dinners almost constantly engaged me.

It was rumoured that Baron Osten paid a great deal of attention to Mrs. Mack and some very wise people imagined that he'd certainly marry her. The old baron is about the very last man to do so foolish a thing, especially as Mrs. Mack is daily increasing in size, and will probably shortly arrive at 17 stone. I wrote an epigram on the report.

May 16.—Called on Colonel Murray and told him that I was anxious to visit home, of course on very urgent private affairs; the colonel in the kindest manner offered to forward my leave of absence.

May 26.—An order arrived for a committee of medical officers to assemble for the purpose of examining those men who had been badly wounded at Bhurtpoor, and such as it was found expedient to move were to be sent by water to the Presidency. I immediately applied to General Reynell, for the command of this detachment, as the boat allowance 500 *rupees*, would almost defray all expenses to Calcutta. General Reynell gave me the command, and told me I should immediately appear in orders. As my leave had been forwarded, and I made no doubt of getting it, I considered myself fortunate in this opportunity.

Whilst paying my farewell visits, Miss Pinkerton asked me to write something for her, and I gave her a charade on her name. Miss Pinkerton is the prettiest girl I have seen in the country.

May 28.—There passed over the cantonments, about 6 o'clock, the most awful storm I have witnessed since my residence in India; large columns of black dust, circling in their progress, were seen regularly approaching from the N. W., producing, as they passed over, a total darkness. This lasted almost two hours. I am justified in applying the epithet awful to a typhoon of this description. Dined at the mess for the last time; and after dinner Havelock proposed my health being drank, as I was about to quit them.

May 29.—Marched from Meerut with my detachment consisting of 21 invalids from the 14th Regiment; all these men had been wounded at Bhurtpoor, and many of them by the blowing up of our mine on the morning of the storm. *Dhoolies* were provided for those who were unable to walk. When I had got them fairly away from cantonments I returned, and spent great part of the day with Enderby. The little woman was carrying on a most decided flirtation with Osborne; before *tiffin* we amused ourselves by writing epitaphs on each other. Mrs. Enderby asked me to write one on her, but she was not at all pleased with the two lines I immediately gave her.

Here lies Mrs. Enderby and she was very small,
She had a pretty little foot, and that's all.

Meerut, in every point of view, is a superior station to Cawnpore; the weather remains temperate a fortnight or three weeks later; the cantonments are much more concentrated, and the society is on a much more sociable footing: and what to me is a great advantage, the easy distance from the hills, on a clear morning, or evening, the snowy range is visible. Left Enderby after *tiffin;* in the evening overtook my detachment and enjoyed my solitary *hookar.*

May 31.—Arrived at Ghurmeekteesah Ghaut on the Ganges, distant about 30 miles from Meerut: the boats were all in readiness, and I was soon joined by Dr. Malloch who is my *compagnon du voyage;* and most fortunate do I consider myself in having his agreeable society.

June 1.—Commenced our passage down the Ganges, the heat very nearly insupportable. Malloch and I agree that if we live through this, nothing but extreme old age can kill or affect us; we find the greatest benefit from a small tent of mine which we have pitched every evening to dine in.

June 5.—Arrived late at Futteyghur, halted the following day and spent it with Peter Labouche. In the evening a delightful shower of rain fell which was beyond measure refreshing. I hope the atmosphere will for a few days be so cooled by it, that I may be able to exist without much difficulty. Labouche was engaged to dine with Colonel Burgh (who distinguished himself with us at Calpee) I accompanied him to the colonel's who seemed to be perfectly *au fait* in his command at the dinner-table.

June 9.—I had very good fun from Futteyghur, shooting at alligators that were lying on the banks of the river; some of these were enormous fellows. In the evening we got to Cawnpore, and I received the heartiest welcome from the Creightons. The 11th Dragoons appear to be as disunited as ever, and party spirit to be raging with so much fierceness that I kept away from the regiment, though I received an invitation to become an honorary member of their mess during my stay. A similar compliment was paid me by the 59th Regiment.

June 19.—The detachment of invalids from the 59th consisting of 20 men who had been badly wounded at Bhurtpoor were delivered over to me. I immediately marched them to their boats, and received orders to proceed the following morning. I was passing my time so pleasantly that I requested Col. Sleigh to delay their departure for one day, which he consented to after a little difficulty. In the evening the 11th gave a large dinner in celebration of the Battle of Waterloo (the 18th happened to be on a Sunday); the dinner was a good one, and the wines, particularly the champagne, were deliciously cooled; but even this could not give spirit to the party, which passed off stupidly. I hurried away from it as quickly as possible.

June 22.—Was obliged to follow the invalids who I had sent on one day in advance. I had spent my time entirely in the society of the Creightons, and never spent a fortnight more pleasantly in my life. I shall always look back to these days with pleasure, and assuredly I shall never forget my visit very late the night before I quitted Cawnpore. I wrote some more verses.

June 26.—Got to Allahabad. Malloch and I received a very pressing invitation to pass the day with George Warde, who I found in deep mourning for his wife's father, Mr. Dashwood who had died suddenly at Canterbury. The city of Allahabad does not make a handsome appearance. The fort is placed at some distance on a tongue of land, one side being washed by the Jumna and the other very nearly approaching the Ganges. It is lofty, and completely commands the navigation of the two rivers. The 3rd side next the land is perfectly regular and very strong. In this fort lies a pillar of great antiquity, cut from one block of marble; its present length is 42 feet, and it is now much mutilated. The characters, which are still visible on this pillar, are unintelligible. In wretched apartments poor Dourjan Sal is confined. I had no wish to see him, and probably should not have been permitted if I had.

June 28.—Before breakfast passed by Mirzapoor on the S. W. bank of the Ganges. This is one of the greatest inland trading towns in Hindostan, and the natives are here more remarkable for their activity than in any part of the Company's dominions. A handsome and durable carpeting, resembling the Persian, is manufactured at this town, as well as various descriptions of cotton goods. The number of boats collected here, proves that it must be a place of considerable traffic. From the river this town has a lively, bustling appearance. In the afternoon passed Chunar, a fort built on a rocky eminence commanding the river. Some State prisoners are here kept in confinement. In the evening dined with William Pattle at Sultanpoor.

June 29.—Arrived early in the morning at Benares, where we found Dr. Langstaff's buggy in attendance to convey us to his house, where we spent the day. The view of this old town, built on steeply rising ground on the N. E. bank of the Ganges, is from the river singular and picturesque. And there is no city in Hindostan held in greater veneration by the Hindoos than the holy city of Benares. The heat during the day was so oppressive as to prevent my visiting the town;

but in the evening Malloch and I drove as far as we could, and then walked through most of the principal streets, which are so narrow, as to prevent the possibility of a buggy being driven through them, and even a *palanquin* would have difficulty in passing.

The houses are generally very high, and the cornices which project over the windows on either side of the street nearly meet. From the vast number of people we met walking, Benares must be very populously inhabited. This place is famous for the manufacture of muslins, worked with gold and silver, and which is beautiful when made into turbans.

June 30.—About 8 *coss* distant from Benares passed the conflux of the River Gumtee, which flows past Lucknow.

July 1.—Soon after we had arrived at Ghazeepoor, Mr. Hunter to whom I had been introduced by the Crightons, came to our boats, and pressed Malloch and me to stay with him as long as we remained at the station. Our host is infinitely good-natured, and obliging, but appears scarcely a remove from an idiot, and I am deceived if his wife does not take advantage of his simplicity. Called on Colonel Carter who is in command of the 44th Regiment, he told me that 68 invalids were to be sent with me; and that as no boats were in readiness, I should be detained some days. The 44th, who were in the *Winchelsea*, kept company for some time with us on our voyage to this country: on their arrival in Calcutta they were a very fine regiment.

It is now melancholy to see the alterations that had taken place in the effectiveness of the corps from the death and sickness that cursed the late war in Arracan. Colonel Carter mentioned that in the month of December last they lost 127 men; and during the war at Arracan (I use his own expression) they had expended upwards of 1,000 men and 40 officers, not one of whom was killed in action. When General Dalzell inspected the corps on its return from the campaign, only 28 men could be produced on parade, and some of these were so weak, as to be unable to bear their arms for more than a few minutes.

July 6.—Left Ghazeepore, and soon found I had a troublesome addition to my detachment. One man by personating another of the same surname, screwed 66 *rupees* out of me. Rather a young trick to be done by a foot soldier.

July 9.—We had just arrived at Dinapore, when we received an invitation to dine with the 31st Regiment who have lately come out to this country; they have been unhealthy, and have already lost double the number of men that the 16th have in four years. It is an Irishism to say the men are all boys, but such is the case. I called to report my arrival to General Dick a regular old dried up *Qui Hi,* should a command of consequence fall on such a man, God have mercy on the expedition, I found the general with nothing on but his shirt, reclining on his couch: I suppose he is incapable of the exertion of rising without assistance, as he did not get up to receive me.

July 12.—Left Dinapore with an addition of 8 invalids from the 31st Regiment, and soon passed the city of Patna, which is not more than 4 *coss* distant, and on the same bank of the river. Malloch and I dined each day with the 31st, who have an excellent mess; but I fear they will soon discover that they are living too freely for this climate.

July 13.—Obliged to bring to at breakfast time, to allow the rear boats to come up; but the wind blew so strongly from the East, that I saw little chance of their accomplishing it. I got on 'The Cheetah' and went out shooting. On my return, near a village called Makharu I met with a people differing in appearance, as well as in language and in the shape of their habitations, from all people whom I have hitherto seen. Their houses, in the shape of a cone, were about 6 or 8 feet high and nearly the same in diameter at the base; the exterior was entirely composed of straw: the only entrance which was at the base was just large enough to give admittance to a man on his hands and knees.

Several of these huts were erected in a grove of trees. My bearer told me these were a race of people who, during the rains, had come down from the hills of Rajmahal, and had made for themselves a temporary residence: that they never tilled the ground, and never entered into any kind of service; that they lived on roots, and what they could pick up. I fancy this must form the principal part of their subsistence: lastly Betchoo said, to use his own expression; "And *Sahib,* they speak no language, neither yours, or mine. What kind of people must they be?" I saw some of the women of this party, who did not endeavour to hide themselves, nor did they appear in any way afraid. I never saw any women so ugly; always excepting those of Car Nicobar—they certainly were fearfully frightful.

July 15.—Early we passed by Monghir and the hot wells at Seeta-coond, and in the evening fastened our boats near to Bhauglipoor. The scenery today was charmingly diversified by a range of wooded hills, which commence at Surajipoor, and stretch for a considerable distance along the S. W. bank of the Ganges. Passed by the rocks of

Jehangara, which rise in the centre of the river; on one of these a Hindoo temple is erected, and has a singularly picturesque appearance.

July 16.—Passed the rocks of Colgong which also rise in the centre of the river, and produce so great a current, that there is during the rains, when there is a great flush of water, considerable danger in passing them. We were taken down the current with great velocity, at a particular spot where a backwater took us; and when I did not feel at all certain that we should not go down, the *gurreyah*—a man who with a long bamboo manages the head of the boat,—kindly told me that two days ago, a cooking boat had gone down precisely in the spot where we then were, and everybody on board of her was lost; with a peculiar nodding of the head, he said: "Such was God's pleasure."

Soon after we had passed these rapids a large snake was seen coming towards the boat; the *daundies* endeavoured to kill it with their oars but missed it. The *gurreyah* who was composedly smoking his pipe seemed to take no interest about it; but presently he came into the apartment where I was writing, and began to look under the beds and trunks. I enquired what he was looking for; he answered, the snake, "*aurkea*," (what else.) I told him the snake could not have got into the boat; he said: "Where else could it have gone?"

The *gurreyah* was right, and he soon found the snake behind a trunk. *Daundies*, servants, and all now came in; but there was such a crowd that nobody could make a fair blow, and he got through the bamboos into the hold, where my *sirdar* discovered him by his eyes. I gave him an old sword; without hesitation he seized hold of the snake by the tail, and keeping it moving from side to side he soon killed him with the sword. I imagine the water snake is never venomous; this must have measured 10 or 12 feet.

July 17.—The scenery today is very beautiful; the formation of the hills reminds me of those so finely wooded in the neighbourhood of Ludlow. The river since leaving Dinapore (just above which station the Gograh and the Saone fall into the Ganges) has increased in magnificence; the breadth in many places must be 7 miles. At Bhauglipoor saw several men floating down the stream, which is here very rapid. I was told some of these had come 8 or 10 miles; they sit on a Kedgeree pot, mouth, of course, downwards; to this I fancy they have a small bamboo attached to support their legs; in a similar vessel they bring milk to sell in the bazaar. Passed Sicri Gully, a beautiful spot, where a bungalow has been erected. When we went up the country, we made a large picnic party and dined here.

I remember on this evening meeting Mrs, Persse who appeared so frightened, that I expected she would faint. I asked her what had alarmed her, she terrified me by saying she had that instant seen a tiger; with a start she said; "Oh, there it is." I looked and saw a little jackal, which had just come out of the jungle.

Wrottesley came up, and we returned together. In the evening we stopped at Rajhmahal. I rode over the town which displays great marks of former magnificence; by moonlight I wandered about the ruins of the palace, which must have been a considerable pile of build-ing. An immense pillar has fallen into the Ganges.

July 18.—The wind blew so strongly from the eastward that at the entrance into the Bhagrattee I was obliged to bring to, that I might allow the rear boats to get up—some did not join us all night.

July 19.—Lagooned our boats at Jungeepoor. Rode the spotted pony through the bazaar, and fancied that the *salaam* which was made to you, was more slavish and abject than that which you receive in the Upper Provinces. Returning to my boat, I was overtaken by a gentleman in his *taujhan*, who entered into conversation with me, and invited me to his house, which, from its appearance, promised excel-lent entertainment, but I did not like to leave Malloch all alone. I now found my friend was the Honourable Allan Ramsay, remarkable for his hospitality. He asked me if I had heard of a duel having been fought at Meerut between Enderby and Osborne, in which the latter had been wounded. The cause of this quarrel, he added, was the captain having intercepted a letter from Osborne to his wife, simply requesting her to leave him—a modest request for a husband to discover. I hope this report is as much exaggerated as rumours in general are.

When I had passed the station Mr. Ramsay's *chuprassees* overtook me, with a present of bread and the most delicious mangoes I ever tasted.

July 20.—My *sirdar* told me the Imaumbara at Moorshedabad was one of the most celebrated buildings in Hindostan. I got my pony out of the boat, and rode to it; as I had not formed an extravagant idea of my *sirdar's* taste I was not disappointed. The Imaumbara is a dirty building of wood, and is in no way deserving of attention or remark. Arrived late in the evening at Berhampoor.

July 21.—Found Chadwick of the 59th at this station, and I spent the day with him. In the evening an entertainment in the name of the *nawaub* was given to the English by the Dewhan, in celebration of the betrothal of his son in marriage. The *nawaub* did not make his appearance. I understand he is a minor, and already combines in his character the worst vices of the natives: he is insincere, inactive, and profligate. The last *coss* into Moorshedabad was lighted by lamps in the shape of those in London; instead of burning oil, a wax candle was placed in each. The supper at this entertainment was quite in the English style: the *nautching* was execrable: nothing recompensed me for a long and very hot ride but the display of fireworks, and this was excellently managed. I returned to my boat very much dissatisfied.

The natives are an inferior race of people in Bengal, both in point of height and muscular appearance, to the men who inhabit the Upper Provinces. The turban is not so generally worn among the Bengalees, and amongst the lower orders, particularly with handicraftmen, it is almost wholly dispensed with: they allow their hair to grow long. At this time of the year they wear on their heads a concave basket about 2 feet in diameter, which is fastened under the chin; this serves as a protection from the rain as well as the sun, which is now more prejudicial than at any other season.

July 23.—Left Berhampore with an addition of 6 men from the 13th Light Infantry, the wind so strong from the eastward that we could make but little way.

July 25.—Passed by Plassey on the east bank of the river this place is celebrated as the field on which Lord Clive gained his decisive victory over the Suba of Bengal. At Cutwah the River Adji flows into the Bhagrattee.

July 28.—Arrived at Chinsurah, and reported myself to Colonel MacGregor who was in command of the depot. This establishment will, I doubt not, be most beneficial to our army, by immediately removing recruits, who arrive in the country, from that sink of unhealthiness and drunkenness, Fort William. I found at the depot some young officers of the 16th who had just arrived in the country; they received me very hospitably. The rain fell in torrents.

July 31.—Lagooned our boats at the Commissariat Ghaut, near the fort, and having procured a *tickha palanquin*, reported my arrival to Captain Greville who was acting brigade major.

Having performed this piece of duty, I called on my old friends the

Parkes who kindly invited me to spend my time with them, whenever I found myself disengaged. *La Champ Elysée*, I thought, had lost her colour; and in consequence of having grown fat, her figure is not so good as it formerly was, but her foot and ankle is still perfect. Parkes is just the same as when I was first acquainted with him.

Augt. 1.—Before sunrise marched the invalids into Fort William, and gave over the charge of them to the brigade-major. I took possession of quarters in the Royal Barracks. As I had heard there was every probability of being detained for some time in Calcutta, I determined of having a home which I could call my own.

Augt. 20.—I was appointed to the command of all the invalids in garrison, though neither honour or profit could be derived from this. I was glad of the appointment, as it gives me a sort of claim to take them home, by which I shall get my passage to England paid for by the company. I now spent my days almost invariably at Parkes; in the evening generally rode with the *Mem Sahib*, or drove her on the course in a buggy; and if not otherwise engaged dined at their hospitable table.

The Dampierss who had lately arrived in Calcutta, took up their residence with the Parkes, and divided the expenses of house-keeping. Mrs Dampier I had known at Cawnpore as Miss Johnson, in the days when she used to flirt with Ellis: then she was a fine buxom girl, with a most beautiful face; but she was a regular hoyden, (boisterous girl), and I could not endure her. Three years has, however, made a great alteration in her; she has lost almost entirely her colour; but what remains is perfectly delicate, and her skin is fair, as the imagination could paint it. You might fancy that a rude gust of wind would destroy her. This fair lady has, however, become a perfect icicle, and received me so coldly, that I was quite delighted that I had not offered her my hand. Dampier I like extremely; he has universally the credit of great talents, with great cordiality of manner; he has a fund of good humour, and his style of conversation is vastly superior to that which is generally met with in society. I look at him as a regular trump.

Sept. 10,—Nothing can be more oppressive than the weather, and I have seen of late in the fort, more hearses and mourning coaches than I quite like. I never though was in the enjoyment of better health; the sun, which I have been very much exposed to, has in no way affected me.

Sept. 18.—Parkes had an official communication that he was appointed Collector of Customs of Allahabad (worth 1,500 *rupees* a month). I am very glad of this, for I am afraid he has gone the pace too fast; and now being removed from the temptation of Calcutta, he will retrieve himself before it is too late.

Oct. 1.—The Dampiers who had removed their things from Parkes' the latter end of the month, get into a house in a very bad situation near Government House. Mrs. Dampier, whose excessive coldness had in some degree thawed, begged of me to spend as much of my time as I liked with them. Though we had constant squabbles, and one fearful quarrel which lasted three days, I now liked her society very much. She reminded me of a wedding which was solemnised at her father's house between Captain Templer and Miss Emma Fontbelle, when she and the Misses Slators declared I should have no dinner till I wrote something on the occasion: it was in vain to remonstrate against this act of tyranny, so I wrote some verses as quick as I could.

These made a laugh for the minute, and we were all in such good spirits that blind man's bluff, hide-and-seek, and other pretty little games were proposed. Col. Johnson thought the room rather too dark, and perhaps the players rather old for these sports. Our amusements were nipped in the bud. The old colonel is, without exception, one of the bluntest and gruffest men I ever met; his regiment was ordered away from Cawnpore; Jackson, a Dandy Ensign in his corps lounging up to him, drawled out, " Well, Colonel, when do you start?"— "When I'm frightened," humph.

Nov. 18.—I crossed the river to Sulkea with Mrs. Parkes, and spent the day with them, at the first bungalow on their march to Allahabad. In the evening they sent their baggage forward on hackeries. In all my experience of marching I never saw any such confusion. About 9 o'clock I left these friends from whom I had received so much kindness and hospitality. I never was so dissatisfied with my quarters in the fort as on my return to them this evening,

Nov. 25.—Dampier is appointed Commissioner of the Sunderbunds, a situation which he had anxiously desired, and one in which, by application and his talents, I trust he will be enabled in three years to pay off his debts, which are at present enormous. There are few things which I should have more rejoiced at than this appointment.

Dec. 1.—Dampier removes to Chowringhee, where he has taken a very good house, and presses me so cordially to become an inmate that I accept his invitation and vacate my quarters in the fort. Calcutta is now at the height of the season, and few evenings pass without an engagement to some party, and the climate is so cool that you can enter into the gaieties which are going forward without inconvenience. The lately-arrived spinsters are in great force and beauty: I have asked the opinion of several married ladies, who universally agree, that the Misses Newcomes of this year are a decidedly bad lot. The young ladies who were consigned per *Duke of Bedford*, were all, I fancy, more or less damaged, and a hasty wedding or two were celebrated when that ship touched at Madras.

I told Dampier who had been acting in the Custom House that he ought not to have allowed the captain of the *Bedford* to land such contraband goods. He replied; "You have entirely mistaken the case. The goods could not have been contraband. I do assure you they were all duly entered."

Dec. 2.—The Calcutta hounds met for the first time this season. Lushington lent me a horse. There was a very good field out. I counted 38 red coats. We soon found a jackal, and killed him after a very short cramped run, but this was quite long enough to convince me that my friend's horse was not worth one shilling: there was not one fence that he did not blunder at. We soon found another jackal, which afforded no sport; the cultivation was so extensive that we could not force him from the rice fields which had not been cut.

Returning to our buggies we had some good practice at banks and ditches. I rode Lushington's horse at one of these, and the beast went at it in such a way as made it evident that he never could get over it. Dewar and several lookers on halloed out, long before the horse offered to take off, "catch the captain's horse; will nobody catch the lancer's horse for him?" This was certainly a little premature, but the event fully justified their foresight, for no horse could have jumped more awkwardly into the ditch than he did. Lushington came up, and asked me if I was hurt, I told him "No."

"Well, then," says he, "just cram him at 4 or 5 fences in the same way, my good fellow I see you'll soon make him jump." As I could not perceive any advantage that I should derive from this, I begged leave to decline it.

Dec. 10.—I went out again with the Calcutta hounds, and got a better mount from Torrens; the hounds appeared in excellent condition and steady, considering it was the commencement of the season;

we had a fair morning's sport, but the country was very bad. After breakfast, chatting with Mrs. Dampier of old times, she gave me two epigrams which I wrote at Cawnpore, and which I had forgotten. The first was on the Miss Slators anxious of visiting the Court of Lucknow, at the time Sir Edward Paget went there; but their uncle, General Thomas who was laid up with the gout, would not consent to this. Ellen, the youngest of the sisters, imagined herself desperately in love with Osborne, who made a fool of her. The other was written on a very pretty, though an extremely affected, young lady, who complained on the hardship of being obliged to accompany her father straight to Benares. Notwithstanding her pretty face, this young lady was not quite straight, for as much as one shoulder in point of height had a great superiority over the other

Dec. 12.—The races commenced, and good running was expected, as some of the best Arabs, that had been in Calcutta for many years, were collected. The sporting men appear to be getting out of the imported English horses, and to be giving high prices for Arabs. The Welter Stakes for maiden Arabs 1¾ miles 11st. 7lbs. was run in less time than it ever had been done with such weights. John Lowis rode 'Esterhazy' like a workman and won in 3 min. 42 sec.

Dec. 18.—Received an official communication that I was appointed to the detachment of invalids that were to be sent in the *Marchioness of Ely*, under the command of Capt. Tomlinson of the 11th Dragoons. Nothing could have suited me better than this appointment. Captain Mangles, who now commands the *Ely*, has the reputation of great liberality; he was 2nd Mate in her when I came out to this country. I shall now get home in a very fine ship, free of expense, and I am, moreover, placed under the command of Tomlinson, who is a man much liked.

This evening the artillery gave a ball at Dum-Dum, and I never enjoyed an evening more; the drive of six miles out, and home, was certainly not the least pleasant part of it. The supper was rather plentiful than elegant. The dishes that were in succession placed before me made us laugh excessively, my partner remarking that the *khansamah* had doubtless been apprised of the extent of my appetite. There first appeared a large tureen of mulligatawny soup, which on being removed was followed by a huge joint of boiled salt meat, and when this was taken away three plum puddings were produced to occupy its place. I sat at one end of a table.

Dec. 22.—Called upon Mrs. Shedden, who had just received from

England a very beautifully bound album. Showing it to me she begged that I would write something in it for her. I gave her some lines.

Dec. 25.—Went to church. I am afraid I did not pray with much devotion, and certainly never sooner forgot the good precepts I had heard.

Dec. 27.—The invalids were ordered to embark at sunrise; and as Captain Tomlinson was on a shipping committee it was necessary that I should go with them. Lately my time had been so pleasantly occupied that I had almost entirely neglected to prepare for my departure, and I was now in no humour to pack up my things. I embarked the invalids and ordered the sergeant to anchor at Garden Reach, and not to remove from thence till the following day, when I would overtake him. I returned to Dampier by breakfast time and gave orders to my servants to have everything packed up. With little exertion everything was ready to go on board in the evening.

Dec. 28.—At 4 o'clock left the Dampiers and at the Coolie Bazaar Ghaut got into a *paunchway*, and soon overtook the brig and sloop which were taking the detachment to the ship at Saugor. I sat up the greatest part of the night, unpacking and repacking my cloaks and linen, and giving the charge of these over to my new servant, Green. I had promised on quitting the Dampiers to return to them the following day, if I could possibly contrive it: and I had fully made up my mind to fulfil this engagement, especially as Mrs. Dampier had asked me to accompany her to a ball at Mrs. Bushby's to which Dampier had not been invited.

Dec. 29.—Left my detachment at Fulta, and about 4 o'clock got back to Dampier, When the sun had gone down the *memsahib* and I went out in the carriage, but had proceeded a very short way when the horses began to kick so violently that I thought the carriage would have been broken all to pieces; it, however, escaped. At night we went to Mrs. Bushby's ball, which was well attended, and passed off pleasantly. I never should have regretted anything more than my not having been able to go to this party.

Dec. 30.—I deferred leaving my friends as long as I possibly could, and instead of again starting to join my detachment, as I had originally intended by the morning tide, I put it off till evening. I never in my life have received more kindness than from the Dampiers, and I never felt more regret at leaving friends. Promising to write to them, and to make their house my home should I ever again come to India, I took leave of them in the evening. About 10 o'clock I got to Fulta, where there is an inn. Here I found Dr. Young, Captain Humphries, and Mr. Alexander staying, waiting for the departure of the *Anne Robertson*, in which ship they had taken a passage to England. I sat up smoking cigars with Alexander, till it was almost time for me to pursue my journey.

Dec. 31.—At 5 a.m. got into my boat, and at 4 p.m. arrived in Saugor roads. I found the invalids lying alongside the *Ely*. As no accident had occurred, my absence from them was not missed. On getting alongside the ship, the *daundies* mismanaged, so that we went adrift, and were going out to sea, and the tide was running like a sluice. The cutter was lowered for me, and I got on board in about an hour, for the men had the greatest difficulty in pulling up against the tide. Neither Captain Mangles or any of the passengers were yet on board, and a worse mess than the 1st and 2nd Mate and the doctor sported, I never sat down to.

Jan. 1, 1827.—The invalids were taken on board. The *Carnbrea Castle* homeward bound, was, lying alongside of us, and got under weigh. I have a bet with Mangles, that she beats us. I thought there never would have been an end of this day. We dined at 1 o'clock.

Jan. 5.—The captain came on board, and the passengers arrived by the steamboat, and enlivened a scene which had been to me beyond measure tiresome. All day long the same discordant sounds were heard, whilst the ship's company were employed in taking in cargo. A boatswain's mate seated on the hammock nettings, with a shrill whistle, and hoist away cheerily, gave the signal to a fiddler, who was seated on a gun, to scrape away *Moll in the Wad*, and away pulled the sailors, vainly endeavouring to stamp in tune, till they had hoisted the bale to a sufficient height; then you heard another whistle, and lower away handsomely, croaked by the same mate instantly finished the tune. The only variation to this incessant noise was the substitute of *Nancy Dawson* for *Moll in the Wad*. I never was so tired and disgusted with anything. Now the captain was on board, a manifest improvement took place in the victualling office. An excellent dinner was placed on the table, and the champagne and claret were both extremely deserving of attention.

Jan. 8.—Mr. McKenzie came down to despatch the ship. We had been all anxiously expecting his arrival. A third of the great cabin, which had been appropriated to Tomlinson and me (and which was all that he had a right to claim), was so small that we should have been greatly inconvenienced during the voyage, if Mangles in the handsomest manner had not offered to give up more room to us. Fulcher, who I fancy is a steerage passenger, had no cabin, the carpenters, which was forward, had not been taken: as I felt confident that Mangles would consent to the arrangement, I proposed that Tomlinson, Fulcher, and I should pay £40 between us which was the sum required by the carpenter. These terms were immediately acceded to, and I now found myself by paying a mere trifle in possession of the midship portion of the great cabin, one of the best in the ship.

The passengers we now had on board were Mr. and Mrs. Sands who look the emblem of good humour and good living; Mrs. Lindsay, the wife of a civilian—her husband is brother to Lord Balcarras. Report says that she is herself a woman of no family, and I should think this is very likely to be true; you cannot look down into the hold without seeing The Honourable Mrs. Lindsay in large characters on brass, and Mrs. Stevenson, the widow of an officer who was in the 59th Regiment. Mr. Almaty, an old civilian, who seems nearly worn out, I expect some fun from him, as I hear that he is a most unaccountably nervous man on board ship, and already he has given evidence of being fidgety. Mr. McFarlan, a lank Scotchman, and a proper long-headed looking fellow, he is a civilian, as well as Ross Mangles, a brother of the captains, who is going to the Cape for the recovery of his health.

With very few exceptions Ross Mangles is the most disagreeable man I ever met in my life; he is stunningly noisy, extremely argumentative, and equally positive in the most absurd opinions; Howard, a son of Lord Carlisle, who has retired from the staff of Lord Amherst on account of ill-health; Neale, of the 10th, who is going home for the same reason; George Mangles, an old Westminster school-fellow of mine; Fulcher, Captain Tomlinson and I form the party. There are on board two very nice children of Mr. Shakespeare's, a child of McKenzie's, Mrs. Lindsay's two children, and a half caste and quarter caste, the undisputed property of a Captain Clarkson. From what I can foresee, I shall not have as pleasant a voyage home as I had to this country. Pilot took charge of the ship.

Jan. 9.—At 12 noon the ship was unmoored. McKenzie left us in the evening to return to Calcutta, having regularly despatched the ship.

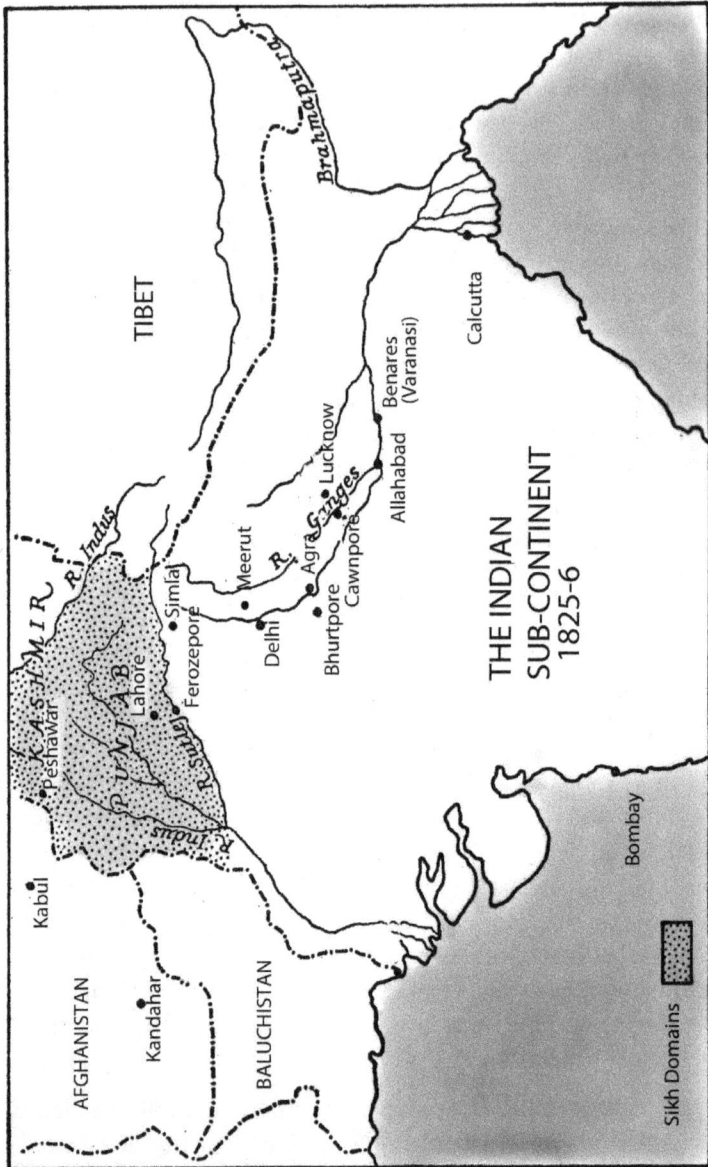

THE INDIAN
SUB-CONTINENT
1825-6

TIBET

AFGHANISTAN

BALUCHISTAN

Kabul

Kandahar

K A S H M I R

R. Indus

Peshawar

P U N J A B

Lahore

Ferozepore

R. Sutlej

R. Indus

Simla

Delhi

Meerut

Bhurtpore

Agra

R. Ganges

Cawnpore

Lucknow

Allahabad

Benares
(Varanasi)

Calcutta

Brahmaputra

Bombay

Sikh Domains

A Brief History of the 16th Lancers in India, 1822-1834

Richard Cannon

In the spring of 1822, the regiment was united at Romford, where its establishment was augmented preparatory to its embarkation for India, to which part of the globe it was ordered to transfer its services.

Having given up its horses to other corps, the regiment embarked in June, on board the *General Hewett* and *Marchioness of Ely* Indiamen, and arriving in the Sanger Roads, in November and December, it was removed into small sloops, and sailed to Fort William, Calcutta, where a camp had been prepared for it on the southern glacis of the fort.

★★★★★★

Names of the officers who embarked with the regiment for India in 1822. *Lieut.-Colonel,* F. Newbery (col.), G. H. Murray; *Major* W. Persse; *Captains* Osten, Luard, Enderby, Byrom, Greville, Ellis; *Lieutenants* Harris, Cureton, Wrottesley, Sperling, McConchy, Crossley, Monteith, Macdowell, Lovelace, Mc-Dougell, Lowe, Armstrong, Douglas; *Cornets* Smyth, Collins, Havelock, Stewart, Osborne; *Pay-Master* G. Neyland; *Adjutant* Hilton; *Surgeon* Robinson; *Assistant Surgeons* Malloch, Murray; *Quartermaster* Pratt; *Veterinary Surgeon* Spencer: *Riding Master* Blood:—352 non-commissioned officers and soldiers.

★★★★★★

From Calcutta the regiment embarked, in January, 1823, in boats, and proceeded up the Ganges about seven hundred and fifty miles, having several men drowned on the voyage up this celebrated stream; it arrived at Cawnpore, a cantonment on the right bank of the river, in April, and received six hundred and fifty horses formerly belonging to the Eighth Light Dragoons, also two hundred and twenty-nine men,

State of H. M. 16th Lancers, and List of Officers.

Colonels	Lieutenant-Colonel	Majors	Captains	Lieutenants	Cornets	Adjutant	Quarter-Master	Pay-Master	Surgeon	Assistant Surgeon	Veterinary Surgeon	Regimental Serjeant-Major	Troop Serjeant-Majors	Serjeants	Corporals	Trumpeters	Farriers	Privates	Horses	Killed	Wounded	Missing
																					Casualties.	
Present.	1	2	6	14	5	1	1	1	1	1	1	1	6	33	31	8	8	529	508		8	2

Rank.	Names.	Remarks.
Lieutenant-Colonel	G. Murray, C. B. . .	Brigadier commanding First Cavalry Brigade.
Major	William Persse .	Commanding the Regiment.
———	Charles King . .	
Captain	W. Osten . . .	
———	John Luard . .	
———	Samuel Enderby .	
———	A. J. Byrom . .	
———	G. M. Greville . .	
———	W. Harris . . .	Major of Brigade to Brigadier Murray, C. B.
Lieutenant . . .	C. R. Cureton . .	
———	C. A. Wrottesley .	
———	A. A. M'Conchy .	
———	John Crossley . .	
———	T. S. L. Monteath .	
———	G. M'Dowell . .	
———	William Hake . .	Brevet-Captain, Superintendant of Semaphores.
———	H. P. Lovelace .	Brevet-Captain.
———	A. C. Lowe . . .	Slightly wounded.
———	T. Armstrong . .	Slightly wounded.
———	Robert Douglas .	
———	J. Vincent . . .	
———	G. Hamilton . .	Brevet-Captain.
———	J. M. Walker . .	
Cornet	J. R. Smyth . .	
———	C. Havelock . .	Aide-de-Camp to Brigadier Murray, C. B.
———	W. Osbourne . .	
———	W. P. Neale . .	
———	W. Penn . . .	
Adjutant	W. Hilton . . .	Lieutenant.
Quarter-Master .	D. Pratt	Lieutenant (half-pay).
Surgeon	J. Robinson . .	
Assistant Surgeon	D. Murray . .	
Veterinary Surgeon	G. Spencer . . .	
Acting Pay-Master	William Williams .	Lieut. and Brev.-Capt. (half-pay) 1st Dragoon Guards.

16TH LANCERS AT BHURTPORE, 1826.

volunteers from the Eighth, and one hundred and seventy-five from the Seventeenth Light Dragoons.

The regiment being thus constituted of men from different corps, required much attention to its formation and discipline, and by the zealous exertions of Colonel Newbery, it was speedily brought into so perfect a condition, that its appearance and performance elicited the unqualified approbation of General the Honourable Sir Edward Paget, G.C.B., commanding-in-chief, at the reviews and inspections in November following.

In December a squadron of the regiment commanded by Captain Greville, accompanied the commander-in-chief, as an escort, on a visit of state to the Nawab of Oude, whose court was held at Lucknow, the capital of his dominions.

The regiment remained at Cawnpore, occasionally suffering very severely from cholera, during the year 1824.

In January, 1825, the right squadron was suddenly ordered to march, under the command of Major Persse, upon Calpee, in consequence of an insurrection having broken out, headed by a petty chieftain; and the British resident, Sir Henry Durrel, and his native guard, were besieged in the residency. After a harassing march of above fifty miles in less than twenty-four hours, the squadron approached the town, when the insurgents dispersed: for two days the Sixteenth halted at Calpee, and on the third commenced their march back to Cawnpore.

While the Sixteenth Lancers were at Cawnpore, the Rajah of Bhurtpore, Baldeo Singh, died in terms of alliance with the British, who had taken his son under their protection. On the *rajah's* death, his nephew, Doorjun Sal, having previously formed a party in the army, excited a rebellion, gained possession of the capital, and seated himself on his cousin's throne. To remove the usurper, and to establish the youthful prince in his possessions, a British Army took the field. The Sixteenth left Cawnpore on the 10th of November, under the command of Major Persse; Colonel Newbery being promoted to the rank of Major-General, and Colonel Murray being placed in command of a brigade. When the regiment was at Etamadpore, General Viscount Combermere passed through the camp on his way to Agra, to assume the command of the grand army assembling on the western frontier, and the regiment turned out and greeted his Lordship as an old Sixteenth officer.

On the following day the regiment crossed the Jumna by a bridge of boats, and joined the second division of the army encamped on a

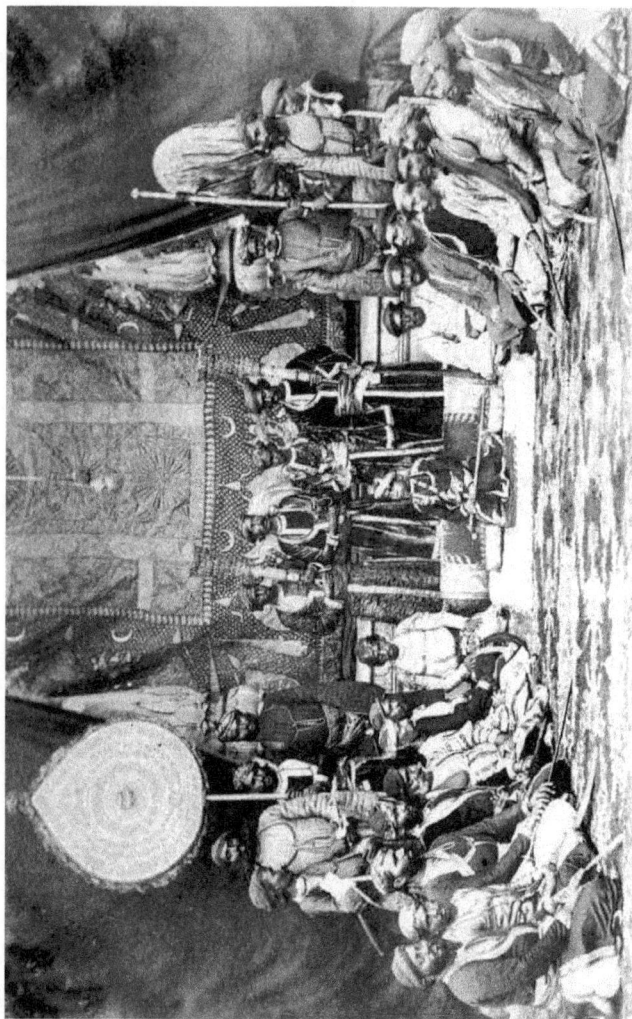

JATS AT BHURTPORE.

fine plain about a league from Agra.

The army advanced, in the early part of December, from Agra and Muttra, to attack Bhurtpore, the capital of the usurper's dominions, a fortress of immense strength, deemed impregnable by the natives, and garrisoned by about twenty-five thousand men, principally Jauts and Arabs, commanded by Doorjun Sal in person. The British forces amounting also to about twenty-five thousand men, arrived in the vicinity of the city of Bhurtpore on the 9th of December. Soon after daylight on the following morning, Brigadier-General Murray's brigade made a reconnaissance towards the *bund*, on the north-west side of the fortress. On approaching this place an encampment of the enemy's cavalry was discovered, with their piquets at a village and their patroles on the skirts of a large wood which extended to the immediate vicinity of the walls.

The skirmishers of the Sixteenth under Captain Luard, and a party of irregular native horse under Major Fraser, made a combined flank movement, and intercepting and charging the Bhurtpore horsemen, as they attempted to escape to an outwork, killed about ninety men. The two supporting squadrons, that of the Sixteenth under Lieutenant Cureton, and of the Sixth Native Cavalry under Lieut.-Colonel Beacher, carried the village in front, and killed several adversaries. The guns of the fortress opened a heavy fire upon the brigade, but with little effect. The conduct of the Sixteenth, on this occasion, was commended by the commander of the brigade; their loss was two horses killed; Lieutenant Armstrong, one sergeant, one rank and file, and five troop horses wounded.

Bhurtpore was invested in a circle of about eighteen miles: the Sixteenth were encamped on a plain to the westward of the city, between the villages of Kunjowbe and Marwurrah: they formed part of the investing force, watched the roads, and pushed patroles forward to the gates of Khambar—a fortress a few miles in the rear of the besieging army.

On the night of the 27th of December, between ten and eleven o'clock, a considerable body of the enemy's cavalry and infantry attempted to break through the first brigade of cavalry, which occupied a front of about six miles; they were checked by the piquets under Captain Luard of the Sixteenth Lancers, and the regiments of the brigade turning out with alacrity, the enemy was repulsed with the loss of thirty men killed, and one hundred and fifty made prisoners. The casualties of the Sixteenth were limited to two private soldiers and

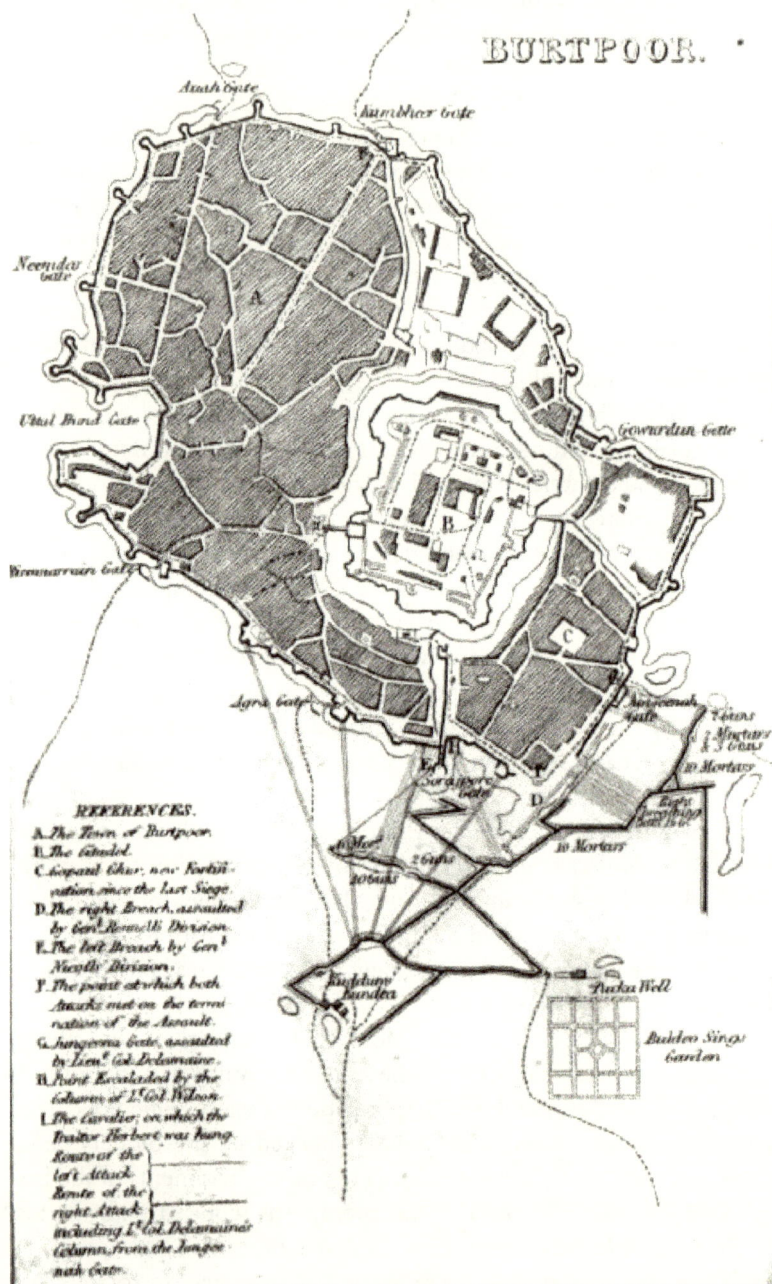

BURTPOOR.

Auah Gate

Kumbheer Gate

Neendar Gate

Uttal Bund Gate

Gowurdun Gate

Verunaraen Gate

Agra Gate

Anteemuah Gate

Seraspere Gate

7 Guns
3 Mortars
2 Guns
10 Mortars

Eight Howitzers

10 Mortars
2 Guns
6 Mor
10 Guns

Kuddum Kundea

Pucka Well

Buldeo Sing's Garden

REFERENCES.

A. The Town of Burtpoor.

B. The Citadel.

C. Soopul Ghur, new Fortification since the last Siege.

D. The right Breach, assaulted by Gen'l Reynell's Division.

E. The left Breach by Gen'l Nicoll's Division.

F. The point at which both Attacks met on the termination of the Assault.

G. Jungeena Gate, assaulted by Lieu' Col. Delamaine.

H. Point Escaladed by the column of L' Col. Wilson.

I. The Cavalier, on which the Traitor Herbert was hung.

_____ Route of the left Attack

_____ Route of the right Attack including L' Col. Delamaine's column, from the Jungee nah Gate.

two horses wounded.

After this action had ceased, a squadron of the regiment, which had been detached to the flank, was fired upon by a regiment of native cavalry, in the dark, and a private soldier wounded, before the error was discovered.

When preparations were made for storming the fortress, a scarcity of European infantry with the army occasioned volunteers from the cavalry to be called for, each King's regiment to furnish three officers, and eighty rank and file. Captain Luard, Lieutenants McConchy and Walker, and the regulated number of soldiers of the Sixteenth, volunteered for this service; but on the arrival of an additional regiment of European infantry at the camp, they were not required; in dispensing with the services of the cavalry volunteers, their readiness to engage in the assault was commended by the commander of the forces.

The city of Bhurtpore was captured by storm on the morning of the 18th of January, 1826. The cavalry were stationed round the city to prevent the escape of the garrison, and crowds of the usurper's legions rushing out were intercepted, cut down, or made prisoners; the Sixteenth, and other regiments of their brigade, slew, or captured three thousand Bhurtpore cavalry and infantry. Among the intercepted fugitives was the usurper, Doorjun Sal, his wife, and two sons, who attempted to escape with a chosen body of horsemen, but were made prisoners. The regiment had four horses killed; Lieutenant Lowe, one sergeant, one private soldier, and one horse wounded. Two soldiers of the Sixteenth taken prisoners by the enemy, during the siege, were recovered.

The capture of the capital, with its magazines and stores, annihilated the military power of the Bhurtpore state; the other fortresses surrendered, and the youthful *rajah* was reinstated in his authority. Thus ended this contest, in which the Sixteenth had performed much harassing duty, occasioned by the small fortress of Khambar, situate a few miles in the rear of the brigade, remaining in possession of the enemy, and from the enterprises of a tribe of freebooters, called Marawatties, who hovered round the camp, and carried off in the night, elephants, camels, and oxen, with inconceivable dexterity.

On the breaking up of the army, the troops were thanked in orders for their distinguished conduct during this short campaign. Prize money amounting to £1500 for each lieut.-colonel, £950 for each major, £450 for each captain, £250 for each subaltern, £12 for each sergeant-major, £8 for each sergeant, and £4 for each rank and file, was afterwards given to the troops. The officers gave the sum of £5000;

£1000 to each of the four widows of European officers killed at the capture of Bhurtpore, and £1000 to be divided among the widows and orphans of European soldiers who fell on that occasion.

His Majesty, King George IV., authorised the Sixteenth Lancers to bear the word "Bhurtpore" on their standards and appointments, to commemorate the distinguished part taken by the regiment in reducing the rebel chief, and in restoring the lawful sovereign of Bhurtpore to his dominions.

On withdrawing from the Bhurtpore territories, the Sixteenth marched to the cavalry barracks at Meerut, which are situated on an extensive grass plain, and are much preferable to the quarters at Cawnpore.

During the following six years the regiment was stationed at Meerut, where Colonel Arnold joined, and assumed the command, in 1827. While at this station it received the expressions of the entire approbation of Major-General Sir Thomas Reynell, previous to his departure for England, in October, 1827; and of General Viscount Combermere, who communicated the high gratification he experienced at finding the Sixteenth in so excellent a state, when making a tour of inspections, in February, 1828.

On the 20th of October, 1829, Field-Marshal Earl Harcourt completed his fiftieth year as colonel of the regiment, and the day was kept as a jubilee by the officers and soldiers. In June of the following year they sustained a severe loss by the death of this highly respected nobleman, who had always evinced a deep interest and a paternal care for the welfare and reputation of the corps, which endeared him to the officers and soldiers, and occasioned his death to be much regretted. He was succeeded by Lieut.-General Sir John Ormsby Vandeleur, G.C.B., from the Fourteenth Light Dragoons.

In October, 1831, nine officers and two hundred and sixty soldiers, of the regiment, commanded by Lieut.-Colonel Arnold, accompanied the Governor-General, Lord William Bentinck, to a meeting with the sovereign of Punjab, Maharajah Runjeet Singh. This detachment returned to Meerut in December, in which month the regiment commenced its march for Cawnpore, where it arrived on the 17th of January, 1832. At Cawnpore the regiment received scarlet clothing, instead of blue, which it had worn since 1784.

A severe attack of the cholera, in August, 1833, deprived the regiment of above sixty men in one month.

On the 15th of December the regiment lost its senior lieut.-colonel, Brigadier-General G. H. Murray, C.B, commanding the Cawn-pore station, who died after a few days' illness. He was an old and distinguished officer of the regiment, served with it in the Peninsular War, and at the Battle of Waterloo, and his decease was much regretted. A handsome monument was erected to his memory, by the officers of the Sixteenth, in the burial-ground at Cawnpore.

The regiment remained at Cawnpore until 1834 January, 1837, when it returned to Meerut, and 1837 occupied the same barracks as on the former occasion when it was stationed at that place.

Soon after its arrival at Meerut, the regiment furnished six of-ficers and one hundred and eighteen non-commissioned officers and soldiers, under the command of Major Cureton, to accompany the commander-in-chief, General Sir Henry Fane, G.C.B., on a visit to Maharajah Runjeet Singh, ruler of the Seikhs, at Lahore, the capi-tal of his dominions. The escort, consisting of the detachment of the Sixteenth Lancers, a party of the Fourth Native Cavalry, Thirteenth Light Infantry, eight flank companies of Native Infantry, and a troop of Horse Artillery, was commanded by Major Cureton, and Lieuten-ant Pottinger performed the duty of brigade-major. After a journey of several weeks, the commander-in-chief arrived at the court of the *maharajah* on the 10th of March, and was greeted by a pompous dis-play of the splendour of the state, for which Eastern potentates have been celebrated. The escort was reviewed, on the 17th of March, by the *maharajah*, and it was stated in general orders:—

> The Commander-in-Chief has much pleasure in communicat-ing to the officers, non-commissioned officers, and soldiers of the escort, that their appearance and steadiness under arms, this morning, met with much approbation, and their performance of the various movements will leave in the Punjub a very fa-vourable impression of their discipline.

The *maharajah* made very valuable presents to the officers, and gave eleven thousand *rupees* (£1100) to be distributed among the non-commissioned officers and soldiers. These presents were allowed to be retained by the escort; but all other persons of the commander-in-chief's suite were directed to return their presents to the British po-litical agent, or to purchase them at a valuation affixed by that officer.

After remaining seven weeks at the capital of Runjeet Singh, Gener-al Sir Henry Fane commenced his journey back to the British domin-ions, and the officers and soldiers of the Sixteenth returned to Meerut.

16TH (QUEEN'S) LANCERS.
1832

The Illustration of the 16th Lancers at Bhurtpore, 1825-6

John H Lewis

This illustration, drawn by John Luard, is particularly interesting since he not only witnessed the event portrayed in it, but was also a principal participant in the action, suggesting it is probable that one of the 16th officers portrayed is Luard himself. Those considerations taken into account (and putting aside the issue of the typical artistic style of the period) mean that within this illustration the viewer is presented with a reliable and authentic insight of what became an important and certainly unique event—the first charge by British Army lancers against an enemy.

Most students of military history know that wooded areas are not the most practicable locations for cavalry actions. However, we have a report from a British cavalryman present at Bhurtpore which clearly describes the country outside the walls of the city. The 16th Lancers was not the only British Army 'King's' cavalry regiment present at Bhurtpore at this time. The 11th Light Dragoons, (later the 11th Hussars (Prince Albert's Own)—the 'Cherry Pickers') which, like the 16th, had also fought through the Peninsular War and at Waterloo was also in action during this campaign.

George Farmer was a trooper of the 11th and has left for posterity an excellent memoir of his service throughout the Napoleonic Wars and afterwards, including at Bhurtpore, which was written on his behalf by G. R. Gleig, who was the author of several first-hand accounts 'ghost' written for less literate soldiers. (This book is published by Leonaur under the title, 'The Adventures of a Light Dragoon'). Gleig, who upon leaving the army became a cleric, also wrote his of own experiences campaigning with the British infantry during the

Bhurtpore, 1826, skirmishes of the 16th Lancers

Peninsular War and in America during the War of 1812 in addition to works of biography and military history from the Napoleonic Wars to the First Anglo-Afghan War.

Of Bhurtpore, Farmer tells us, 'The town and fort of Bhurtpore are planted in the very heart of an enormous wood, of which the outskirts approach within five or six hundred yards of the defences of the place. The wood is intersected in all directions by roads or passes; and while the infantry worked in the trenches and pushed their saps, we, that is the cavalry, had it in charge to guard these passes so as to prevent both ingress and egress to the garrison. We were not always permitted to effect this, or to do the ordinary duty of outline picket, without molestation, as well from the enemy's guns, as from attacks by their very active and vigilant cavalry.'

In a later passage, Farmer tells us, 'The wood which surrounded Bhurtpore was so dense, that in spite of constant service at the outposts, a good while elapsed ere I succeeded in obtaining of the place such a view as could be said to allay my very natural curiosity. It was only, indeed, by riding to the far extremity of one of the avenues, that you could hope to see a yard beyond your own ground; and this, for some reason which was never explained to us, we were particularly cautioned from hazarding'.

Need it be said, in company with a comrade, Farmer ignored this instruction. He continued, 'Suddenly we found ourselves on the edge of the open country; and the formidable appearance of the place against which our operations were directed I shall not soon forget. There seemed to be no limits to the succession of redoubts and batteries which covered it on every side'.

The accuracy of Luard's drawing compared to Farmer's written description needs little emphasis. The scene very closely resembles Farmer's description of the forest, particularly at its extremities where the trees peter out before the glacis of the citadel. Indeed, to the right of the image the edge of the tree line reveals a glimpse of the fortified walls of Bhurtpore, and though they are in the distance, examination by comparison with photographs and other illustrations clearly identifies them.

Let us turn to John Luard's description of these events taken from an extract of his journal. 'On the 10th', he wrote, 'Colonel Murray who commanded our brigade with four guns of horse artillery turned out at half past 3 a.m. The infantry remained in camp. We proceeded to Sesma, then brought our left shoulders up and led straight for Bhurt-

MOUNTED UNDRESS UNIFORM.
Note the similarities in dress with the officers of the 16th Lancers portrayed in the John Luard illustration of the skirmish at Bhurtpore.

THIS ILLUSTRATION OF A *SOWAR* OF NATIVE CAVALRY.
Dressed very similarly to the figures in Luard's drawing and indeed originate from the same period. The soldier is wearing walking out trousers whereas the mounted figure in Luard's rendition is wearing high cavalry boots. Note the holstered pistol.

pore.' Earlier he informed his readers that 'the balls were taken off the points of the lances', which is an interesting detail demonstrating that for safety purposes and presumably to ensure it remained sharp, the steel tip of the lance was habitually protected by a ball. Luard continued, 'Colonel Murray chequered the troops by placing alternately a troop of the 16th Lancers and a troop of 6th Native Cavalry.' These would have been the 6th Bengal Light Cavalry.

This 'chequering', as Luard termed it, was common practice when taking a mixed force of 'King's' (and later in the Victorian era, 'Queen's') regiments into the field to work in concert with the native troops of the Honourable East India Company. The reason was a straightforward one. On occasion the native troops could work extremely well and behave courageously, but equally experience had demonstrated they might not reliably stand or press forward when ordered to do so and thus British army regiments, though invariably fewer in number than native regiments when serving with them on campaign, were positioned among the native troops as 'stiffeners'. The concept was to ensure the native regiments remained functioning in good order by their own examples and to ensure at all perils that the 'line', essential to the preservation of all, was not broken.

This practice was employed up to the outbreak of The Indian Mutiny of 1857 and subsequent creation of the Raj—including for infantry in line—and many references to this practice can be found relating to the engagements of Anglo-Sikh Wars which brought an end to large scale pitched battles in India. The mutiny of 1857 which broke out in Meerut among the 3rd Bengal Light Cavalry, upon spreading, principally involved native troops from the Bengal presidency. This resulted, after its bloody conclusion, in the decision no longer to recruit troops from Bengal to serve in the Indian Army of the Raj period, which was thereafter comprised almost entirely of troops raised from the martial races of the sub-continent.

'I was ordered to command all of the skirmishers,' Captain Luard wrote, 'having Lieutenant Armstrong of the 16th Lancers and Lieutenant Farrar of the 6th (Bengal Light) Native Cavalry under my command. I was ordered by Colonel Murray to cut off any enemy I could. I led the skirmishers close under the walls to the right, while Skinner's Horse under the command of Mr. Fraser, a civilian, made a sweep to the right'.

Examination of Luard's illustration reveals representatives of the three regiments he describes moving from left to right. On the ex-

WILLIAM FRASER.
As he appeared some twenty years before the campaign at Bhurtpore. He had already adopted an Indian lifestyle as can be seen by
the *alkaluk* coat he is wearing.

treme left of the drawing we can see two mounted *sowars* of the 6th Bengal Light Cavalry dressed as we might expect to see them. These are regular Indian Honourable East India Company troops of the Bengal Presidency serving under British officers and their uniforms emulated in measure, perhaps, unwisely, those of European troops of the period. Of course, this was entirely unsuitable uniform for Indian soldiers (and for Europeans, in point of fact, given the Indian climate, but inevitably few concessions were made on that score) since it was alien to their normal manner of clothing themselves in every way. This convention did not apply to irregular Indian troops who usually wore looser clothing in the Indian manner.

These troopers would be wearing the 'French blue' uniform jacket which immediately identified them. It may be a coincidence that these Indian cavalrymen are advancing with drawn horse pistols rather than with the sabre. However, examination of another illustration of these troops in the uniform of this period shows a trooper with a huge horse pistol (which rises up under his arm-pit) in a holster on his belt. This together with the two pistols on the saddle (one of which can be clearly seen in Luard's drawing) suggests these men carried three pistols. This in turn possibly suggests that the use of pistols was a first recourse in offensive or defensive action.

The introduction of 5-round Colt Paterson revolvers ten years later, in 1836 in America brought about the innovation of effective fire-power from the saddle initially demonstrated in a military situation most notably and effectively by John Coffee Hays and his Texas Rangers against Mexican forces and native American Indian tribes. By the time of the American Civil War, 1861-65, skirmishing and even charging cavalry was employing pistol fire in preference to closing with the sword. Could it be, for reasons of expertise, reliability or lack of dependable willingness to close with an enemy armed with edged weapons, these troops—at this earlier period—also used several pistols to the same effect? As it transpired, the 6th Bengal Light Cavalry also mutinied in 1857 and was accordingly disbanded.

'Some of the enemy's horse encamped under the walls retired', wrote Luard, 'as we advanced, but another party encamped further out were attacked by Fraser (with Skinner's Horse) and driven towards one of the gates of the fortress while I galloped on with my skirmishers, and intercepted them as they approached the gate of the fort. We killed and wounded about fifty (of them) and took one hundred horses. Mr Fraser was wounded by a sabre (cut) in the face and Lieutenant

COLONEL JAMES SKINNER OF
SKINNER'S HORSE (1778-1841)

A *SOWAR* OF SKINNER'S HORSE.
Wearing the distinctive uniform
of his corps including a helmet.

SKINNER'S HORSE AT EXERCISE.
Demonstrating their expertise in all arms as mounted warriors.

Armstrong (was wounded) by a musket ball (fired) from the walls'.

Readers may have already noted as peculiar that Skinner's Horse was commanded on this occasion by Mr. Fraser, a civilian. William Fraser (1784-1835), served in the Honourable East India Company's Civil Service and, though he was not a full-time soldier, had a passion for the military life (particularly if action was promised) which prompted him to volunteer for service with Skinner's Horse on several occasions, since he was a long standing friend of Colonel Skinner, the unit's commanding officer and founder. Luard referred to Fraser as, 'an uncommonly good fellow and always ready for a dash at the enemy'. That view seems to have had some provenance because whilst acting as an agent to the Governor General in 1814, Fraser accompanied the army to act against the hill fortress of Nalapani at Khalanga in the foothills of the Himalayas near Dehradun, strongly held by Nepalese forces. He was wounded twice in this action (though General Robert Rollo Gillespie was killed) and thereafter had the local rank of major conferred upon him.

At Bhurtpore, it has been claimed he struck the first blow. Fraser was a confirmed Indophile who dressed and lived in the Indian style and actually kept a *harem*. He was murdered by being shot to death in 1835 by an assassin in the pay of the Nawab of Ferozepur near to his bungalow in Delhi. Both the murderer and the *Nawab* were hanged for the crime. Lieutenant Thomas Armstrong, who is a candidate for depiction in the Luard illustration, was an Irishman, the son of Lieutenant-Colonel James Armstrong, and in his 28th year at the time of the Bhurtpore engagement. He retired with the rank of Major and died in England in 1861.

In the left background of Luard's illustration we can see advancing Indian irregular cavalry and though they are too far in the distance to discern much detail in the pages of this book, a very much enlarged image reveals them to be, as may be expected, Skinner's Horse wearing the distinctive metal helmets which typified their dress of this period. A much-enlarged image reveals that several of the troopers are firing long-barrelled firearms (possibly matchlocks) from the saddle which was something of an accomplishment to achieve a degree of accuracy. Whilst most Indian irregular cavalry was quite similarly dressed in *alkaluks* in a variety of colours, there was no mistaking James Skinner's elite, 'Yellow Boys'. Dressed in bold mustard yellow, oranges and reds, embellished with furs which extended to their saddle cloths, these dandies of the irregular cavalry were expert horsemen, consummate warriors, skilled in every aspect of mounted warfare.

The wearing of chain mail and steel '*mughal*' style steel helmets was common and images exist that show them armed with *tulwars*, lances and muskets. The regiment was formed in 1803 as an irregular cavalry unit of the Honourable East India Company, though its founder had long experience as a freelance in the pay of Indian rulers prior to that time. Notably, Skinner's Horse remained loyal to the British during the Indian Mutiny and indeed, with a long and distinguished record to its credit, exists to this day in the Indian Army as the senior regiment of the Armoured Corps, second only to the President's Bodyguard.

Luard continued in his journal in reference to the 16th Lancers under his command at this time, 'Our left squadron under the command of Captain Cureton came up in support and charged a party more on our right and had two men wounded, three horses killed and three (horses) wounded'

Charles Robert Cureton (1789-1848), who is possibly one of the officers in Luard's drawing, had a colourful career. He was born the son of a gentleman and held the rank of lieutenant in the Shropshire militia, but his youthful financial extravagances led to a pursuit by his creditors which compelled him to fake his own death by drowning and in 1808 he joined the ranks of the 14th Light Dragoons under the assumed name of Charles Roberts. He served throughout the Peninsular War taking part in the battles of Talavera, Busaco, Fuentes d'Onor, Badajos, Salamanca and Vittoria rising to the rank of sergeant, whilst being wounded several times by sabre cuts and shots.

As the campaign moved into the south of France, Cureton was recognised by a comrade from militia days who was by that time on Wellington's staff. Cureton became attached to the staff as a sergeant and in 1814 he was gazetted under his own name and without purchase as an ensign in the 40th Regiment of Foot. He served in the infantry for the battles of Orthes, Tarbes and Toulouse. In late 1814 Cureton exchanged into the 20th Light Dragoons (originally raised in Jamaica) and promoted to lieutenant and adjutant, but the regiment was disbanded soon after the close of the war with France and so he bought into the 16th Lancers as lieutenant and adjutant in early 1819.

As we know, he sailed to India with the 16th in 1822, rising in rank incrementally to regimental lieutenant-colonel in 1839 and brevet colonel in 1846. By this time, he had fought in the First Anglo-Afghan War, The Gwalior War and had commanded the cavalry at the Battle of Aliwal during the First Anglo-Sikh War in January, 1846. In the Spring of 1846, the much-decorated Cureton was appointed Adjutant-General of the Queen's Forces in the East Indies. In 1848 he marched to war for the last time in the Second Anglo-Sikh War. It is commonly reported that at Ramnagar (Ramnuggar), in command of the cavalry division and three troops of horse artillery, leading the 14th Light Dragoons-the regiment he joined as a trooper—to support the 5th Light Cavalry he was killed in action. Edward Joseph Thackwell, son and *aide-de-camp* to General Joseph Thackwell (Colonel of the 16th Lancers), who was present, in his history of the war, tells a different, somewhat less glorious, story. According to him, Cureton, inappropriately acting as his own *aide-de-damp*, was on his way to check on the 14th when he rode close to an enemy matchlock man secreted in a *nullah* who opportunely fired upon him striking him in the heart.

'The guns from the fort', continued Luard, 'now opened up on our brigade, but killed only one horse. The skirmishers were then called in. Had I been supported by infantry, I could have galloped into the fort with the retiring enemy horse'. Perhaps, fortunately for Captain Luard, his final comment remained hypothetical, since claims such as this are not uncommonly attributed to enthusiastic officers' post-mortem.

In the centre of his illustration we can see the 16th Lancers, lances couched, at the charge and their appearance is worthy of examination. In contrast with the pale blue jackets of the native regular cavalry, the 16th wear the dark blue uniform jacket introduced for the first regiments of light dragoons to be converted in lancers. In fact, rather than 'introduced', it would be accurate to acknowledge that with the exception of the Polish style *chapka* head dress, the lancer uniform had changed little from the light dragoon uniform that had been worn during the Waterloo campaign. The jacket had a plastron front in the facing colour boldly identifying the regiment, which in this case was red, though since the figures are drawn in profile that contrasting detail is not visible. Indeed, in this early period of lancers' introduction into the British Army the words 'Light Dragoons' still appeared as part of the official title of the regiment. It is clear that the troopers are wearing this uniform with no allowance made for climate.

The shabraque on the trooper's horses appears to be the regulation one with the light border and royal cipher suggested if not visible in detail. Worth noting is the, presumably, all black lancer cap. A few representations of this coloured *chapka* appear in illustrations of the time, though in the case of tropical service a pale coloured sun cover is most usually depicted. For example, aquatint etchings published by Ackermann of the charge of the 16th Lancers at Aliwal during the later First Anglo-Sikh War appear with the regiment wearing light coloured or black headdress'. Oil-skin covers were well known from periods before this one as a weather protection and an example of a light-weight pattern lancer cap which is black certainly exists. It is not clear what version is to be seen in the Luard illustration, but both the troopers and the officers can be seen wearing this cap, and that would have included the artist himself, so we may take it this is not an artistic error regardless of whether it was a possible deviation from regulation.

Examination of the two mounted officers of the 16th is possibly more revealing and provides the viewer with a particular sense of time and place. Both men, it will be noted, are mounted on lightly framed grey horses with docked tails. Worthy of note are the shabraques on the horses ridden by both officers which appear to be plain coloured (dark blue) and not accompanied by a sheepskin. A print of a mounted officer of the 13th Light Dragoons by Mansion and St. Eschauzier of this period in undress (included in this book for reference) also illustrates this shabraque although, unlike the officer of the 13th, the 16th officers do not carry portmanteaus presumably because these operations were being carried out only a short distance from their encampment. It may be noted that the 13th Light Dragoon also wears an unadorned black headdress though, naturally, of the bell-top shako pattern worn by his regiment.

Both officers appear to wearing the undress jacket of the period, but neither wear small epaulettes. Equally, neither man is wearing a banded girdle around the waist (the same applies to the officer of the 13th) which is present when one examines the troopers, who presumably had less recourse to personal choice on the matter. Indeed, examination of the figure on the right of the illustration clearly shows the reverse detail of the bottom edge of the jacket which, for obvious reasons, is rarely seen in illustrations. The similarity in appearance of these two officers, in the absence of regulation uniform speaks of a degree of concerted action.

However, whilst both men appear to be wearing the blue/grey 'Cossack' style trousers these may be slightly different. Examination of the figure in full profile reveals that the stripe on the leg is lighter in tone than the trouser colour itself. The colour on the collar of the jacket (under the band of regimental lace) is demonstrably darker and we know that this must be red since it is the facing colour. So, we can reasonably deduce that the stripe is broad, single and yellow and that, indeed, is possible, though undress uniform usually shows the stripe as double and red. It is, admittedly, very difficult to see the trouser stripe on the figure that is a rear view, but it does appear (to this viewer) to be darker than the blue/grey cloth upon which it runs which suggests it is red, though single and quite narrow.

Neither writer nor reader should allow themselves, of course, to become too obsessed with matters of uniform in reality compared to that of regulation. For the soldier in the field the availabilities and practicalities of time and place combined with personal preference invariably decide these matters. It has been many years since this writer, examining an early photograph of a large gathering of officers of the Bengal Artillery during the Indian Mutiny noted with some surprise that not one of them was dressed in the same manner as another. Equally, the 16th had been in India for four years before the Bhurtpore action, which was ample time for variations of clothing and equipment to be commissioned from local suppliers. It is quite plausible that these two officers decided to be quite literally 'stripped down for action', a detail which makes the illustration only more interesting and appealing given the nature of the engagement it portrays.

Finally, we should remember that it is entirely possible that John Luard drew himself into this illustration. He was thirty-six years old at the time of the action at Bhurtpore. Originally, he chose the Royal Navy as a career and served as a sailor for seven years until 1809 when he became a cavalryman joining the 4th Dragoons (his father and two uncles had served in that regiment) as a cornet. In 1814, having served in the Peninsular War since 1811 and by then a lieutenant, Luard transferred to the 16th Light Dragoons. He saw action at Waterloo and ultimately became Lieutenant-Colonel of the 10th Foot. Whilst indisputably an able military man, what distinguished John Luard from his peers was his abundant creativity. He wrote well and engagingly in his own journal, but also became the author of a 'History of the Dress of the British Soldier', a once well-known and regarded book on the subject which he also illustrated.

His time on the sub-continent became the subject matter for much of his fine work, 'Views of India, St. Helena and Nicobar', which includes superb drawings of the notable sites, architecture and people of those places, though Luard appeared to be perpetually making sketches of everything he witnessed from maritime scenes and landscapes to natural history studies of animals and birds. Having retired from the

OFFICER OF THE 16TH LANCERS, BHURTPORE, 1825-6. J.H.L.

army in 1838, Luard accepted the post of military secretary to Sir Jasper Nicholls, Commander in Chief of the Madras Army (subsequently Commander-in Chief, India) which took him back to India, though his campaigning days were over.

Luard's second son, John Dalbiac Luard inherited his father's artist talent, arguably with a greater sophistication of technique. His first career was also a military one serving in the 63rd and 82nd Foot, but in 1853 he left the service to focus on his art and studied at The Royal Academy under John Phillip R.A. However, he joined his older brother, Major (later Lieutenant-General) Richard Luard serving with the 77th in the Crimea in 1855-6 and subsequently created, 'The Welcome Arrival' a work with a Crimean War theme which enjoyed some public popularity. This painting is interesting since it portrays the arrival of 'welcome' provisions which are being unpacked in a makeshift campaign shack by three 'officers', two of whom are in uniform. It has been suggested that the central figure is Richard Luard and the figure seated with his back to the viewer is the artist.

Unfortunately, John Dalbiac Luard died young, aged just 30 years, before realising his full potential as an artist. John Luard senior died in 1875 in his 85th year. Richard Luard's son, Edward incidentally, served in the First World War and was killed in Ypres sector in 1916 whilst another son, Charles, served in Mesopotamia and Egypt becoming Commander of British Troops in South China after the war.

An Overview of the Siege of Bharatpur, 1825-6

Evelyn Wood

This powerful Jat fortress had, in 1805, been attacked by Lord Lake, but being staunchly held by numerous defenders, he was obliged to withdraw his army after suffering heavy losses. Bharatpur had thus, among the natives of India, acquired the character of being impregnable.

DISSENSIONS IN BHARATPUR

In the later years of the life of Runjeet Singh, (this prince not to be confused with the Sikh Runjeet Sing, "The Lion of the Punjab") the *rajah* who had successfully defended his stronghold against Lord Lake, that ruler had maintained pacific relations with the British Government. On his death, however, internal dissensions arose in the Bharatpur State. His successor, Buldeo Singh, apprehensive of the ambitious designs of his younger brother, Doorjun Sal, applied to Sir David Ochterlony, British Agent at Delhi, to recognise, in the name of the British Government, the heirship of his son, Bulwunt Singh.

After some consideration, Sir David Ochterlony invested him with a dress of honour, and acknowledged him as the heir-apparent to the *musund*. Soon afterwards Buldeo Singh died, not without suspicion of poisoning, and the troubles which had been apprehended broke out in the fashion so common in Eastern states. Doorjun Sal grasped the rule of Bharatpur. The citadel was seized, the young *rajah*, Bulwunt Singh, was thrown into confinement, and English influence was defied.

Lord Amherst, the then governor-general, forbade the British Agent at Delhi to support the *rajah* who had been recognised.

In 1825 the Indian Government was at war with Burma. Its mili-

THE 16TH LANCERS AND SKINNERS HORSE DRIVING THE JATS
INTO BHARATPUR. DECEMBER. 1825.

tary operations in that country had not always been successful, and exaggerated stories of failure had reached the chiefs and peoples of India. Speculations even were afloat as to the possible impending downfall of the company's *raj*, and upon the urgent advice of Sir Charles Metcalfe, the successor of Ochterlony at Delhi the serious task of crushing Doorjun Sal at Bharatpur was at length decided upon. If this usurper's defiant attitude had not met with condign punishment the prestige of English power might have been most gravely compromised. Although Sir David Ochterlony had collected a strong force, it was considered that, now that Doorjun Sal had had time to consolidate his power, such force was insufficient for the purpose required, and orders were issued for the preparation of a powerful army to be at the disposal of Sir Charles Metcalfe, in whose hands were placed the issues of peace or war.

LORD COMBERMERE

The commander-in-chief in India at that time was an old officer, in infirm health and unfit to take the field, who had long wished to resign. The intelligence of the probable necessity of war with the State of Bharatpur had reached the Court of Directors in England, and, in the appointment of a new commander-in-chief, it was above all things necessary to select a soldier who could be trusted. The choice fell upon Lord Combermere, who, as Sir Stapleton Cotton, had been the able and daring leader of the British cavalry in the Peninsula, and who had served in India in the last war with Tippoo Sultan, including the taking of Seringapatam. With regard to Lord Combermere's selection, a deputation of East India Company's directors sought the Duke of Wellington, in order that he might indicate to them a commander likely to accomplish what even General Lake had been unable to effect. In answer to their inquiries as to whom the great Duke considered the most fitting person, he replied:

> You can't do better than have Lord Combermere. He's the man to take Bharatpur.

It was well known that the Duke's opinion of his cavalry general's capacity, despite his great services, was not high. When he named Lord Combermere, therefore, the astonished deputation could not help remarking:

> But we thought that your Grace did not consider him a man of great genius.

"I tell you he's the man to take Bharatpur," exclaimed the Duke, who rightly appreciated Combermere's determination. After this emphatic recommendation there could be no further doubt about the appointment, and in June, 1825, Lord Combermere sailed for India.

SITUATION OF BHARATPUR

Bharatpur is situated about thirty miles west of Agra, and is surrounded by a wide, sun-baked plain, whose surface is broken by a few insignificant eminences and some low rocky ridges. In 1825 the town was about eight miles in circumference, enclosed by an enceinte of 35 semi-circular bastions Connected by curtains. These fortifications were built of clay mixed with straw and cow-dung, and as this composition had been put together in layers, each of which was allowed to harden in the sun's rays before another was added, while the whole was strengthened by rows of tree-trunks buried upright, it was considered almost impossible with the artillery of that time to establish a practicable breach in the city walls. From the construction of the bastions, enfilade was also difficult in many cases.

On some of the bastions there were cavaliers, and the body of the place was completely commanded by a citadel of great strength, rising to a height of 114 feet above the level of the ground. Since the attack by Lord Lake many additions had been made to the defences. Outside the enceinte was a strongly revetted dry ditch 115 feet broad and 50 feet deep, which could be filled with *water* by cutting the bund, or embankment, which separated it from the Moti Jheel (the Pearl Lake), situated a short distance from the place. The garrison numbered 25,000 men, belonging to some of the most warlike races of India. Strong in position, armament, resources, and, above all, in the proud remembrance and prestige of former victory, Bharatpur stood a formidable antagonist, challenging the supremacy in India of England.

COMBERMERE'S ARMY

The army of which Lord Combermere was about to take command had been assembled at Agra and Muttra. It was composed of nearly 30,000 men of all arms. including a powerful siege-train, and drawn from the European and Native armies. Major-General Reynell commanded the right wing then at Muttra, and Major-General Nicholls the left at Agra. Everything that foresight could devise as necessary for the operations in view was carefully prepared, and the whole force was animated by the most confident spirit.

On December 5th Lord Combermere was joined at Muttra by Sir

Charles Metcalfe, who, having exhausted all peaceful means to induce Doorjun Sal and his followers to give way, now used the authority vested in him to set the army in motion, and placed the further conduct of affairs in the hands of the commander-in-chief. He accompanied the army as a spectator of its operations. The movement from Agra and Muttra commenced on December 8th-9th. General Nicholls being directed to take up a position on the west of Bharatpur, while General Reynell was to establish himself opposite the north-east angle.

The first object to be secured was the safety of the *bund*. It was known that the enemy would at once cut it as soon as Bharatpur was seriously threatened, so as to let the waters of the Pearl Lake into the ditch. To frustrate such an attempt, the success of which would have added greatly to the difficulties of the siege, General Nicholls sent forward an advanced guard of the 16th Lancers and Skinner's Horse, supported by the 14th Regiment. This detachment arrived as the enemy began to make an opening, through which the waters of the lake were beginning to flow. Skinner's Horse was at the head of the advanced guard, and without hesitation charged the Jats, who, taken by surprise, resisted obstinately but were driven back to the town.

They were followed so close by the Irregular cavalry and the 16th Lancers that the enemy shut the gates upon their own men, for fear that their pursuers might force their way in with the crowd of fugitives. Meanwhile by great exertions, the engineers managed to close the gap which had been made in the *bund*, and General Reynell stockading it, made it a strong military position. When Lord Lake attacked Bharatpur, he erred in thinking that the defences could be carried at once by assault, and Lord Combermere, with this warning before him, resolved not to break ground until a careful examination had been made of the obstacles to be overcome.

After the investment was completed on December 11th, therefore, the following nine days were employed by him and the engineer officers under his command in reconnoitring every part of the fortress. The prolonged reconnaissance in different directions had besides the useful effect of diverting the enemy's attention from the point of attack eventually selected, and were profitably employed by the troops in making many thousands of gabions and fascines. On the 20th, the examination of the scene of action was complete, the siege-train and engineer park were all present, wanting in nothing, and Lord Combermere decided that the north-east angle of Bharatpur's defences should be the point of attack.

It was true that here the defenders would be able to concentrate the fire of the largest number of their guns, but this fire would only be effective while the besiegers were still at a distance from the ditch. As they approached closer the guns on the fortifications could not be depressed sufficiently to reach them. The great points in favour of selecting the north-east angle were that here the defences were un-flanked, the ditch was more shallow than at other parts, and there was a ravine communicating with the ditch, which would give good cover to any parties who might have to descend into it.

The point of attack having been determined, it became necessary to seize two positions, hitherto held by the enemy. 800 yards from the place and the same distance from each other—the village of Kullum Kundy and the pleasure-garden of Buldeo Singh. This was done with little loss, and both positions were strongly fortified and stockade to serve as flanking supports for the line to be occupied by the work-ing parties. The line of investment was drawn closer round Bharatpur, and, on December 23rd the first parallel was traced about six hundred yards from the ditch.

Heavy gun and mortar batteries were now constructed, and, from the morning of the 24th, shot and shell were poured on the defences and into the town of Bharatpur. Offers had been made to Doorjum Sal of permission for all women and children to quit the doomed town under safe conduct, but it was not till the 25th that the rebel chief allowed all the women not belonging to the royal family to depart, and they were suffered to pass through the besieger's lines un-scathed and unsearched.

From the 25th till the 31st the siege works were steadily and rap-idly carried forward to the great ditch, till at last the counterscarp was crowned, and the last breaching-batteries contemplated by the engineers were established. The operations were daily covered by sharpshooters, principally taken from the Goorkha Sirmoor battalion. Whose fire was so constant and accurate that scarcely a single enemy dared to raise his head over the parapet of the city's ramparts, and the musketry fire of the defence was thus subdued. The results of the un-remitting discharge of the siege artillery were, however, not encourag-ing. So strong was the construction of the fortifications that but little effect was produced upon them, and the prospects of taking the town by breaching alone seemed to become more and more remote. Efforts were redoubled, and a great gap was at last formed, which, as it was

Long Necked Bastion.

Breach at which General Nichol's division entered Bhurtpore..

seen from the counterscarp, appeared to offer a way for a storming party. So practicable did it seem that Lord Combermere ordered an assault on January 7th, but this was cancelled, and recourse had mines.

Continuous Battery

The history of the siege after January 7th is a record of continuous battery and bombardment, and of constant and persevering effort in mining and countermining. There was opportunity for many gallant deeds and many gallant deeds were done.

An exploit performed by Captain Carmichael, of the 59th Regiment, deserves more than passing notice on account of the soldierly spirit which dictated it, and the brilliant completeness of its execution. A report had been brought by spies into the camp that the Bharatpureans had cut trenches across the breach opposite to General Nicholls's division, and had otherwise so fortified it as to make it impregnable to a storming party. General Nicholls was anxious to obtain exact information as to the truth of the report, but this could only be gained by personal inspection, in broad daylight and under the observation of the numerous defenders, whose muskets and spear-points could be seen glinting on the ramparts.

Captain Carmichael's intrepid spirit prompted him to volunteer to lead the small party which would undertake to clear up the well-guarded secrets of the defence. It was the high-noon of the sultry Indian day, the hour when it is the native custom to yield for a time to sleep and when the extreme vigilance of the enemy might be expected to be somewhat relaxed that he chose for his heroic enterprise.

Captain Carmichael's Exploit

The grenadiers of his own regiment and some Goorkhas were on duty in the advanced trenches. No need to call upon such men for volunteers to follow him and share his adventure. All sprang forward, eager to be chosen, and the only difficulty was to keep the numbers employed within the desired limits. The total number taken was only twelve, half of whom were 59th Grenadiers and half Goorkhas. Captain Davidson, of the Bengal Engineers also joined the little party, which headed by Carmichael, stole quietly out of the trenches. With breathless anxiety their rapid rush across the ditch to the foot of the breach was watched by their comrades left behind. At every pace it was feared that a hail of bullets would pour from the ramparts and sweep them away. But no, either drowsy or careless, the Jats gave no heed.

Carmichael and his men cleared the wide ditch unnoticed, and

SKINNER'S HORSE TRAINING.

found themselves at the foot of the pile of stones and dried mud, where the strong wall of the fortress had been shattered. They commenced the steep ascent and, scrambling on hands and knees, in a few moments stood within the fortification which they had so long watched from a distance. Startled into wakefulness by the sudden appearance of their foe so close to them, whom they doubtless took to be the head of a storming party, the Jats seized their arms and gathered for resistance. Carmichael's followers took full advantage of the surprise and deliberately fired a volley into the dense cluster of men in front of them. Then as the smoke cleared away, they carefully surveyed the interior of the fort and noted all its features. The Jats realised at last how feeble was the party that insulted them, and rushed forward to punish their temerity.

Carmichael's object had been gained, however, and he plunged down the breach in retreat. There was a rush, in pursuit, of the exasperated enemy to the top of the breach, and the little reconnoitring band was in deadly danger from the many weapons about to be pointed at them. But the muskets in the English trenches were ready and aimed. Fingers were now on the triggers, and the first crowd of the enemy was swept away by the calculated discharge before they could use their matchlocks.

The places of the first that fell were quickly supplied, but ever the heavy and well-aimed fire from the trenches flamed forth with crushing effect, and, covered by the friendly storm which hurtled over their heads, Captain Carmichael and his men regained the shelter of their lines almost unscathed. The sole casualty was one grenadier, struck dead and falling into the advanced English trench, so nearly had he achieved safety. The result of the daring adventure was the knowledge that the breach, though a formidable obstacle, was not impregnable, a knowledge which was soon to be of inestimable value.

On January 17th the engineers reported to Lord Combermere that the mines on which the issue of the siege depended would be ready that night. They were three in number: one under the angle of the north-east bastion, loaded with 10,000 pounds of powder connected by a train 300 feet long leading under the ditch; another, less heavily loaded, destined to improve and extend the breach; while a third, still smaller, was to blow in the counterscarp. Orders were given for the assault on the following day. Two columns were formed for the service, placed under Generals Reynell and Nicholls respectively. General Nicholls attacked the left-hand breach. Brigadier Adams had command of a reserve formed in the trenches, in case the assault failed.

At half-past four on the morning of the 18th the troops silently entered the trenches, where they were to remain hidden till the signal for assault was given. The most advanced parallels were not occupied, as it was feared that the debris of the exploding mines would cause many injuries to people within their influence. The commander-in-chief himself inspected each column, made sure that his orders had been carried out and that every precaution had been taken to keep the assemblage of soldiers hidden from the enemy with whom they were so soon to grapple hand to hand. Not a head was raised, not a bayonet was to be seen over the trenches, not a sound was to be heard in the still morning but the low hum rising from a mass of men quivering with excitement and with difficulty restraining their pent-up feelings.

A little after eight o'clock an engineer officer reported to Lord Combermere that the mines were ready, and the order was given that they should be fired. Every eye was turned to the points of the expected explosions, and followed with keenest suspense the lightly curling smoke which showed the gradual ignition of the trains. At last with a mighty roar the two lesser mines exploded, doing all the work that had been expected from them. Alarmed by the sudden and mighty shocks, and fearing an immediate assault, the garrison crowded to the angle of the bastion, the sunlight gleaming on their white garments their armour, and waving weapons. Little did they think that death was even now leaping towards them, and that their time on earth was to be counted by seconds.

Even as they gathered and shouted defiance there was the convulsion of the great mine's explosion. The whole bastion heaved and rent. An ear-splitting crash like loudest thunder shook the air, and where the bastion had been, a dense cloud of dust and smoke arose, mingled with the bodies and limbs of the ill-fated wretches, with stones, timbers, masses of earth, and indefinable debris. To the authors of that terrible destruction the spectacle was appalling among the sufferers by this gruesome expedient of cruel war were scattered broadcast confusion, dismay, and death in its most horrible forms.

Nor were the effects of the great explosion confined to the defenders of Bharatpur alone. Even more far-reaching than was anticipated spread the shadow of death. Scattered fragments of the upheaval were hurled into the English trenches where the stormers were lying ready for action and Lord Combermere himself was present in command. Two *sepoys* standing close by the commander-in-chief were killed. Brigadier McCombe was struck down and Brigadier Patton, with Captain Irvine. Lieutenant Daly of the 14th, and twenty men of the 14th, were either killed or wounded. When the echoes of the mighty crash had ceased, the whole scene was still hidden by the thick cloud of smoke and dust which hung like a veil over rampart, ditch, and trenches.

As it slowly cleared away the Grenadiers of the 14th and 59th were seen charging impetuously up the steep faces of the breaches. Staggered as the enemy had been by the mine, they yet gathered bravely in defence, and poured a heavy fire of grape and musketry on the attackers. Major Everard, who led the 14th, made good his ascent, and in a few moments the colours of the regiment were seen floating on the summit. The 59th were equally successful. Their band played the stirring strains of the "British Grenadiers" as they left the trenches. The breach was steeper, the fire to be encountered heavier than at the main attack, but, unchecked for difficulties, undismayed by the fierce resistance, they pressed stubbornly on till they also stood triumphant within the enemy's works.

The remainder of the columns directed by Generals Reynell and Nicholls followed where the 14th and 59th had led the way. There was a moment of hesitation in one native infantry corps, but when General Reynell himself, standing on the top of the mined bastion, exposed to the heavy fire from the citadel, called out to them to follow him, they answered to the appeal and plunged with confidence into the fight.

As had been directed in orders, the head of General Reynell's column turned to the right to clear the ramparts as soon as the breach had been crowned, while the native infantry penetrated into the town and moved through it parallel to the storming party. The Jats rallied gallantly and, facing Everard and his grenadiers in hand to hand conflict, disputed every inch of ground. There was no time for the actual combatants to load and fire. The struggle was between *tulwar* on one side and bayonet and musket-butt on the other. Matchlock fire from the adjacent houses told heavily on the English, but still the 14th fought their way on, driving their enemy before them. And of that enemy many brave men died where they stood rather than step one backward pace. The gunners in particular would not forsake the pieces which they had served so well, and, at the close of the fight, were almost to a man found lying dead, sword in hand, round their loved artillery.

Lieutenant-Colonel Delamain had led a column to the attack of a breach near the Juggeenah gate on the right of General Reynell's main assault. He had won his way into the town, though with heavy loss, as a mine had been fired by the enemy beneath the feet of his stormers and blown up many. His success was complete, however, and clearing his path to his left along the fortifications he met Major Everard. who was coming in the opposite direction. And now one of the most terrible catastrophes of the day happened to the defeated but still desperately fighting Jats. Between Colonel Delamain and Major Everard there yawned a steep and narrow gorge, about sixty feet deep, and the two bodies of English troops arrived at the opposite side of this gorge, simultaneously pressing their foes before them.

From both sides the Jats were driven backwards at the point of the bayonet towards the abyss and, making a frantic leap for safety, were buried in its depths. In a few minutes several hundred lay piled at the bottom of the gorge, a helpless, groaning mass. To add to the horror of their condition many of them wore armour of quilted cotton, impervious to sword-cut and even to musket-ball. This armour had in many cases been set on fire by the close discharge of musket or pistol and the wretched wearers were slowly roasted till death came as relief to their inconceivable torture. A noble attempt was made to rescue some of them, and a few were extricated, but time and means were unavailable for the work of mercy, and, a few hours later, nothing was left but "a confused mass of burned and burning bodies."

All the storming parties were now in Bharatpur. The fighting, which continued from house to house took a heavy toll of loss from Lord Combermere's army.

The Summons to Surrender

The commander-in-chief had himself shared the dangers of his army, and that he was not the first to mount the breach was less due to his own prudence than to the more than verbal dissuasion of his staff. He made his way to the glacis of the citadel and summoned it to surrender. As no reply was given, he sent for a couple of twelve-pounders to blow open its gates, while some field-guns which had been dragged up the breach opened fire.

By 3 o'clock in the afternoon the twelve-pounders had arrived, and everything was prepared for blowing in the gate when a deputation came out with an offer of unconditional surrender. The 37th Native Infantry was sent for to take possession, and after brief delay they entered and the King's colour of the regiment was hoisted on the battlements of the citadel—a sight of joyous triumph, for it told the completion of the day's stern work.

Capture of Doorjun Sal

Shortly afterwards the news was brought in that Doorjun Sal had been captured by the cavalry, which hemmed in every outlet from the town. When he saw the fortune of the day going against him, he had collected a vast amount of treasure, and with his wives and children, at the head of a picked body of horsemen he had thought to cut his way out. But he had to yield to the 8th Light cavalry. Every horseman of his escort had from 1,200 to 2,000 gold *mohurs*, equal to from £1.920 to £3,200, sewn in the lining of his saddle.

The loss of the garrison of Bharatpur is estimated at about 13,000 killed and wounded during the siege, of whom 4,000 were slain in the assault. Most of the remainder were taken prisoners, the cavalry alone having captured 6,000 or 7,000 after the town was stormed. The British casualties during the siege and in the assault amounted to 1,050 killed, wounded and missing, including 7 officers killed and 41 wounded.

BHURTPORE.

a. Jungeenah Gate.
b. Anargur D^o.
c. Nuttra D^o.
d. Terruckpore D^o.
e. Uttulbund D^o.
f. Mewdar D^o.
g. Puth D^o.
h. Khumbur D^o.
k. Gourelica D^o.

1. Main Breach, Maj.' Genl. Reynell. C.B.
2. D^o D^o Nicolls. C.B.
3. Escalade D^o L.' Col.' Cartwright.
4. Jungeenah D^o Paterson.
5. Buldeo Sings's Gurden.
6. Rudram Bustee.

LEONAUR
ALSO FROM LEONAUR
AVAILABLE IN SOFTCOVER OR HARDCOVER WITH DUST JACKET

ZULU:1879 *by D.C.F. Moodie & the Leonaur Editors*—The Anglo-Zulu War of 1879 from contemporary sources: First Hand Accounts, Interviews, Dispatches, Official Documents & Newspaper Reports.

THE RED DRAGOON *by W.J. Adams*—With the 7th Dragoon Guards in the Cape of Good Hope against the Boers & the Kaffir tribes during the 'war of the axe' 1843-48'.

THE RECOLLECTIONS OF SKINNER OF SKINNER'S HORSE *by James Skinner*—James Skinner and his 'Yellow Boys' Irregular cavalry in the wars of India between the British, Mahratta, Rajput, Mogul, Sikh & Pindarree Forces.

A CAVALRY OFFICER DURING THE SEPOY REVOLT *by A. R. D. Mackenzie*—Experiences with the 3rd Bengal Light Cavalry, the Guides and Sikh Irregular Cavalry from the outbreak to Delhi and Lucknow.

A NORFOLK SOLDIER IN THE FIRST SIKH WAR *by J W Baldwin*—Experiences of a private of H.M. 9th Regiment of Foot in the battles for the Punjab, India 1845-6.

TOMMY ATKINS' WAR STORIES: 14 FIRST HAND ACCOUNTS—Fourteen first hand accounts from the ranks of the British Army during Queen Victoria's Empire.

THE WATERLOO LETTERS *by H. T. Siborne*—Accounts of the Battle by British Officers for its Foremost Historian.

NEY: GENERAL OF CAVALRY VOLUME 1—1769-1799 *by Antoine Bulos*—The Early Career of a Marshal of the First Empire.

NEY: MARSHAL OF FRANCE VOLUME 2—1799-1805 *by Antoine Bulos*—The Early Career of a Marshal of the First Empire.

AIDE-DE-CAMP TO NAPOLEON *by Philippe-Paul de Ségur*—For anyone interested in the Napoleonic Wars this book, written by one who was intimate with the strategies and machinations of the Emperor, will be essential reading.

TWILIGHT OF EMPIRE *by Sir Thomas Ussher & Sir George Cockburn*—Two accounts of Napoleon's Journeys in Exile to Elba and St. Helena: Narrative of Events by Sir Thomas Ussher & Napoleon's Last Voyage: Extract of a diary by Sir George Cockburn.

PRIVATE WHEELER *by William Wheeler*—The letters of a soldier of the 51st Light Infantry during the Peninsular War & at Waterloo.